CONSUMER REDRESSAL SYSTEM AND CONSUMER PROTECTION IN INDIA

CONSUMER REDRESSAL SYSTEM AND CONSUMER PROTECTION IN INDIA

(An Inter-disciplinary Study of Issues, Challenges and Opportunities)

Edited by

MC Paul

Foreword by

Justice JD Kapoor

KALPAZ

ISBN: 978-93-5128-094-1

Price : ₹ 990

First Published, 2015

Published by

Kalpaz Publications
C-30, Satyawati Nagar,
Delhi – 110052
Ph.: 9212142040
E-mail: kalpaz@hotmail.com

Lasser Type Setting : Quick Media, Delhi
Printed at : Chawla Offset Printers, Delhi

Cataloging in Publication Data—DK
Courtesy: D.K. Agencies (P) Ltd. <docinfo@dkagencies.com>

Consumer redressal system and consumer protection in India
: an inter-disciplinary study of issues, challenges and opportunities / edited by MC Paul ; foreword by Justice JD Kapoor.
pages cm
Includes bibliographical references (pages) and index.
ISBN 9789351280941

1. Consumer protection—Law and legislation—India. I. Paul, Madan C. (Madan Chandra), 1955-, editor.

DDC 343.54071 23

DEDICATED

To billions of consumers whose rights are yet to be protected; who suffer endless market injustices silently; it is with a hope that they become aware of Upobhokta Adhikar (consumer rights) rightfully given under the Consumer Protection Act of 1986 and would rise up by shedding the victim-syndrome to organise themselves to usher in a new era rather than becoming pawn and silently suffer in the hands of thousands of dubious/unscrupulous profit-hungry busineses and trades. And especially to those Vyaparis who believe and follow ethical business and fair trade practices as well as to those well-intended quasi-judicial Consumer Fora officials. Their pro-consumer approach could make the consumer really a 'King' of the market. They follow the true spirit of Consumer Protection Act, 1986 despite limitations in doing so against the wrong-doers of market.

Editor

CONTENTS

Foreword

The book edited by Prof. M.C. Paul of Jawahar Lal Nehru University, New Delhi opens with a pithy and insightful analysis of the present existing scenario of the disputes redressal for a and uncovering whole gamut of issues and challenges that has been found to have crept in under various circumstances over the year. It offers us opportunities to search for pragmatic and effective remedy and other complimentary arm to tackle the ever rising market menace of injustice as well as to strengthen the unique quasi justice delivery system set up under Consumer Protection Act 1986, enacted for protecting the interests of consumer by providing speedy, inexpensive and efficacious remedy for redresal of grieances of consumers and populace at large by doing away with evils of ordinary court system and thereby help protect and strengthen the consumer rights in the country. As said, the essay in this volume discuss several vital issues and highlight pragmatic options and/or solution considering the weaknesses of the present system, namely the Court annexed mediation system, not as an alternative but as complimentary to fulfill the objectives of the Act in right earnest (by amending the Act) to reduce to agonizing delay in deliery of justice to the aggrieved consumers who approach the quasi-judiciary body with tremendous hope and expectations that cannot be allowed to be undermined or belied under any circumstances considering the very spirit of the Act. There are no two minds that the policies of economic liberalization and globalization and the consequent economic surge have given us choices but this scenario also forced billions of consumers confront daily various kinds of disgruntled powerful opponents who help perpetuate market injustice on the run for sheer profit. It is only in this regard that the quasi-judicial redressal body has tremendous role to play by pro-actively balancing their act together against the violators with heavy hands. This singular act by the disputes redressal fora can certainly pass a strong and effective message to violators of the consumer rights; force them to put their house in order to check the rising menace of market injustice. Thus the quasi-judiciary has the power to make a difference to the prevailing situation that would generate enough hope and confidence to the consumers at large. Unless timely redressal of grievance of consumers and that too efficacious and less costly is ensured the faith and confidence of citizens in the mechanism of redressal of their grievance through consumer fora cannot be restored.

Thus this publication, "Consumer Disputes Redressal System and Consumer Protection in India: An Inter-disciplinary Study of Issues, Challenges and Opportunities by Prof. Paul is a meaningful contribution to the public debate and discourse on an important subject that demands urgent attention to make the Act more fruitful to serve the purpose for which it had been brought to force by August House of Indian Parliament as per the guidelines of UN in 1986. The contributory experts rightly approach with insights the problem of consumer right protection issues from multi-disciplinary perspective concertedly to benefit the billions of consumers whose rights are under siege by the disgrountled free-market economic forces.

I am very sure the compilation will prove valuable to all the stakeholders who are desirous to fight the menace of market injustice in our country to usher a new era upholding the law of the land.

Sd/-

Justice JD Kapoor

Former President
Delhi State Consumer Disputes
Redressal Commission
Former Judge, Delhi High Court.

Introduction

Every one among us is consumer one way or the other in the market-driven and consumer-oriented society. As consumers we all have to buy goods or avail of services for our living. Consumerism refers to economic policies placing emphasis on consumption and/or pre-occupation with acquisition of consumer goods and services made available by the business. A tendency of people to identify strongly with products or services they want to consume including conspicuous consumption. Thus, the consumerism culture is permeated and led by free-market forces whose ultimate aim is profit. But it seems that the emerging free-market economy in India is yet to whole-heartedly adopt responsible business ethics and social norms to protect consumers rights. Even in developed market economies of US, the President John F. Kennedy gave four basic rights to US consumers in 1962. He equated the rights of the consumers with national interest because they are recognised as the largest economic group in the country's economy, affecting and having affected every public and private economic decision. He remarked: "If a consumer is offered inferior products, if prices are exorbitant, if drugs are unsafe or worthless, if the consumer is unable to choose on an informed basis, then his money is wasted, his health and safety may be threatened, and national interest suffers."

Twenty-five years ago a major step was taken by the General Assembly of United Nations which resolved by consensus to rightly adopt the "UN Guidelines for Consumer Protection (UNGCP)" on 9th April, 1985 (*General Assembly Resolution* No. 39/248). It was nonetheless a bold step that made concerned world leaders to take initiative in regards to enactment of Special Act to protect consumer rights in the market economy. The Year 2010 was celebrated as the Silver Jubilee year as it was on 9th April, 1985 that the UN Guidelines for Consumer Protection was issued.

In pursuance of the above UN Resolution did the Government of India, in the following year in 1986, clain that she became one of the first countries to have specially enacted the progressive Consumer Protection Act to protect the "little *aam* consumers" who have been the most unprotected lot in the hands of market forces. This landmark Act is considered as the most benevolent and revolutionary Act ever legislated by the Indian Parliament with the noble aim to protect better the interests of consumers; and for that purpose made provisions for the establishment of Consumer Councils and other authorities for the settlement of consumers' disputes and matters connected thereto. Para 4 of the Statement of Objects and Reasons, appended to the Bill, reads: "To provide speedy and simple redressal to consumer disputes, quasi-judicial machinery is sought to be set up at the District, State and Central levels. These quasi-judicial bodies will observe the principles of natural justice and have been empowered to give reliefs of a specific nature and to award, wherever appropriate, compensation to consumers. Penalties for non-compliance of the orders given by the quasi-judicial bodies have also been provided."

Subsequently, in 1991 the Government of India had initiated economic reforms by phasing out Licence-Raj and started de-regulatory regime freeing the market economic forces as a part of liberalisation agenda under the global economic dictum. As we know, since then the free-market forces have been expanding exponentially with growth potential encompassing many new areas and sectors of goods and services unseen before by the consumers. But despite the operation of the revolutionary Consumer Protection Act specifically enacted to serve the interest of the consumers the new evolving free-market economies seminally fail to respect the Act in true spirit on this count. This is the inconvenient truth that the consumers are, by and large, forced to encounter multiple violations of their rights in the market arena. The billions of consumers are yet to be reassured and rekindled the much-needed hope to protect their rights by the powerful business and network of market forces. The ethics and equity are yet to seriously take roots in the vocabulary of Indian business and even the so-called Corporate Social Responsibility is so narrowly defined that it is considered primarily as charitable or philanthropic activities but not protection of consumers' rights *per se*.

The mammoth goliaths of business is very well aware that without consumers they cannot possibly sustain and grow, so it is to this end that they must owe certain responsibility while doing business in customer-centric goods and services as a part of their primary duty to protect consumer cause. They must be made aware that buyers and sellers relationship is symbiotic in nature. So a new slogan *'Jago Vyapari Jago Upabhokta Adhikar ko Apnalo'* needs to be forcefully disseminated to make them aware of their responsibility to the billions of consumers in their own interest as consumers are the backbone of business. Mere *'Jago Grahak Jago'* sloganeering by the Ministry of Consumer Affairs in different Mass Media incurring billions of Dollars alone will have no meaning or any impact unless the *Vyaparis* are forced to adopt mandatorily the fair business ethics to protect consumers' rights. It may be apt here to highlight what Father of the Nation, Mahatma Gandhi, long back emphatically held that "a customer is the most important visitor on our premises. He is not dependent on us. We are dependent on him. He is not an interruption in our work he is the purpose of it. We are not doing him a favour by serving him. He is doing us a favour by giving us an opportunity to serve him." The Sooner the *Vyapari* realises the Gandhian talisman in true spirit, better it is for every consumer as well as the nation. In fact, the renowned economist and Padma Vibhushan John K. Galbraith, once said that "The notion that consumer is a sovereign influence in the market economy will serve only those who believe in fairy tales." This seems to be the starkest reality in the new age of globalised India since 1991 with deterioration in quality and purity, shortcomings in quantity, glut of adulterated and sub-standard articles in the market, fraudulent practices, deficiency in services rendered, unscrupulous manipulation of prices, over charging, uncontrolled price-rise, massive misleading and unethical advertisement galore, etc., with the vast expansion of business and trade where the consumer rights protection and principle of consumer sovereignty are found to be disrespected and/or neglected/under-estimated or inapplicable. Whether it is in variety of consumer goods sector and host of service sectors like insurance, transport, housing, entertainment, finance, banking, telecom, etc.

(*Lucknow Development Authority vs. MK Gupta, AIR 1994 SC 787*). It is unfortunate that even after about 25 years of passing of the Consumer Protection Act of 1986, and after more than 16 years of passing of the said Ruling, the echo of the unfair scenario still found to be prevailing in the market arena as highlighted in the said historic Judgement of the Hon'ble Consumer Commission in Lucknow in 1994.

Thus, protecting *Upabhokta Adhikar* (Consumers' Rights) is a crucial challenge for the ubiquitous *aam* consumers all over the country who feel concerned about the rampant consumer rights abuses in the market and, by and large, there is glaring apathy to respect consumer's rights issues by the business. It is a fact that the business cannot acquire goodwill and loyalty of the consumers for their products and services unless they respect the consumer rights issues. The government must also not shy away to exercise tough options to tackle the consumer rights violations while simultaneously encouraging the responsible fair free-market business. This is also equally true for most of the Ministries both in the Centre and the States as they also do produce and market many goods and public utility services to respect consumer rights as model.

On 14th December 2010, while inaugurating the India Corporate Week 2010 at Vigyan Bhavan (New Delhi) even the then Prime Minister of India, Manmohan Singh had to candidly remind the business houses the genuine need for ethical and responsible behaviour. He aptly said, "Ethics encompass a wide sphere of actions, economic, social and human, involving the consumer, labour, society at large and the Government." He also referred what Mahatma Gandhi repeatedly emphasised on the importance of not only good ends but also of the use of fair means to attain them by the business. (*The Pioneer*, New Delhi, 15.12.2010, p. 5). However, there are other broader issues that also need serious consideration like global warming induced by climate change due to irresponsible, unsustainable patterns of consumption worldwide at the behest of unregulated free-market activities. In 1999, the UN General Assembly also revised the United Nations Guidelines on Consumer Protection to include sustainable consumption in the Objectives and General principles.

It is no exaggeration that the little *aam* consumers cutting across all barriers, in general, find instances galore in the market of the violation of consumers' rights provided under the

Consumer Protection Act, 1986. The average consumers feel helpless when the Government enforcement agencies also fail to enforce law or take stringent actions against many ingenious unethical, unfair and exploitative trade practices by various unscrupulous business groups including the policy of making hay when the sun shines. This is particularly true in the case of people belonging to middle and lower socio-economic strata of our multi-lingual and multi-cultural society having less purchasing power, who are neither aware of consumer rights under the Consumer Protection Act, nor they know how to protect and where to go when their rights are breached and violated; nor do they have time, energy and money to fight with powerful traders/ 'business'. The menace of exploitative and unethical trade practices of powerful Mobile phone service companies are examples which we all are very aware of. This is, undoubtedly a pathetic situation when the disgruntled free-market forces take the vulnerable consumers for a ride in several ways. Thus, in a scenario when the spirit of Consumer Protection Act, 1986 is respected or undermined it only strengthened the powerful business who feel empowered to exploit more and/or grow at the cost of consumers only. That it is certainly a biggest challenge and cause of great concern where Government's intervention is highly required.

But the most unfortunate part of the challenge is also to experience the fact that even the supposed to be pro-consumer juristic three-tier quasi-judicial Consumer Settlement machineries established under the Consumer Protection Act of 1986, which are empowered to solely redress consumer grievances have failed to perform its sacred duty as expected to deliver just, speedy and equitable justice to the aggrieved consumers who dare to complaint against violation of consumer rights and other market injustices as a last resort. By and large, these disputes settlement machineries have much to their credit of rendering some good work despite several inherent limitations, but some good things do also go wrong. The absence of effective pro-consumer quasi-judicial leadership in these Consumer Fora has also compounded the consumers' sufferings and mental agony which often lead to 'double-victimisation syndrome' to a large number of aggrieved consumers. First, the consumers suffer varied exploitations in the hands of unjust market forces and second, in the Consumer Fora as complainants. The latter suffer unreasonable delay--no quick delivery of justice, irregular attendance and absence of punctuality of functionaries, cumbersome legal procedures and technicalities, involvement of lawyers like in the Civil and Criminal Court proceedings, adjournments, etc. The situation, by and large, is found to be no way different in Consumer Fora for the consumers as they face the proverbial 'devil and deep sea' syndrome between the rising menace of market injustices engulfing the society and the insensitiveness of Consumer Fora where often the helpless consumers suffer "miscarriage of justice" as it renders them helpless and, hopeless whereas big market shirks get away. As we all know that as per law simple and quick justice delivery is a critical component of consumer right protection but the ground reality shows otherwise. The functioning of Fora needs to be tremendously improved with appropriate training and orientation programme to not only strengthen consumer rights protection but also to ensure much of its credibility and effective-ness as a faster delivery system.

Over the years the confidence of *aam* consumers who approach Fora as a last resort is found to have eroded and as a result the credibility of court is questioned by the aggrieved consumers. These are some of the crucial issues and challenges that have cropped up over the last two decades or so and need serious consideration demandily an urgent pragmatic solution to protect the vulnerable consumers. There is no doubt today that getting justice by the aggrieved consumers in the country, by and large, is a far cry and it has become a far more frustrating and expensive affair to pursue justice with equity in Consumer Fora. As said, the statistics do show the disposal rate of the Consumer Fora is very good but increasing number of consumer-victims is not satisfied. We are yet to see the fast development of separate consumer jurisprudence like the Civil Jurisprudence. It can be made possible only when the Consumer Fora quasi-judicial trained functionaries truly believe and adopt a fresh and unconventional approach while interpreting the provisions of law and providing pro-consumer justice as per the said Act. In this context it may be apt to quote what Justice MB Shah (Former Judge of Supreme Court of India and Former President, National Consumer Disputes Redressal Commission) in his *message* penned down for the book titled, *Consumer is King!!* by an equally concerned Member of

NCDRC (Retd.), Rajyalakshmi Rao. He candidly emphasised that "For deciding the matter under the Consumer Protection Act, we have to step into the shoes of a consumer. If that is done, the decision would be just and reasonable. We have to imagine the plight of a consumer:

- Who has lost his entire factory premises in fire and yet the insurance company is not reimbursing him;
- A widow, who is claiming the insurance amount as per the policy on the ground that her husband met accidental death and the insurance company is not paying the amount;
- In a shop, there is dacoity and the insurance company refuses to reimburse the person on the ground that the insurance policy covers only theft by breaking open some part of the premises;
- Similarly, a surgeon, who commits a blunder and the patient dies on the operation table and the legal heirs file complaint for compensation for the negligence of the surgeon;
- Builder fails to deliver possession of the flat/bunglow despite receipt of full amount.

On occasions, decisions are rendered without realising the ground reality. There is some observation in one of the decisions rendered by the Supreme Court that before entertaining the complaint, a consumer has to obtain expert doctor's opinion and thereafter only notices can be issued. These observations are without considering the reality of life that a patient or his legal representatives are in no position to obtain the expert opinion. For this, they have to spend a large amount. Secondly, experts are reluctant to give any such opinion even if there is negligence. Further, there is neither any such provision in the Civil Procedure Code or in the Criminal Procedure Code or in the Consumer Protection Act. To lay down such rules is the function of the Legislature.....in such cases. Consumer Fora has to render equitable justice. For this purpose, 199th Report of Law Commission observed—"For grant of equitable relief, consumer fora shall take into consideration the following guidelines—The consumer, a weaker party, has no bargaining power with big insurance companies, big service providers or well-known hospitals. In a contract with such companies many terms or exclusions are added so as to deprive the consumer from getting relief of the reimbursement in case of contemplated peril...."

All the above remarkable facts highlighted by the judicial mind do glaringly show urgent requirement to be followed by the quasi-judicial functionaries while delivering speedy justice to help the *aam* consumers from the growing challenges thrown open by fleecing unscrupulous market forces under the liberalisation agenda. The consumers are increasingly experiencing heart-rending unfair deals. The Consumer Courts are yet to follow uniformly throughout the country in true spirit of the Consumer Protection Act. 1986 to tackle seriously the menace of market injustices. That is by adopting a pro-consumer approach in the Consumer Fora proceedings which should be non-adversarial in nature. It will then only go a long way in translating the Act into practice and help tackling the growing menace of market injustice and wrong-doings that intimidates the lay consumers who have the temerity to file a case. The spirit is lost if those sitting in judgement miss the spirit of the enactment and prefer instead to go by technical hair-splitting and legerdemain from lawyers as in the conventional court of law. The problem is not the law, its absence or limitations; the real problem is the lack of commitment to public accountability even among those appointed to interpret and uphold the law as the Consumer Acts and Fora are meant for the aggrieved consumers.

The Consumer Protection Act is a unique enactment where a consumer is not only told of his rights but can also enforce the same in specially created consumer disputes redressal agencies by bringing under its ambit a vast variety of subjects which affect the consumers in his day to day life; be that purchase of goods or hiring of services. Thus, the Act was passed with high hopes to get quick justice. Many times it is found that the cases were not adjudicated speedily and properly for years together due to various factors. It is possible only when the courts adopt a fresh and unconventional approach while interpreting the provisions of law providing consumer justice as Justice Shah. Former President of NCDRC has said 'that the proceedings in Consumer Fora are not to be adversarial in nature. For breach of certain obligations, there has to be consumer factor or consumer surplus, as one may like to call, to which a consumer should be entitled'.

Lack of adequate knowledge and application of provisions by the court functionaries who are mostly brought in after retirement from Civil Court with not much experience in consumer jurisprudence is creating the avoidable hurdles in this era of consumerism. As it is said, 'the Act has to be construed in favour of the consumer to achieve the purpose of enactment as it is social benefit-oriented legislation. The primary duty of the court while construing the provisions of such an Act is to adopt a constructive approach subject to not having violated the language of the provisions and not contrary to the attempted objective of the enactment.'

But there are varied experiences the consumer victims face or suffer in the Consumer Fora despite many success stories in its credit. We also come across facts that the Fora are not always in a position to serve or play their pro-consumer role effectively as expected under the Consumer Protection Act, 1986. There are various issues, challenges and opportunities that the Consumer Disputes Redressal system in India encounters which need serious consideration, so that the agonies of the consumer victims are minimised if not absolutely eliminated. However, the present scenario has to be changed and/or remedies found in the light of growing market violations and it also equally offers tremendous responsibilities to consumer Fora all over the country as the cases of disputes are getting piled up; increasing the burden on the system, and thereby the purpose of the Act is undermined or defeated. The inherent weaknesses or fallibility of the Fora are certainly the biggest challenge which renders them weak to keep up the expectations and it also offers opportunities to think of certain appropriate ADR mechanism like in the developed economies where the ADR system is followed to redress the disputes faster and where the civil society is increasingly allowed to involve in the mediation process. Similar ADR system, keeping in view the multi-lingual and multi-cultural background of different sections of our society, could help bring much solace to the affected consumers. It has to be court-annexed to give a tooth to bite and it should act as complementary rather than having a separate structure as it is opened by the Delhi Government; then the justice delivery will be faster and cheaper as enshrined in the CP Act, 1986. Many models may exist but what is required is honest effort to implement many of these. Of course, it is not one way road but two way roads. Policy reform alone cannot be the only solution unless it is seen to work on the ground. Public Private Participation (PPP) model with NGOs can probably work wonders as in developed countries.

However, certain weaknesses or fallibility of the Fora are certainly the biggest challenge which I believe offer us opportunities to think of certain appropriate ADR mechanisms like in the developed economies where the ADR system is followed, and where the civil society is increasingly allowed to involve in the mediation process. Similar, ADR system keeping in view the different sections of society belonging to multi-lingual and multi-cultural background could help bring much solace to affected consumers. It is probably then the justice delivery will be faster and cheaper as enshrined in the CP Act.

This volume consists of several insightful articles that highlight several issues, challenges and opportunities related to role of consumer courts and whether court-annexed mediation system can be suitably brought-in to strengthen consumer rights protection. These articles are penned down by well-informed and spirited persons, well-known practitioners and eminent experts in this field. I am sure most of these articles would help enrich the concerned people who are interested to protect and strengthen consumer rights as well as to know more the various issues and challenges in the areas of consumer rights protection in India. The volume also has articles by Malaysian and German activist-experts.

The editor is very thankful to the contributors for readily agreeing to contribute for this volume their thought-provoking articles based on their informed-knowledge and long-five years of expertise on the subject, deep understanding of the ground reality and their innovative ideas to tackle challenges in this emerging multi-disciplinary areas of protection and strengthening of consumer rights. However, the book stands on its own merit. The efforts of the editor would be heightened if the concerned people, court functionaries, practitioners, the policy-makers as well as researchers and students become more aware about the innovative ideas, suggestions and recommendations highlighted in this volume and apply them in tackling the various types of exploitations of ever-increasing number of gullible consumers, who are increasingly falling victims to all kinds of wrong-doings perpetrated in regards to varied goods and services marketed by the global free-market forces in India.

It won't be fitting if I don't extend my heartfelt thanks to my wife and children who were bearing with me the pain at every stage of completion of this volume. I owe a great deal of sincere thanks to the Justice JD Kapoor, Former President, Delhi State Consumer Disputes Redressal Commission for kindly agreeing to pen down a suitable Foreword for this volume. Last but not the least, I record my deep appreciation to Kalpaz Publication, New Delhi for readily agreeing to publish this volume in right earnest.

New Delhi **MC Paul**

1

Consumer Protection Law and Redress Mechanisms in Asia—An Overview

RSN Sharma

"The consumer protection and law programme under Consumers International supports the development of legal structures for consumer protection in countries where there are none and strives to strengthen the existing laws which are weak. The services include advice on drafting or reform of consumer protection legislation, advice on enforcement mechanisms and accessible redress mechanisms."

Introduction

The goal of consumer protection laws is to place consumers, who are average citizens engaging in business deals such as buying goods or borrowing money, on an even par with companies or citizens who regularly engage in business. Globally, consumers have eight fundamental rights. It is the responsibility of all Governments, the business community and civil society in respective countries to ensure that these through the development of an appropriate legislative framework are protected through effective implementation and enforcement measures. In any country, consumer protection laws are designed to ensure fair competition and the free flow of truthful information in the marketplace. The laws are designed to prevent businesses that engage in fraud or specified unfair practices from gaining an advantage over competitors and may provide additional protection for the weak and those unable to take care of themselves. Consumer protection laws are indeed legislated to protect the interests of consumers at large and are linked to the idea of "consumer rights" and to the formation of consumer organisations which help consumers make better choices in the marketplace.

Asia comprises of a great variety of political and legal systems. These have been going about the business of consumer protection at different speeds, with different degrees of rigour, using a variety of techniques. In many of these countries consumer protection law and redress mechanisms are still very rudimentary; some have made significant progress, and in a few spectacular and novel approaches have been adopted. To attempt generalisations for such a diverse group of countries is a difficult task. This paper highlights some salient features of consumer law and redress mechanisms in Asia. The information provided in this paper has been collected from different sources including my professional experience.

Consumer Protection: Concerns and Challenges

During the 1980s, trade relations between the developed and developing countries underwent significant changes. Developing countries opened their markets to imports and investment and strove to become successful exporters. Under unrelenting pressure from developed countries they accepted a greater degree of openness in their trade regimes and rapidly became integrated into the GATT system. Such liberalisation was carried out without the developing countries receiving any concessions from developed-countries. Managed trade, regional agreements and ingenious non-tariff restrictions by the developed countries imposed greater burden on the new entrants to multilateral trade. The developing countries did not withdraw, but instead made greater efforts to become successful exporters. Their emphasis was and still is on attracting foreign investment. One consequence of this in many developing countries was the removal of what little consumer protection measures existed, or their non-enforcement, so as to make them more competitive in attracting foreign investment. Increased intra-trade and more complex forms of market penetration occurred. Developing countries were forced to accept new rules in areas previously out of bounds to international negotiations.

Apart from the above, regional integration of economies led to a concentration of economic power and the transformation of private monopolies and duopolies where public monopolies existed. The possibility of collusion has also increased with liberalisation among private sector operators through various business houses such as producer associations, sector and industry associations, business chambers and similar manner of like-minded businesspersons. While the ostensible reason and objective of such business associations is to safeguard and further the mutual business interests of the concerned economic operators, collusion by way of price fixing, market segmentation, production limits or quotas cannot be ruled out. In countries with weak regulatory environments, stiffer competition arising from liberalisation has also led to a rampant disregard for consumer welfare. Product standards easily fall below acceptable minimum levels, proper labelling of products is seen as an unnecessary cost, to the extent that even the practice of changing or hiding the product expiry date with the product already on the shelf is not a fairy tale. Inconsistency of product quality is a major concern, especially consistency in quantity (underweight products are not unknown), contamination of consumer goods and inconsistent composition of ingredients are equally not unknown problems. Another concern for consumers is product safety and manufacturer's liability. Manufacturers taking liability for any accident or harm that a consumer may suffer from the use of their product is rarely heard of. Worse still are those recalls of products that are found to be faulty while already on the market is beyond consumer's dreams.

Attempts have been made in few countries to make manufacturers accountable for distributing contaminated products. A case in point relates mainly to soft drinks, mineral water, toilet soaps, beauty products and others.

Consumerism in Asia

Amongst the developing countries in the world, Asia is the fastest growing region with 33 per cent of the world's GDP and 50 per cent of its population, emerging as a rapidly growing force in the global economy. Consumerism in Asia dominates the minds of the middle class. To Asia and outside, it is a market to make money out of. And the governments encourage it, for more consumer goods means more that the middle class have to buy and they work very hard to achieve it. And the middle class falls for it. It is perhaps in the commercial and retail area where the most absurd and insidious western influence is seen. Despite its impressive growth figures, the living standards and sustainable lifestyles of the people in this region are still far lower from those in the already developed economies which now register less impressive growth. Developing countries in Asia are prone to growth and inter-generational equity and it should be remembered that growth does not in itself mean well being; at best growth is only a movement towards well being. Growth statistics only measure certain aspects of change; they do not reflect the negative impacts. Rapid growth can, and often does, result in the exploitation of vulnerable groups. Growth, without appropriate policies to ensure socio-economic equity, can so marginalise them that they have no hope to partake in the fruits of the growth. Rapid growth can demean the social structures and interpersonal relations. It can even lead to a celebration of conspicuous and wasteful consumption leading to resource depletion and the devastation of the environment and further sacrifice inter-generational equity.

Absence of a Consumer-friendly Legal Protection Framework

These issues are compounded by the absence, in most countries, of a legal framework that readily allows consumers to seek redress in cases where they perceive to have suffered injury or an infringement of their rights. Very few countries in Asia have competition laws, let alone consumer protection laws. In countries where competition laws have been enacted, consumer protection is but a small appendage to the competition law provisions. Other agencies such as the Office of the Ombudsman, the Investigator-General, Human Rights Commissions, all seem to concentrate on other human rights issues and invariably ignore consumer protection issues and do not consider them as human rights *per se*. The lack of information and low awareness among consumers themselves of their rights compounds the problem. Where a consumer purchases an expired product, very rarely would one contemplate taking it back for a replacement or a refund of his/her money! In most cases, they would hope they would be more careful the next time round and check the expiry date. They ignore the fact that it is the responsibility of the manufacturers and seller to ensure that all expired goods are removed from the shelf. In cases where enlightened consumers take cases to court, the legal proceedings are so expensive and time consuming that most consumers cannot afford both in monetary terms and in terms of the time required for the case to conclude. Some cases have been known to take a few years. With inflation and other economic factors, even the compensation that one may get at the end of court proceedings is greatly devalued. Some examples of comprehensive consumer protection measures include the legislations of Australia (Fair Trade Practices Act), India (Consumer Protection Act), and the UK which have been emulated as basis or foundations for consumer laws in other countries.

Constitutional Provisions on Consumer Protection in Asia

An aspect in which modern constitutions differ from the earlier genre is that they explicitly confer a wide range of human rights. They specify not just civil and political rights but a range of economic, social and cultural rights. Since the 1980s consumer rights have been recognised as human rights and have been included in the constitutions of many countries. A study by Consumers International reveals that the Constitutions of at least 24 countries worldwide provide for consumer protection. Of these, the countries in Asia with Constitutional protection for consumers are South Korea (1980), China (1982), the Philippines (1987), Vietnam (1992), Cambodia (1993), and Thailand (1997). An analysis of these constitutional provisions indicates great differences in content and form. Conflations of the aspects they cover indicate an emphasis on four aspects:

1. The basic consumer rights that are to be protected by law;
2. The areas of economic activity to be regulated to provide for these rights;
3. The freedom to form independent consumer associations and confer them with the required legal standing *(locus standi)* to represent that interest in the courts;
4. The creation of an agency of State to protect the interests of consumers.

Some Salient Features of Consumer Protection Laws in Asia

Consumer law here is defined to mean the legal manifestation of the desire to protect the consumer interest. Till the late 1960s, no statute in any Asian country defined the term "consumer" or included it in any laws. However, though consumer protection law is often regarded as a modern phenomenon, many of what we regard as laws with an emphasis on consumer protection have their origin in much earlier laws. In fact, most countries already had laws on weights and measures, contracts, sale of goods, food and sanitation and such financial services as money lending, pawn broking, hire-purchase, banking and insurance. These laws were motivated by three principal considerations:

1. Protect honest traders from their dishonest competitors, the emphasis being on fair trading;
2. Facilitate the development of financial institutions often to the advantage of the colonial powers that ruled these countries; and
3. Provide for a minimum of health and sanitation of the general population.

With increased demand for consumer protection, efforts were made to obtain greater enforcement of these laws; where they were seen to be not particularly helpful to consumers, amendments were sought. A feature of these earlier laws is that they did not distinguish between different categories of buyers-consumers were treated in the same manner as commercial buyers. A major step was made when provisions were inserted into existing laws to distinguish consumer purchases from those of commercial buyers and to extend greater protection and rights to the former. An example of this is the Sale of Goods Acts of various countries.

The Malaysian Sale of Goods Act, for instance, provides for implied terms as regards quality, fitness for purpose, and conditions applicable to sale by description or by sample. However, these may be excluded by way of express provisions in the contract of sale and purchase. This was also the case in Hong Kong, until the Sale of Goods Ordinance was amended in July 1977. The Hong Kong Sale of Goods Ordinance now provides that the implied terms relating to quality, fitness for purpose and the conditions implied in a sale by description or by sample cannot be excluded in the case of a consumer sale. The focus in the early phases of law formation was still very much the buyer and seller of goods and services. No responsibility to the consumer was imposed on the manufacturer and importer of goods, and, no protection was extended to the user of the goods and services and other affected persons if they were not the buyers or purchasers of the goods and services concerned. It was a considerable period of time before the Acts would begin to remedy the seller-buyer focus and instead deal with the producer-consumer relationship. In Malaysia, for instance, the term consumer first entered the statute books only in 1991 and that by way of an amendment to the Hire Purchase Act, 1967. In time, the campaign shifted towards obtaining new legislations that focussed on specific problems such as trade descriptions, advertising in specific trades (pharmaceuticals, food, financial services, housing etc.) door-to-door sales, distance selling, and safety of particular products (electrical goods, children's products, household goods etc.). Consumers were given added protection in these Acts.

Piecemeal legislation, however, has severe limitations. New problems keep coming to the fore and the law focussing on specific areas is inadequate to deal with the new problems. For instance, legislation specifically crafted to deal with door-to-door sales cannot curb malpractice in mail order sales or electronic media sales. In the area of consumer credit, for instance, the piecemeal approach focussing on such areas as money-lending, pawn-broking, hire-purchase, etc., has resulted in separate Acts that lack any functional basis, and distinctions between one type of transaction and another are drawn on the basis of legal abstraction rather than on the basis of commercial reality. More significantly, such piecemeal legislation fail to extend consumer protection to many forms of credit transactions, for example, credit and charge cards, installment payments, and revolving credit and confusion arises as to what law applies to many consumer transactions.

Consumer protection in many Asian countries, including Malaysia, Singapore, and Hong Kong is still very much in this phase. One area of consumer protection in which progress has been particularly slow in coming is the area of product liability. In many countries, it was possible on the basis of contract law to make the seller strictly liable for damage caused by defective products. Liability was for personal injury and death of the buyer, damage to her property and such consequential loss as she may have suffered. However, there was no contractual relationship between the manufacturer and the buyer, and other users of the product. It was, therefore, not possible for the buyer or other users of the product to sue the manufacturer for breach of contract. Similarly, there was no contractual relationship between the seller and users of the product who were not the buyers. Again, it was not possible for the other users to sue the seller on the basis of contract law.

In some countries, especially those that have inherited the English tort law pertaining to negligence, it is possible for an end-user and a buyer to bring an action against the manufacturer, or indeed any party whose negligence causes personal injury or death or consequential loss. But the law of negligence requires the "fault" of the negligent party to be established and this the injured consumer finds particularly difficult. It was to overcome these particular difficulties that a new product liability law was enacted in the European Community and many other OECD countries.

The novelty of the new product liability laws is essentially two folds. The first is that they extend the protection afforded by the concept of strict liability, already a feature of contract law which governed the buyer-seller relationship, to all users of the goods, i.e., to all consumers. The second is that the liability is not confined to the seller of the goods and services, but is extended also to all those involved in the production and sale of the product. No longer is it necessary for the consumer to rely on the fault-based law of negligence to impose liability on the producer. The new product liability laws have not been introduced in the vast majority of Asian countries because of objections from producer interests, though its introduction in Philippines in 1991, in Japan in 1994, and in Malaysia in 1999 has served to increase demands for such laws in other countries. Since 1968, several Asian countries have enacted statutes specifically titled as Consumer Protection Acts:

1. ***Bangladesh:*** The Act titled, Bangladesh Consumers' Rights Protection Act 2009 was passed by Parliament on 2nd April 2009. The Act reflects the central premise of many consumer laws. The Act focusses on three areas of consumer protection: product labeling, misleading advertising and mandatory product and service standards.
2. ***China:*** The Law of the People's Republic of China on the Protection of Consumer Rights and Interests was adopted on 31st October 1993 and came into force on 1st January 1994. The law enumerates consumer rights and the obligations of business dealers and enjoins state organs to punish the criminal offences of business dealers who violate legal consumer rights and interests.
3. ***Hong Kong SAR:*** Though Hong Kong does not have an omnibus statute on consumer protection, it does have consumer protection legislations on various areas including smoking and Health Products Safety, Drug Safety, Trade Description, Sales of Goods, Control of Unconscionable Contract Terms, just to name a few.
4. ***India:*** The Consumer Protection Act 1986 provides for the regulation of trade practices, the creation of national and state level Consumer Protection Councils, consumer disputes redress forums at the National, State and District levels, class actions and for recognised consumer associations to act on behalf of consumers.
5. ***Indonesia:*** The Law on Consumer Protection 1999 came into force on 21st April 1999. The law specifically regulates unfair competition, standard clauses, warranties and guarantees, advertisements and product liability.
6. ***Japan:*** The Consumer Protection Fundamental Act 1968 is a directory of laws clarifying consumer protection policy and specifying the administrative framework to implement that policy. It sets out the need for and measures to be adopted by government, business and consumers for consumer. The Act itself does not specify any penal sanctions.
7. ***Macau SAR:*** The Protection of Consumer Law (Decree-Law No. 12/88/M) was promulgated in 1988. It provides for the recognition of consumer rights and the establishment and functions of the Consumer Council.

8. ***Malaysia:*** The Consumer Protection Act 1999 came into force on 15th November 1999. It provides for areas of consumer protection not already covered in other Acts and covers the following: misleading and deceptive conduct, false representations and unfair practices; safety of goods and services, etc.
9. ***Nepal:*** The Consumer Protection Act, 1998 of Nepal came into force on 13th April 1999. It establishes the Consumer Protection Council whose duties and powers include advising the government on matters relating to the protection of the rights and interests of consumers, prices, quality, disseminating information, conducting studies, etc.
10. ***New Zealand:*** The Act relating to consumer protection in New Zealand is the Consumer Guarantees Act 1993, the Fair Trading Act 1986, the Lay by Sales Act 1971 and the Hire Purchase Act 1971. The Consumer Guarantees Act deals comprehensively with and provides for fixed guarantees for goods and services in trade. The Fair Trading Act deals with certain conduct and practices in trade, provides for the disclosure of consumer information.
11. ***Pakistan:*** The Islamabad Consumers Protection Act 1995 took immediate effect upon its enactment and extends only to the Islamabad Capital Territory. The Act provides for the promotion and protection of the interests of consumers.
12. ***Philippines:*** The Consumer Act of the Philippines 1990 came into effect on 15th July 1992. It provides for consumer product safety and quality; food, drugs, cosmetics and devices; deceptive, unfair and unconscionable sales acts and promises; price tagging; labeling and packaging; consumer credit transactions; consumer complaints handling, etc.
13. ***Singapore:*** The Consumer Protection (Fair Trading) Act, 2003 of Singapore.
14. ***South Korea:*** The Korea Consumer Protection Act was enacted in 1980 and wholly amended in 1986. The Act enumerates broadly cast rights - safety, information, choice, representation, compensation and, consumer education, organisation and participation.
15. ***Sri Lanka:*** The Consumer Protection Act *1979* came into effect on 1st January 1979. The Act provides for consumer protection, regulation of internal trade and the establishment of fair trade practices.

16. *Thailand:* The Consumer Protection Act 1979 is set out in four chapters, comprising altogether 64 sections. It is one of the earliest consumer laws to be enacted in the Asia Pacific region. It came into effect on 4th May 1979. Amended in 1998, it provides for the creation of a Consumer Protection Board, which regulates advertisements, labels, and contracts.

Though the Acts of each of these countries has the same name they each are vastly different in content. Some of these Acts are a disappointment as they provide little improvement over the situation prior to their enactment. However, several of these new genres of Acts have introduced a number of very progressive features. These are as follows:

1. Some of these Acts state the rights of consumers as rights that are protected in law - rights such as that for safety, choice, information, education, fair price, representation and redress.
2. They define the term 'consumer' broadly. They cover three categories - the purchaser, the user and the innocent bystander. For example, Thailand, which previously provided for a "consumer" to mean a person who buys or obtains services from a businessman or who has been offered or invited by a businessman to purchase goods or obtain services, has after the amendment of 1998, provided for the first two categories.
3. They frequently cover the delivery of both consumer goods and services, and some even include the provision of professional services (doctors, dentists, engineers, architects, etc.).
4. They create consultative bodies comprising of government, industry and consumer representatives to proactively address systemic consumer problems, recommend legislation and other consumer protection issues.
5. They address issues relating to product and service safety. In relation to products, they provide for standard setting, notification of unsafe products and recall of defective products.
6. They facilitate compensation of consumers for defective products by introducing the principle of strict liability where products have caused personal injury or death to consumers.

7. They vest existing or newly created agencies with rule-making power to enable a swift response to evolving malpractice. In some instances, the rule-making power is vested in the executive branch of the government, but advisory committees comprising both consumer and industry representatives are permitted to formulate recommendations of the regulations to be promulgated.
8. A very important development has been the creation of special tribunals with simplified rules of procedure and evidence is created to hear consumer complaints.
9. The Acts permit individual consumers to seek redress. Importantly, they confer upon a public officer (such as the Director of Trade Practices, etc.) and in some instances social action groups such as consumer organisations, the right to commence litigation on behalf of a consumer or a group of consumers.
10. A range of remedies, including rescission, the right to damages and, injunctive and declaratory relief are provided for. This is in recognition of the fact that the absence of a full, balanced and flexible range of remedies has the effect of emasculating the rights that such Acts seek to confer upon the consumer.
11. They provide for the appointment of an official of Government (a Commissioner, Director, etc.) to exercise a range of administrative functions. In at least one instance, i.e., in Sri Lanka, the efficacy of the Commissioners operations are enhanced by conferring her with powers to enforce directions to and undertakings by manufacturers and traders. Such directions and undertakings may be made by trade associations (in which case it would be to all traders of that particular class) or individual rogue traders. Breach of a direction or undertaking is an offence under the Act.
12. Some of the Acts establish Consumer Protection Funds into which specified fines, allocations by government and donations by private individuals and corporations are to be paid. The funds so established are meant to support consumer education programmes and the activities of consumer organisations.

Consumer Redress, Access to Justice–Mediation, Standing to Sue and Class Action Provisions

The wide array of consumer redress mechanisms is available in Asia. Notably these include ombudsman schemes, industry specific self-regulatory schemes, and complaints handling services operated by government agencies, and by consumer organisations. In general, consumer disputes are quite common in modern business world. Finding an effective consumer dispute resolution mechanism is, therefore, very much a need of the modern society. The availability of effective dispute resolution and redress mechanisms can increase consumer confidence and trust in the marketplace. They encourage fair business practices, too. Notionally, "dispute resolution" refers to the use of mechanisms designed to provide compensations to the consumers who have suffered "economic harm" resulting from transactions involving goods and services. It is important that the national system of any country should provide cost effective and simple procedures to its consumers to enable them to obtain "redress" for the economic harm suffered. According to the *OECD* recommendations, "redress" refers to compensation for economic harm, whether in the form of a monetary remedy (e.g., a voluntary payment, restitution, or other monetary relief) or a conduct remedy with a restorative element (e.g., exchange of a goods or service, specific performance or rescission of a contract).

Access to consumer redress mechanisms can be understood from two perspectives, when -

- Consumers are acting individually; and
- Consumers are acting collectively.

When consumers are acting individually to resolve their individual disputes, it is expected that the redress mechanisms be cost effective, user-friendly, less formal, and speedy. When a number of consumers allege that "they have suffered economic harm as a result of the similar conduct of the same entity or related entities, and it is not practicable or efficient for them to act individually to resolve their disputes, those consumers should have access to mechanisms that provide for the collective resolution of those disputes." It is expected that collective redress mechanisms be transparent, efficient and fair to both consumers and businesses.

The underlying principle of consumer redress is that if a consumer actually sustained any loss or damage, he/she should be entitled to compensation. Consumer protection laws of various countries, therefore, include within their ambit a very clear set of remedies to compensate economic harms suffered by their consumers. Though in several Asian countries redress mechanisms have been introduced this has not been uniformly the case. In several others though redress mechanisms are existent they have been put in place without significant improvement in substantive rights. Redress mechanisms cannot provide, except as charity, what is not a substantive right. In other countries, procedural rights do not match substantive rights and redress is therefore still illusory. Unless, there exists a comprehensive range of substantive rights matched by a full range of procedural rights, redress will not become a reality. Some jurisdictions in Asia, where consumer organisations play an active role helping consumers to seek redress are listed below:

In Hong Kong, the Consumer Council handles all consumer complaints that come its way. Consequently 1/3rd of their 130 staff are devoted to this function alone. FFC in Thailand takes a smart approach, once a problem has been identified; it organises public interface sessions at various parts of the country so complainants may come forward. In so doing, the time of ascertaining the breadth and depth of the problem is compressed, it also brings a soothing effect to complainants that their grievances are being addressed. Similarly, the National Consumer Complaints Centre (NCCC), in Malaysia is providing valuable services to consumers in seeking redress.

One-stop Service–from Conciliation to Arbitration

Success of the conciliatory service provided by consumer organisations depends on a willingness by the consumer and business to settle their differences. Should such an attempt fail, consumers will have to resort to other dispute resolution mechanisms such as small claims courts or higher levels of the judicial system. To facilitate consumers' access to justice, China has come up with a one-stop service to assist consumers to seek binding outcomes. The system relies on consumers associations at state level setting up arbitration centres at their premises.

The centres are operated as separate entities in accordance with international arbitration practice and China's Arbitration Law. At least one staff from the consumer association acquires the requisite professional training to become an Arbitrator. The one stop service providing conciliation service through to arbitration befits China's unique circumstances as not many of its states have Small Claims Courts and normal courts have long queues.

Legal Assistance and Standing to Sue on behalf of Consumers

Seeking redress through the judicial process is prohibitive to most consumers as the loss suffered by them individually is small, although in aggregate it can be enormous. Consumers' fear of the legal system, their lack of legal knowledge and expertise and the long span of time for court hearings are great hurdles. The greatest obstacle of all is the rule in some jurisdictions that require the losing party to shoulder substantial legal costs, such as all costs incurred by the winning party plus liquidated damages. Consequently, only those who have deep pockets will dare take the risk. The following measures could help alleviate the situation:

- Giving consumer associations the standing to sue;
- Designated funds to finance legal actions;
- Representative actions and a class action regime; and
- Empowering regulators to take action on behalf of consumers.

Such regimes will not succeed in the absence of sufficient financial resources and the necessary legal backing to the consumers association. In the UK, this has been given a super-complainant status and standing to sue on behalf of consumers. In Indonesia, YLKI has had a number of successful cases acting on behalf of consumers, acting as plaintiff. YLKI challenged the uncontrolled promotional activities of two of the largest cigarette manufacturers in Indonesia in court and won. The move also established YLKI's significant role counteracting the negative effects of tobacco in Indonesia.

In Japan, as a result of a Consumer Contract Act amendment in 2007, Consumer groups certified by the Prime Minister are given standing to sue on behalf of consumers as parties to injunction actions. Causes of action include inappropriate solicitations targeted at unidentified and large numbers of consumers as well as contractual clauses that will unjustly harm the interest of consumers. On the other hand, FFC in Thailand, Hong Kong Consumer Council, Consumers Foundation of Chinese Taipei, China Consumer Association and Consumers Korea do not have standing to sue. These organisations rely on providing funds and/or legal assistance for worthy private action cases. The model in China, Chinese Taipei and Korea deserves special mention in that the consumer associations are supported by a large group of reputable lawyers who offer their service on a pro bono basis. Consumers associations are then free from cost worries to bring worthy cases to court. Furthermore, their chances of winning are enhanced because top notch lawyers consider it their duty and honour to serve the consumer interest.

The legal system in Korea further alleviates cost worries as the plaintiff consumers who have lost a case need not pay for costs of the defendant, nor would they be required to pay court charges. CACPK won the hearts of Koreans when it successfully challenged Nestle in court for depriving Korean consumers of the essential information on food ingredients as given for the same product in the US. The case was an important milestone in Korea's consumer protection history.

Representative Proceedings and Class Action Regime

Representative proceedings and class action regimes facilitate access to justice of deserving cases and overcome cost-related hurdles. These also increase the cost-effectiveness of the court's procedures, because cases with similar facts can be grouped together and represented by one test case. This redresses the imbalance of power between the consumer and the party being sued; typically big corporations or the government. Despite the perceived benefits, class action regimes have limited presence in this region.

In Australia, the Commonwealth and Victoria have a specific piece of legislation on representative proceedings. Recognising the problems of consumers in pursuing small claims in courts and tribunals, the Productivity Commission has given a green light to allow regulators to take representative actions on behalf of consumers and to examine the workability of private class action arrangements. Such a welcome development sets a good example for other jurisdictions to follow.

Hong Kong and Singapore have rules governing representative proceedings and are examining the feasibility of introducing a class action regime. For example, the Law Reform Commission of Hong Kong has set up a committee to examine class actions, and in Singapore, the Final Report of the Committee to Develop the Singapore Legal Sector (2007), recommended that consideration be given to allowing class actions in appropriate cases.

In China, there is no single piece of legislation governing the conduct of class actions but it is provided for under the Civil Procedural Law. It has been reported that 117 families have lodged a class action suit seeking compensation of 12.4 million renminbi from Senlu Milk Company in China. In this biggest food safety scandal uncovered so far, 16,000 children were found to have kidney stones and other complications from taking milk products contaminated with melamine. It was recently announced that the government has promised life-long free medical service for these victims.

YLKI in Indonesia should be justly proud with its success in a class action suit: The Central Jakarta State Court favoured YLKI backed consumers in a class action against the state-run Oil Company Pertamina, for an abrupt increase in the price of Liquefied Petroleum Gas (LPG). Pertamina was urged to cancel the price increase and to compensate consumers. The case implies that government's price related decisions will have to go through a process of public consultation.

Likewise, some Lehman Brothers victims may also benefit from a class action regime. US lawyers have approached victims in Hong Kong and Singapore to join their class action suit to be lodged in the US courts. Despite the obvious benefits in facilitating access to justice and increased judicial economy, class action regimes have been criticised for promoting unnecessary and unmeritorious legal proceedings; and are strongly resisted by the private sector. Concerns have been expressed that entrepreneurial lawyers under a 'no win, no fee' scheme will drive class action suits to obtain fees rather than acting in the best interest of their clients. It is my humble view that consumer protection frameworks must support class action schemes, as the benefits outweigh the perceived disadvantages. To address concerns over the 'no win, no fee' arrangement, governments can always outlaw lawyers accepting contingency fees arrangements, rather than depriving consumers of a class action regime altogether.

The Task Ahead for Consumer Protection in Asia

The vast majority of Asian countries have now provided for framework laws for consumer protection. The laws themselves are not identical; they are very different in form and content. Unfortunately, their existence has in most cases brought little improvement to the status of a consumer. A number of factors account for the failure of consumer law in achieving its purposes. Four of these are especially critical—their limited scope, the failure to put into place the requisite implementation rules, the failure to enforce the law and, the limited avenue for redress.

(a) Scope: The framework laws are invariably all titled Consumer Protection Act/Code but they are substantially different in content. It is necessary to focus on the detail of each statute and propose the kind of amendments that need to be made to make them more complete. A notable omission in almost all of the framework laws is that even though they may deal with the goods and services bought on credit, they do not deal with the credit transaction itself. Our studies indicate that consumer and household credit are increasing rapidly in almost all Asian countries and indebtedness plagues many homes. Impulse buying, overspending, deceptive advertising, lack of information about alternative sources of credit, one-sided standard form contracts, harsh and ruinous rules governing default both on borrowers and guarantors, and harassment of defaulters are but some of the problems confronting consumers. The problem has become especially pronounced with the advent of various new forms of credit. Yet, the vast majority of Asian countries rely on outmoded credit laws which the suppliers of credit avoid or even ignore with impunity.

Another important area of importance not within the ambit of these laws is e-commerce, a subject matter that is growing in importance especially in the more rapidly developing countries of Asia. Many of the framework laws are also largely reactive in their approach; reactive to breaches specified in the law. They do not permit for the prescribing producer conduct that prevents losses to consumers. Consumer protection would be better served if there are provisions that permit the prescription and enforcement, amongst other matters, of safety standards, product recalls, adequate labeling of the contents of products, display of prices and unit pricing.

(b) Implementation Rules: As noted earlier, most of the so-called comprehensive laws are merely framework laws that call on the appropriate legislative or executive authority to provide for subsidiary laws. There has not been a sense of urgency in achieving this. An area of special concern is the specification of standards for the safety of the goods and services supplied to consumers. Decisions will have to be made to ban, restrict or specify the manner in which particular goods and services may be supplied. Consumer protection and other specialised agencies that have to determine standards have to agree on the approach to be adopted and the principles that will govern their tasks. A number of terms are currently in vogue to describe the guiding principles - paternalistic, cost-benefit analysis, risk analysis, hazard analysis, precautionary, bodies-in-the-street, and even consumer self protection. It is unclear whether consumerists and even consumer lawyers in the countries of Asia have begun to focus on the manner in which standards are set and the principles that govern standard setting.

Decision-makers should be guided in the approach they adopt and urged to improve the quality and transparency of their decisions. Much work in this area of defining the approach and refining the guiding principles is being undertaken at the Codex Alimentarius Commission. The decisions arrived at there will inevitably influence standard setting in Asian countries. It is critical that we are part of that discussion. A related matter of concern is that governments appear to have been influenced by industry to adopt the "consumer self-protection" approach. In effect, this is a dereliction of duty; a refusal to grant substantive rights that in particular adversely impacts vulnerable groups - children, the aged, the illiterate and the economically deprived. It is unfortunate that governments, thus, surrender the principal reason for their existence, the protection of its all its people and especially the weak amongst them.

(c) Enforcement: In many of the countries in which the framework laws have been enacted there has not been the concomitant enforcement to give the laws effect. Lack of capacity is not the only factor for this. Governments may actually have an undeclared policy of non-enforcement because of the insidious influence of industry or because it is assumed that industry would be stifled or would migrate taking in its wake valuable employment opportunities for the local population and potential foreign exchange earnings. There has been an apparent decline in the will to enforce especially since the recent Asian Economic Crisis. To this must be added the debilitating effect that corruption has on the will to enforce.

(d) Limited Avenue for Redress: There is a further concern that needs to be focused on. The new redress mechanisms appear to have not benefited those who do not have, or are unable to excess, redress mechanisms. Those who already enjoy a disproportionate share of rights and the state's resources appear to have hijacked them. Consumer activists and academic lawyers are best placed to assess the efficacy of the new mechanisms established and to propose the reforms necessary.

Conclusion

There are a number of basic consumer protection measures that are necessary to create consumer confidence, whether the marketplace is local or global; traditional or electronic, where all stakeholders need to play an important role. Much has been achieved over the years, and continues to be achieved in the development of consumer protection regimes in Asia. To a large extent these mirror the basic safeguards that are enshrined in the UN Charter of Consumer Rights, and also recognise specific needs within particular cultures. However, there is also a need to recognise that there is a cross-over between the formulation of consumer policy and social policy. The consumer problems that we as professionals discuss and attempt to address, are problems faced by individuals whose needs change in the course of their lives, or who cannot be considered within a broad and anonymous grouping of consumers. Moreover, their well being in terms of how they deal with the perils of the marketplace is a matter that policy makers need to consider in terms of curbing social unrest, not merely addressing a case of market failure.

2

Status and Position of Consumer Disputes Redressal Mechanism in India: Issues and Challenges

MC Paul

In India "consumerism" in terms of consumption of goods and services at a higher rate, is likely to dominate for a long time to come thanks to the 1991 economic reforms adopted in de-regulating and freeing the markets along with several agreements signed under the World Trade Organisation[1]. With the free-market globalisation process, personal relations between the buyer and the seller are very difficult to experience in the market now unlike in the past. This also ushers a transition from a predominantly "sellers market" to a "buyers market" syndrome with unbridled consumer culture promotion whether we like it or not[2]. Under this circumstance, the producers/sellers increasingly are becoming more organised, stronger, and highly profit-oriented, where the buyers feel weak since they are not yet organised to tackle many of the market injustices at different levels of market arena. Moreover, in the era of revolutionised information technology and emergence of e-commerce related innovations, the vulnerable consumers are prone to be further deprived of their rights to a great extent, due to increasing use of deceptive methods and hi-tech promotional tactics applied by the companies for selling products and/or resorting to unrestricted hype about their products and services through diverse advertisement methodologies. As a result very often unsuspecting buyers are misled, duped and deceived in the market as it becomes very difficult to discern the quality of the goods and services marketed by the business[3]. Moreover, the choice exercised by the consumers to buy product and services is increasingly influenced by the pricing policy including the media-based advertisement policy and product promotion, packaging, technology used, etc. Secondly, in the absence of appropriate consumer awareness as well as the pro-active consumer movements increasing number of consumers cannot even apply rational decision-making while buying product and services from the diverse markets. However, in this regard the role of regulatory authority with specific enforcement powers cannot be under estimated to offset the deceptive practices of pricing, promoting shoddy and unsafe products through misleading/deceptive advertisements, etc[4]. But things are yet to be settled at different levels of the Government, business and civil society for the benefit of the consumers.

As we know that the pro-active consumer movements and high-level of consumer awareness can play a critical role in empowering the consumers to protect them from the onslaughts and/or blatant violations of consumer rights in the market while doling out new consumerism culture which the global free-market nurture, practices and/or believes in offering variety of products and services some of which even at the cost of environment[5]. It is in this regard, it may not be out of place to mention what the Consumers International, an organisation that links, supports and represents consumer groups around the world said since every consumer has responsibility to use their power in the marketplace to "drive out abuses, encourage ethical practices and support sustainable consumption and production"[6]. This can help achieve good governance, evolve fair and effective markets and protect the environment. Therefore, informed, aware, active and concerned consumers can play vital role in paving the way and forcing the business to adopt better ethical practices while marketing their goods and services. Under this situation, though consumers cannot vote but their decisions about what to buy, when to buy and what not to buy can influence the business practices; because it is one of the ways of expressing their views on a range of consumer products as well as much desired global and ethical issues.

Since the era of liberalisation global business leaders are attracted to India as it has vast plethora of opportunities and magnitude of consumers in the world and is also the second fastest growing economy after China with an average GDP growth rate of 8-9 per cent plus for the last few years, and to tap this huge market potentials and consumers, a large number of national and international marketing companies are entering India in flocks to operate in financial, insurance and banking sectors, consumer goods and durables products and services including information and communication sectors, etc.[7] Most of these companies have grown fat in terms of profitability, sales revenue line and even market growth share.[8] But some of the relevant issues that have been bothering the consumers in India are:

Deceptive Practices of Marketing: Deceptive practices adopted by dubious business class which fall into three groups; pricing, promotion, and packaging of products and services;

High Prices: High prices without checks and balances by the Government make many companies to resort to profiteering and exploitation of the consumers. Often this is due to high cost of distribution; incurring high cost of advertisement by roping in celebrities from film world, sports, etc., including other costs related to promotion and excessive mark-ups;

High Cost of Distribution: Ultimately it is the consumers who have to pay for excessive advertisement and distribution costs; this includes also the costs, if there are too many, intermediaries, inefficiency and duplication of services;

Spurious and/or Unsafe Goods: Often goods and services offered to consumers lack the requisite quality standard and/or fail to perform than the promises made including the poor after-sale service;

Product Safety: This concerns the production of flawed products due to company indifference, increased product complexity, and poor quality control and assurance standard. Many companies are found to be producing poor quality products in the backdrop of rising consumerism in India. Many a time we find quality of same products vary from one market to the other particularly in markets of developing and developed societies.

Harmful and Low-benefit Products: Producing harmful products like baby milk-products, lead-based toys, tobacco-based *Gutka*, cigarettes, alcoholic drinks and genetically developed products are a concern just as promoting products that lack nutritional value like carbonated drinks, noodles, potato chips, chocolates and even junk food, fast food, etc.

Planned Obsolescence: Increasing competition makes some companies/producers follow a programme of planned obsolescence to have competitive edge over others; causing popular products to become obsolete before they actually should and thereby create a situation when replacement and/or repair become difficult or impossible in the absence of spare parts of the marketed model that were compulsorily made out-dated;

Poor Service to the Disadvantaged: It has been observed that the consumers particularly the illiterate and poorer sections and disadvantaged consumers often become the victims of poor products and services as due to their poorer purchasing power they also end up buying inferior goods/services at higher prices from retail outlets like in *Haats* and/or mobile vendors/ shopkeepers. In rural areas, spurious goods are often passed off as original by retailers as consumers, particularly the unaware and illiterate sections of society and other vulnerable ones who are neither aware of the product quality and/or service conditions. They often fall victims and are exploited like people belonging to backward classes, the poor elderly, ethnic and minorities, people living in periphery of the border or interior areas, hilly tracts far away from the mainstream society where rule of law hardly respected. They are being charged often higher prices, interests, premiums with suspecting quality, etc[9].

These are some of the instances, vividly describe how these work against the vulnerable and unsuspecting consumers in many parts of the country day in and day out without much remedy. As said, the choice exercised to buy goods and services by the consumers make them fall victims as they are usually influenced by the market strategies adopted by companies, producers, sellers, dealers and/or their intermediary agents. Thus, what is urgently required is the need to protect consumers legally from unbridled unethical practices by the free-market forces at different levels in our society. Increasing number of consumers are encountering several types of market violations of consumer rights in the era of global free-market consumerism culture promoted by them. However, it is to be noted that accepting consumer welfare as the responsibility, the Government of India had taken pro-active role in this regard and enacted in the Parliament the Consumer Protection Act, 1986, to ensure and protect consumer rights from various types of market injustices resorted and/or perpetrated by the market forces.[10] As per this Act, a separate Department of Consumer Affairs was created in the Central and State Governments to exclusively focus on protecting rights of consumers as enshrined in the Consumer Protection Act, 1986. This Act has been regarded as the most progressive, comprehensive and unique benevolent piece of legislation ever enacted by Indian Parliament exclusively for the consumers. In fact, the Act was described as one "which has set in motion a revolution in the fields of consumer rights, the parallel of which has not been seen anywhere else in the world."[11] But unfortunately, millions of Indian consumers are not aware of the clauses of this Act; and they are yet to be sufficiently made aware to reclaim their rightful consumer rights from the violators in the market.[12] As we have seen how in Indian market umpteen number of disgruntled marketers doing business without caring and/or violating consumer's rights day in and day out in high magnitude unlike in the developed market economies and societies.

Consumer Protection Act, 1986: The Consumer Protection Act rightly defines the consumer as one "who purchases goods and services for his/her use. The user of such goods and service with the permission of the buyer is also a consumer. However, a person is not a consumer if he purchases goods and services for resale purpose". The Act covers all "products and services".[13] The products are those which are manufactured or produced and sold to consumers through wholesalers and retailers. The services are of the nature of transport, telephones, electricity, constructions, banking, insurance, medical treatment, education, etc. The services also include those services provided by professionals such as doctors, engineers, architects, lawyers, etc.

The Act postulates establishment of Central Consumer Protection Council and the State Consumer Protection Councils for the purpose of spreading consumer awareness. Central Council is headed by minister-in-charge of the Consumer Affairs in the Central Government and in the State it is the Minister-in-charge of the Consumer Affairs in the State Government who heads the State Council. A separate Department of Consumer Affairs was also created in the Central and State Governments to exclusively focus on ensuring the rights of consumers as enshrined in the Act.

Amendments: The Act was amended in 1991 mainly to incorporate provisions for the quorum of District Forum, appointing persons to preside over State Commission/District Forum in case of absence of the President to enable the court function uninterruptedly. In 1993, the Act was again amended exhaustively to make it more effective and purposeful.

The Government has formulated comprehensive proposals for amending the Consumer Protection Act mainly based on the recommendations of the Working Group and Expert Group set up for the purpose and the wide-ranging consultations it had with the representatives of consumer interests, presidents of the national and state commissions and Central Government Ministries and Departments. These amendments are mainly aimed at facilitating quicker disposal of complaints, enhancing the capability of redressal agencies, strengthening them with more powers, streamlining the procedures and widening the scope of the Act to make it more effective to protect the consumers' interest.

The Consumer Protection (Amendment) Bill, 2001 introduced in the Rajya Sabha on 26th April, 2001 among other things addresses the issues of quicker disposal of complaints, widening the scope of the Act, strengthening the Consumer Courts, streamlining the procedure and a proposal to strengthen the consumer movement. It is also proposed to establish a Consumer Protection Council in every district in order to strengthen the consumer movement at the grassroots level. Enactment of the Amendment Bill will not only further strengthen the consumer movement in the country but also help the large number of consumers in securing speedy and effective redressal of their complaints.

This Act, as said, has been regarded as the most progressive, comprehensive and unique piece of legislation[14] but to protect and implement the Act are the government, the regulatory authorities for goods and services and the Consumer Fora especially set up to redress the grievances of consumers in areas highlighted above. Though there are consumer movements in many parts of the country but there are few who are pro-active in this regard to protect the consumers in comparison to the might of the well-organised trade, industry and service providers. The law-makers and those in charge of implementation of the laws and rules though powerful but often fail to perform on the ground that makes the scenario pathetic because rule of law sometimes fall victims and voluntary non-government consumer organisations also feel helpless under the circumstances.

Consumer Disputes Redressal Forums

Any way under tremendous pressure, particularly Common Cause, from NGO sector, the government has expeditiously set up quasi-judicial machinery under this Act at each District, State and National levels, namely, District Consumer Disputes Redressal Forums, State Consumer Disputes Redressal Commission and National Consumer Commission respectively with the hope that these set ups would deliver cheap, speedy and simple redressal to consumer disputes without going into much technicalities unlike the civil courts in the country. There are 627 District Forums (out of which eight are non-functional), 35 State Commissions at states and Union Territories and an apex body of National Consumer Disputes Redressal Commission (NCDRC) having its office at *Janpath Bhawan, A Wing, 5th Floor, Janpath*, New Delhi. The National Commission was constituted in 1988. It is headed by a sitting Retired Judge of Supreme Court and other members chosen by Government in consultation with its Chairperson. Similarly, the State Commission is headed by a sitting retired High Court Judge with at least three Members. Similarly, District Consumer Forum is headed by District Court Judge with at least three other members. As a rule, in all the above-mentioned tiers, one Member must be a woman.

The Disputes Redressal Mechanism: A written complaint, as amended by Consumer Protection (Amendment) Act, 2002, can be filed before the District Consumer Forum (value up to Rupees twenty lakhs), State Commission (value up to Rupees One crore), National Commission (value above Rupees One crore) in relation to a product or in respect of a service, but does not include rendering of any service free of cost or under a contract of personal service. Proceedings are summary in nature and endeavour is made to grant relief to the parties in the quickest possible time keeping in mind the spirit of the Act which provides for disposal of the cases within possible time schedule prescribed under the Act, preferable within 90-150 days. These Fora are supposed to discourage the presence of lawyers who usually believe more in technicalities than substance. If a consumer is not satisfied by the decision of the District Forum, she can challenge the same before the State Commission and against the order of the State Commission a consumer can come to the National Commission.

In order to attain the objects of the Consumer Protection Act, the National Commission has also been conferred with the powers of administrative control over all the State Commissions by calling for periodical reports regarding the institution, disposal and pendency of cases. National Commission is empowered to appropriate issue instructions regarding adoption of uniform procedure in the hearing of the matters; supply of prior service of copies of documents produced by one party to the opposite parties; speedy grant of copies of documents; and generally over-seeing the functioning of the State Commissions or the District Forums to ensure that the objects and purposes of the Act are best served without in any way interfering with their quasi-judicial freedom.

Where to File Consumer Complaint?

Before rushing to file a complaint, a consumer must know that s/he cannot file complaint in any or every consumer court. The Act has prescribed certain restrictions in this regard. The consumers can have their grievances redressed only in a court which has jurisdiction to try their complaints. Jurisdiction means the power of the court to hear the consumer grievance and determine a cause to adjudicate or exercise any judicial power in relation to it. Section 11 (2) of the Consumer Protection Act, 1986 (amended in 2002) deals with territorial jurisdiction of a District Forum and prescribes that a complaint shall be instituted in the District Forum within the local limits of whose jurisdiction the opposite party actually and voluntarily resides or has a branch office or personally works for gain or where the cause of action wholly or partly arises.

So consumers have to ascertain the exact forum where s/he can file a complaint and that is within whose jurisdiction the cause of action has arisen. Regarding the cause of action, the Supreme Court has laid down that the facts in dispute must arise within the jurisdiction of the relevant court. It is observed that "each and every fact pleaded by the respondent in the application does not *ipso facto* lead to the conclusion that those facts give rise to a cause of action within the court's territorial jurisdiction unless those facts pleaded are such which have a nexus or relevance with the list that is involved in the case."

Analysis of Registered Consumer Dispute Cases in India

The statistical data in Table-1 depicts that 67,764 complaints were registered since inception up to January 2011 with the National Commission out of which 87.29 per cent cases were disposed of, while 12.71 per cent were still pending with the National Commission.[15] Around 11.014 cases were registered with the National Commission during one year period between 2007 and 2008. In case of State Commission, 5,27,963 cases were registered since inception up to January 2011 and 80.48 per cent cases were disposed off. Around 79,265 cases were registered with State Commission during last one year period between 2007 and 2008. A staggering number of 29,29,466 cases were registered throughout the District Consumer Forums in the country and performance of District Consumer Forums was better as 91.45 per cent cases were disposed off. Significantly around 3,41,766 cases were registered with the District Consumer forums during 2007-2008 period. This indicates that consumer redressal system is now being slowly utilised at the district levels only in our country of billions of consumers, which is a positive sign of generated awareness to seek dispute redressal but still it is only a minuscule of our vast population. We also included graphical presentations at the end of the paper for better understanding of the reality of Consumer Fora. (See also the Appendices-IV to XI for better picture about the performance of the Consumer Justice system at District, State and National Level till 2011.

Table 2.1: Number of Cases Filed/Disposed in Consumer Fora of India since Inception

Period	*Cases Filed*	*Cases Disposed*	*Cases Pending*	*Percentage of Cases Disposed*	*Percentage of Cases Pending*
National Commission					
Up to 30.6.2004	34512	26370	8142	76.40	23.59
Up to 19.1.2006	40645	32911	7734	80.93	19.07
Up to 19.1.2007	45907	33743	8654	73.50	26.50
Up to 19.1.2008	56921	47304	9617	83.10	16.89
Upto 17.1.2011	67764	59151	8613	87.29	12.71
State Consumer Commission					
Up to 30.6.2004	319219	209890	109329	65.75	34.25
Up to 19.1.2006	378657	262986	115671	70.98	29.02
Up to 19.1.2007	386778	277636	109142	71.78	29.22
Up to 19.1.2008	466043	354863	111360	76.14	23.89
Upto 17.1.2011	527963	424895	103068	80.48	19.52
District Consumer Forum					
Up to 30.6.2004	1944692	1709563	235129	87.90	12.10
Up to 19.1.2006	2128712	1903521	225191	89.42	10.58
Up to 19.1.2007	2288814	2066372	222442	90.28	9.72
Up to 19.1.2008	2630580	2393708	236872	90.99	9.00
Upto 17.1.2011	2929466	2679051	250415	91.45	8.55

Sources: Annual Report 2008-09, Ministry of Consumer Affairs, Food and Public Distribution, Government of India; National Consumer Disputes Redressal Commission, 2011.

A State-wise analysis indicates (see Table 2.1) significant variations in the number of cases registered and per cent cases disposed by the State and District Consumer Forums. Although the magnitude of cases registered up to January 2008 was higher for Uttar Pradesh followed by Rajasthan, Maharashtra, Haryana and Delhi, but number of cases registered per "000" urban households was higher for Himachal Pradesh followed by Rajasthan, Haryana, Kerala, Delhi and Uttarakhand. Thus, it signifies consumer awareness is associated with civil society movement as in case with Rajasthan and literacy rates as in case with Kerala, Himachal Pradesh, Uttarakhand and Delhi. (Refer Table 2.1). An analysis of the data from the consumer courts in different States shows that there is a direct relationship between literacy and consumer awareness. Statistics relating to Kerala and

Bihar will justify this. The question to be considered is that there is a greater need of intervention by the Government to improve the position further through innovative multi-prone strategies including mass consumer movements keeping in view the our most heterogeneous, multi-lingual and multi-cultural population groups of country who are at different stages of socio-economic development parameters? Only "*Jago Grahak Jago*" slogan will have no meaning to them when the *Vyaparis* are not forced to follow the law and rules of the land. The Government has to take a pro-active role in enforcing the law, increasingly encourage consumer education and awareness, training and research including the upgradation of infrastructural and training needs of the consumer courts and its functionaries with adequate funding provision. However, it is not always easy to get adequate budget allocations for obvious reasons. The best way appears to be to work out methods by which the Central Consumer Welfare Fund is augmented with a similar fund set up at State level too. It is gratifying to note that some action has been initiated in this direction and hope the future of consumer rights protection will be better.

Table 2.2: No. of Cases Registered and Literacy Rate

States	*Registered Cases Per '000 Census HH*	*Registered Cases Per '000 Urban Census HH*	*Literacy Rate*
Andhra Pradesh	9.38	37.88	60
Assam	2.04	14.11	63
Bihar	4.44	46.97	47
Chandigarh	121.9	136.3	82
Chhattisgarh	5.61	29.51	64
Delhi	65.67	70.34	82
Goa	18.81	37.93	82
Gujarat	11.87	30.47	70
Haryana	43.1	141.5	68
Himachal Pradesh	34.94	302.94	76
Jammu and Kashmir	12.39	49.27	56

Jharkhand	0.82	3.77	54
Karnataka	9.43	27.11	66
Kerala	22.66	96.46	91
Madhya Pradesh	9.79	38.25	64
Maharashtra	9.25	21.85	77
Odisha	8.31	60.17	63
Punjab	23.16	66.31	70
Rajasthan	24.71	105.65	60
Tamil Nadu	5.63	13.63	73
Uttar Pradesh	15.76	78.52	56
Uttarakhand	17.36	70.61	72
West Bengal	3.73	12.89	68

Source: Census General Population Tables 2001.

The percentage of cases disposed off both by the State and District Consumer Forums also depicts regional variations. States with poor disposal system were North Eastern States, Assam, Haryana, Jharkhand, Uttar Pradesh at the State Commission level. However, performance of District Consumer Forums was better across the states except for Jharkhand. (Refer Table 2.3)

Table 2.3: Number of Cases Registered/ Disposed and Registered Per 1000 Urban Households

States	*Cases Registered in State Consumer Forum*	*Cases Registered in District Consumer Forum*	*No. of Cases Registered per '000 Urban HH in District Consumer Forum*	*Percentage of Cases Disposed of in State Consumer Forum*	*Percentage of Cases Disposed of in District Consumer Forum*
Andhra Pradesh	19382	158133	37.88	86	97
N-E States	500	5675	56.87	52	91
Assam	2070	10094	14.11	52	90
Bihar	11393	62127	46.97	66	83
Chandigarh	3569	24613	136.3	97	83

Chhattisgarh	3569	23297	29.51	87	90
Delhi	25532	167755	79.34	92	93
Goa	1790	5253	37.93	90	83
Gujarat	24178	114522	30.47	85	84
Haryana	31161	152147	141.5	57	88
Himachal Pradesh	4890	43355	302.94	87	93
Jammu and Kashmir	5020	19239	49.27	87	87
Jharkhand	607	4001	3.77	52	39
Karnataka	21278	96514	27.11	95	96
Kerala	20481	149511	96.46	80	94
Madhya Pradesh	24560	106915	38.25	90	93
Maharashtra	34988	176364	21.85	56	91
Odisha	15433	65423	60.17	55	94
Punjab	17551	98789	66.31	72	94
Rajasthan	35994	230916	105.65	78	94
Tamil Nadu	18200	80403	13.63	84	91
Uttar Pradesh	48129	406003	58.52	31	80
Uttarakhand	2630	27553	70.61	82	92
West Bengal	9693	58729	12.89	92	94
India	**386778**	**2288814**		**72**	**90**

Source: Annual Report 2007-08, Ministry of Consumer Affairs, Food and Public Distribution, Government of India.

However, the latest data compiled by NCDRC show that a total of 66,914 cases were registered since inception in National Commission till 12.11.2010 and out of these 58,341 cases have been disposed of and the rest 8573 cases are waiting to be adjudicated. So, the disposal rate stands at 87.19 per cent is slightly better than what it shows in Table 2.1. Whereas a total of 5,19,942 cases were filed in various State Commissions of the nation and out of these only 4,12,493 cases got adjudicated, and 1,07,449 cases are yet to be disposed of. Thus, the rate of disposal comes to about 79.33 per cent. In the case of District Forums a total of 28,94,173 cases were registered and out of which only 26,44,860 cases were disposed of and the rest 2,49,313 cases are yet to be adjudicated. The rate of disposal comes to about 91.39 per cent. If we calculated the total number of cases filed in all the three-tier consumer courts the total number of cases filed stands at 34,81,029 and out of these only 31,15,694 cases were adjudicated/ disposed of (the rate of disposal comes to about 89.50 per cent). The rest of 3,65,335 cases are yet to be disposed of. Thus, the overall percentage goes marginally up by 2.56 points from 83.41 per cent to about 86 per cent. By Indian standards and keeping in view several limitations like varying and poor pay structure/ honorarium, poor infrastructure, poor manpower and training, insufficient annual budgetary provision, etc., the scenario in regards to disposal of cases in consumer courts, unlike in civil courts, is no mean achievement, though marginal in overall improvement of disposal rates by all the three-tiers but it is more in regards to the National Commission and the State Commissions. In regards to the District Fora the scenario is not a happy one and a lot more needs to be endeavoured to improve the justice delivery at this level since it is where a majority *aam* consumers belonging to middle and lower level grievances/cases with lower compensation amount are usually filed for justice/redressal. But what is vital is that this scenario has to be improved further to keep the objective of delivery of justice within 90-150 days which is but a rare occurrence as cases are dragged on for years due to one reason or the other. Secondly, since these consumer courts deal exclusively with consumer issues unlike the civil courts the pro-active actions by the functionaries in regards to disposal of cases could be expedited. The time of disposal also can be shortened so as to generate hope among the consumer-victims who often had to go through long process and technicalities like filing several replies/affidavits, etc. This will definitely go a long way in passing a message to the violators of the consumer laws as well as generating the much-desired confidence among the justice-seekers in consumer courts. It must not be as frustrating like in civil/criminal courts. Unfortunately, it is an accepted and well-recognised fact that the process mainly being adopted from the day it is filed to the final adjudication by the functionaries of the Consumer Fora who man these consumer courts are selected invariably with civil court backgrounds. And they invariably fall back habitually on their past baggage of experiences of using/applying rules of civil court procedures. It is in this regard a a pro-consumer mindset is required to be brought at different levels urgently. This should start from the Ministry onwards like in Malaysia the Minister who takes special extra care and dynamism adopting transparent policies and procedures for the benefit and welfare of consumers.

India is growing at a faster pace in terms of higher GDP with heightened market activities but unfortunately pro-active policies of consumer rights protection issues have not yet been fully understood by the functionaries of consumer courts. There is a serious need to hammer into the heads of functionaries that consumer rights laws and procedures are different in many ways than the civil and criminal jurisprudence, it is very vital for them to know pro-consumer law better and practice the same for the benefit aggrieved consumers who go to consumer forums for prompt justice without considering technicalities as in civil/ criminal courts. Moreover, the existing personnel manning the consumer courts have to be given appropriate training and orientation. Many of them have to de-learn the past learning and re-learn afresh the benevolent pro-consumer laws so as to do justice as per the spirit of Consumer Protection Act. This will enable them to pro-actively apply and deliver pro-consumer justice or evolve a new set of cadre of professional dispenser of justice and functionaries who would be well-versed with benevolent consumer jurisprudence law. Thus delivering 'speedy, simple and inexpensive justice' becomes the norm without resorting to adjournments as envisaged in the Consumer Protection Act. Resulting in a more consumer-friendly manner where the consumer complaints can be adjudicated considering less the technicalities. This will generate tremendous confidence and hope among the ever-growing aggrieved consumers in this era of global free market scenarios.

However, it is very agonizing to note and also several studies do indicate that consumer rights or redressal awareness is limited to few urban pockets/areas of India only. This has been reflected by fewer number of cases registered every year in majority of the District Consumer Forums across the country in comparison to the population size of the districts. For example, there is a high need of opening of consumer courts in different parts of the country and also an urgent need of filling up of vacancies in large number of District Consumer Forums and the State Commissions expeditiously in order to dispose the increasing number of cases filed with the gradual awareness of consumer rights against the rampant violations of consumer rights in the market arena all over the country. Since one of the major objectives of these consumer redressal forums was to deliver simple, speedy and inexpensive justice to the consumers within a stipulated period of 90-150 days, a policy has to be seriously taken so that the vacancies are filled-in immediately with experienced pro-consumer persons so that the consumers are encouraged to approach the Fora and file cases for disputes redressal.

Unfortunately, the Government takes longer time to fill-in the vacancies in these courts. It is in this regard that we need to relook the whole gamut of evolving consumer issues and huge challenges the consumer face in the market. Moreover, since the consumer protection law is a new area so the special consumer jurisprudence laws are to be urgently introduced and incorporated in the course curriculum in the law colleges and universities to produce trained cadre of pro-consumer functionaries. These trained people well versed with consumer jurisprudence law can properly man and deal with increasing number of cases filed in the consumer courts because the violations of rights are becoming a menace in India. Unless we take pro-active actions and appropriate strategies at several levels, the fate of the aggrieved consumers can be easily imagined as they will have no other way to combat the organised business class who adopt several unethical business practices violating consumer rights in the absence of stringent checks by the government agencies due to one reason or the other.

Secondly, it becomes heart-breaking when the consumers are made to wait for long years and/or forced them to suffer inordinate delay in delivering judgment. Most of the consumer courts at different levels at District, States and national level failed to adjudicate cases within the stipulated time-frame of 90-150 days as envisaged in the Consumer Protection Act, 1986. In this scenario the consumers suffer from double-victim syndrome: once in the hands of market and again in the hands of court when the justice was not delivered speedily but delayed inordinately. It is a fact that cases are piling up in several District Consumer Fora and State Commissions in different parts of the country; backlog of cases are yet to be cleared within the stipulated time frame especially in those districts and/or states which have large consumers (Population Size). For example, the graphs and figures show that less than one-third of total cases, that is, only 31 per cent cases, registered with State Commission has been disposed off within the stipulated time period of 90-150 days and the rest have been dragged much beyond the stipulated time-frame. This scenario makes many aware and informed 'consumer-victims' fear to approach the consumer courts even if they want to file cases against the growing number of violators of their rights in the market. The data reveal significant state-wise variations which exist in disposing of consumer disputes cases within the stipulated time. Most poor performance was observed in the case of States of Bihar, Assam, Haryana and Kerala. However, states like Punjab, Chandigarh, Orissa and Rajasthan were better performers. (See Table 2.4)

Table 2.4: Selected State-wise Number of Cases Disposed in State Consumer Forum (within 90-150 days and after 150 days) in India 2000-2005

States	*Cases Registered/ Disposed*	*Cases Disposed within 90-150 days*	*Cases Adjourned or disposed after 90-150 days*	*Percentage Cases Disposed within 90-150 days*
Bihar	8181	1042	7139	12.73
Orissa	17186	7673	9513	44.64
Haryana	18282	3684	14598	20.15
Rajasthan	171241	68708	102533	40.10
Karnataka	82801	27570	55231	33.29
Andhra Pradesh	15843	5740	10103	36.23
Pondicherry	527	164	363	31.11
M.P.	40053	10908	29145	27.23
Punjab	15789	10545	5244	66.78

Uttaranchal	5131	2177	2954	42.42
Kerala	6106	1399	4707	22.91
Assam	9218	1260	7958	13.66
Goa	595	251	344	42.18
Chhattisgarh	2741	663	2078	24.18
U.P.	251666	65433	186233	25.99
West Bengal	52027	13800	38227	26.52
Chandigarh	6220	4235	1985	68.08
Delhi	837	135	837	9.78
Lakshadweep	45	21	24	46.66
India	**704489**	**225273**	**479216**	**31.97**

Source: Comptroller and Auditor General of India.

State-wise Funds Released for Consumer Forum Awareness

Funds released for Consumer Forums during 2007-08 have shown significant increase over the years, reflecting increasing attention given by the government for creating appropriate consumer awareness. But there are significant variations among the states in terms of grants released by the governments creating tremendous constraints in streamlining and strengthening the consumer rights protection activities in right earnest. However, the State of Gujarat has released significant amount for the Consumer Forums followed by Uttar Pradesh and West Bengal where, by and large, the consumer rights protection and awareness have taken an upswing. But majority of states still do not attach appropriate attention to consumer rights protection and awareness creation. Author's own study funded by the Ministry of Consumer Affairs also shows much is desired to be done in this regard. (Refer Fig. 2.1).

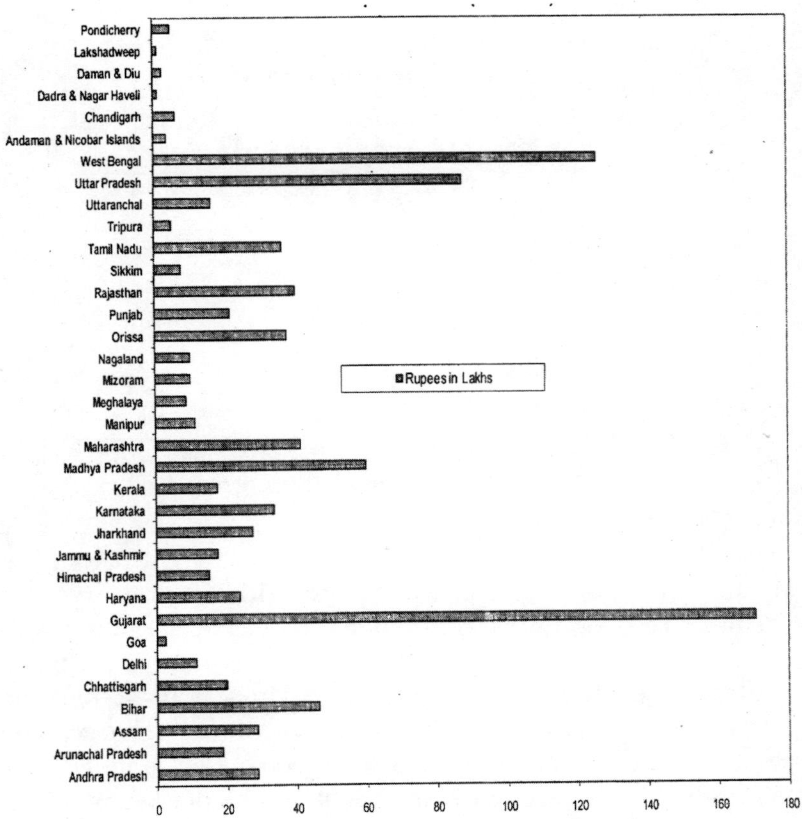

Fig. 2.1: State-wise Amount Released for Creating Consumer Awareness Rupees in Lakhs (2007-2008)

There is a Consumer Online Research and Empowerment (CORE) Centre set up in collaboration with Consumer Coordination Council (CCC) to provide the most scientific and effective system of collection and dissemination of consumer related information to generate consumer awareness and empowerment of all sections of the society.

A total of 20,919 complaints were registered through CORE during 2005-2006. The results indicate that government needs to change the focus of its consumer rights protection and awareness campaign as services, and not product related problems, are currently troubling the Indian consumers more. (See Table 2.5)

Table 2.5: Nature of Cases Registered in Consumer Online Research Empowerment Centres (CORE) 15th March 2005 to 31st December 2006

Nature of Cases	*Number*	*Percentage of Total Cases*
Products	4449	21.27
Services	6937	33.16
Banks	3815	18.24
Telecom	4829	23.08
Miscellaneous	889	4.25
All	20919	100

Source: Annual Report 2006-07, Ministry of Consumer Affairs, Food and Public Distribution, Government of India.

Considering the above challenges and increasing number of cases filed by the aggrieved consumers in different parts of the country in different Consumer Fora with different types of disputes related to different products and services as well as the serious concern for the long delay in redressing these cases in different courts, we need to take certain serious actions and strategies to protect and strengthen the consumer rights activities in a concerted manner. This is required to be attempted early since the violations of consumer rights in the market are on the rise. Moreover, high proportions of consumer disputes are also on the rise as there is paradigm shift in the exploitative behaviour of marketeers of various products and services whose only goal is to earn more and/or fast profit out of the deal at the cost of consumers. This trend is being seen of late by the increasing use of several types of ingenious and novel methods or strategies to exploit the vulnerable consumers in the market. Even the competitions in expanding sector of consumer goods and services like mobile telephony failed to check the exploitation of consumers and individual mobile telephone subscribers still at the receiving end.

Unless the business learns and/or makes a collective effort and endeavour to respect and protect consumer rights like in developed economies, the present scenario will give rise to more consumer dissatisfaction that may lead to more consumer disputes cases with the rising consumer awareness and rights movements in the country. It is against the backdrop keeping in view the various types of exploitative practices resorted to by the market forces as well as the increasing awareness of consumer rights and rising number of aggrieved consumers filing cases in different Consumer Fora for redressal, that there is an urgent need to strengthen consumer rights protection activities as well as to find immediate solution to make the functioning of Consumer Forums more consumer-friendly with appropriate strategies to deal with rising number of cases filed as well as to protect the consumers as per Consumer Protection Act, 1986.

It is in this context and to cope with the problems of 'pending justice' we may have to think of an alternative court-annexed justice delivery system namely, Alternative Dispute Redressal (ADR) Mediation system. It would be a complementary alternative system under the present circumstance to tackle the rising disputes and consumer rights violations in the market. This will not be an additional system but complimentary to the Consumer Disputes Redressal Fora, as a added arm to the existing consumer courts. The ADR system should be court-annexed. Otherwise the mighty 'exploiting marketers' will care less and/or not bother to listen to any consumer disputes brought to them. The ADR system will substantially reduce the burden of the Consumer Fora all over the country and thereby reduce the period of delay to a large extent in delivering the timely justice as prescribed in the CP Act to bring relief to the harassed consumers, rather than making it a parallel system with separate controlling authority and with separate budgetary provision, etc. There is another area where the government has a big role to play and this is in regard to vast majority of illiterate and poorer sections of people who often fall victim to exploitative market forces as they neither have adequate resources and purchasing power nor knowledge to protect their rights.

Millions of them do dream and/or aspire to enjoy the consumerism culture like the 'other better-off' sections but unfortunately they are caught in between devil and deep sea because they don't have the adequate purchasing power. By and large, they find it tough to manage their life and try to solve every day basic needs of *Roti, Kapda* and *Makan* within their means only. So whatever they buy in the market whether goods or services the quality or standard is always in accordance with their socio-economic standards only because their meager purchasing power cannot allow them to have anything best in quality whether it is related to goods or services. Thus, it is anybody's guess what they must be purchasing from thousands of small hawkers, vendors, neighbourhood *Kinara Shops, Bazaar* or Weekly *Haats/ Bazaars* where quality is in accordance of one's purchasing power. Thus, they become victims of low quality products and services. The businessmen will not compromise or forego their profit and thus they fix lower prices of their goods and services to attract the poor consumers. Often the dubious and disgruntled marketers resorted to unfair trade and unethical practices in order to earn fast bucks which are at the cost of poor illiterate consumers.

Daily experiences of poor consumers in the hands of many such local vendors, weekly neighbourhood *Haats /Bazaars* can be the eye opener. It is seen to be believed how the 'poor souls/ consumers, suffer the 'unjust deal' in terms of quality, pricing, weight and measures, etc. Moreover, most of them buy daily consumption goods in small quantities as per their economic capacity. The sample testing of quality of many such goods at road-side *Haats /Bazaars,* eateries and *Dhabas* and vendors or hawkers of goods sellers and/or service providers can gauge the actual reality. Thus, what is required is the stringent pro-active Government actions in terms of bringing standard and quality control mechanism to help the Indian consumers like in developed countries. We have enough laws but what is needed is the strict law enforcement system. It will only then quality products and services to Indian consumers particularly for the poorer sections of society can be ensured. Just the mere slogan through various channels of mass media, incurring billion Dollars: *Jago Grahak Jago* will not probably help much unless enforcement of law against the violators of consumer rights is earnestly taken. In fact, it may not be out of place here, to mention that for millions of poor and illiterates the much touted slogan and periodical advertisement *'Jago Grahak Jago'* can hardly have any value and/or meaning; and as such it has failed to make any difference to them. The author's own study has found out it has least impact. The policy-makers must activate the enforcement machineries with strict surveillance and control mechanism to check the rampant unfair/unethical trade practices and/or wrong dealings including many other violations and injustices to the unsuspecting consumers in the market.

Under the aegis of globalisation the market is becoming more complex and complicated with e-commerce, etc. This is also true for many unorganised sector markets. Moreover, it is a known fact that our Indian market is full of duplicate, spurious, fictitious, look-alike products with varying degrees of quality and quantity, etc. and the vulnerable and unsuspecting consumers are getting trapped daily to many ingenious methods adopted by many dubious businessmen. Unless these rampant violations of consumer rights are controlled or checked, millions of consumers including the unaware consumers belonging to lower sections of society will always fall victims to disgruntled marketeers of goods and services. Secondly, even if the consumer-victims want to take action or want to get justice they cannot easily do so. Millions of them are not even aware and/or don't know how and where they have to go to protect their consumer rights given to them through the benevolent Consumer Protection Act, 1986? What we suggest is that rather than spending billions of Rupees in slogan like *Jago Grahak Jago*, what the government must do seriously is to pass a strong message to the marketeers of goods and services to follow strong ethics of fair business practices as a part of mandatory duty and responsibility. Probably a slogan like this: *'Jago Vyapari Jago, Grahak Adhikar Ki Raksha Karo'*. This single slogan and act on the part of government can make a difference to the business when they know that they have to respect the consumer's rights as mandatory requirement and then only we can save millions of vulnerable consumers. The business class needs to be made aware about Gandhiji's saner words, whether they are manufacturers, producers and distributors of goods and services: "A customer is the most important visitor on our premises. He is not dependent on us. We are dependent on him. He is not an outsider on our business. He is part of it. We are not doing him a favour by serving him. He is doing us a favour by giving us an opportunity to do so". If enforced properly it can have a salutary effect on the business community. It is only then there is a possibility that the globalised free-market activities under economic reforms can become a boon to everyone irrespective of race, class, status otherwise free-market economy under economic reforms will be a curse for millions of consumers. Further, by just giving consumers the best consumer rights under the Consumer Protection Act cannot provide much help and solace because at best it is seen only as paper tiger without any tooth to bite in the light of several growing challenges of unfair trade and unethical practices by the unbridled free-market forces bleeding the consumers everywhere every day.

Conclusions and Recommendations

The Consumer Protection Act, 1986 has been regarded as the most progressive, comprehensive and unique piece of legislation. The choice exercised by the consumer will be influenced by the level of consumer rights awareness and Market Strategies adopted by sellers/manufacturers of goods and services. It is true to protect Consumers from the different challenges of consumer rights violations that the Government of India had promulgated Consumer Protection Act in 1986 whose aims are to ensure various types of rights under the Act. The stakeholders who have to protect and implement the Act are not only the government but also the voluntary non-government consumer organisations, the regulatory and enforcement authorities for goods and services in a competitive economy, the consumer courts, organisations representing trade, industry and service providers, the law-makers and those in charge of implementation of the laws and rules. A separate Department of Consumer Affairs was also created in the Central and State Governments to exclusively focus on ensuring the rights of consumers as enshrined in the Act. The Act postulates establishment of Central Consumer Protection Council and the State Consumer Protection Councils for the purpose of spreading consumer awareness. Central Council is headed by minister-in-charge of the Consumer Affairs in the Central Government and in the State it is the minister-in-charge of the Consumer Affairs in the State Government who heads the State Council.

The Act defines the consumer as one who purchases goods and services for his/her use. The user of such goods and service with the permission of the buyer is also a consumer. However, a person is not a consumer if he purchases goods and services for resale purpose. Hence, the Act covers "Products and Services". The products are those which are manufactured or produced and sold to consumers through wholesalers and retailers. The services are of the nature of transport, telephones, electricity, constructions, banking, insurance, medical treatment, education, etc. The services are, by and large includes those provided by professionals such as Doctors, Engineers, Architects, Lawyers, etc.

It is imperative that the government of India brings the Consumer Disputes Redressal Fora under the Concurrent List of the Constitution and take adequate measures including the amendment of the Act so as to make the provisions of the benevolent Act work on the ground and does not stand on the paper at the cost of the consumers. It is here that concerted actions and strategies can work wonders bringing enough confidence to the aggrieved consumers. Some of the recommendations highlighted here can help removing the bottlenecks in regards to improvement of the functions of these Fora. For example, since the violation of consumer rights are rampant and thereby the aggrieved consumer population is also increasing, opening of more Consumer Disputes Redressal Forums and strengthening the existing ones will be a great help. Secondly, selection of pro-consumer Presidents and members having adequate knowledge and understanding of consumer jurisprudence are a must, and those having inadequate knowledge and experience must be given appropriate training and orientation in this regard to help rejuvenate the revolutionary redressal system ever legislated for the welfare of the consumers in this country. The Presidents including functionaries of these quasi-judicial Fora must act as facilitators rather than as Judges and Court functionaries (but without robes technically). It will only then help generate adequate confidence among the ever growing consumer-victim population as we all are aware how the whipped up crass *consumerism culture* presented on a shinny platter in different garbs by the global free-market forces who have least respect for the consumer rights can only bring more pain than worldly pleasure the former seek to buy.

Moreover, most consumer forums do not generate a sense of confidence as they are mostly located in a hopeless shabby remote obscure corner of a dark room/building; at a far off distance place away from locality having no sign boards/signage to find them, crowded by lawyers who try to fish in troubled water with more reliance on technicalities as usual. This is particularly true by the lawyers of opposite parties standing and arguing against the consumer-complainants; and often the Presidents of the Fora do rely more on the lawyers than on consumers. The presence of lawyers do vitiate the atmosphere as they play more on technicalities to mislead the court proceedings, delay the matter with adjournment requests, etc. Unfortunately, the habitual reliance on lawyers by some of the consumer Fora functionaries having Civil Court background and mode of thinking is also seen to be believed. These scenarios highlighted above do generate a sense of anxiety and hesitation to the growing number of consumer-victims who daringly approach these forums for justice delivery. Moreover, these redressal forums need proper resources to spruce up with improved infrastructure along with adequate manpower, IT-support system and fitting budgetary provisions to perform its role. It is found that the existing functionaries are not given adequate salary/honorariums uniformly and the vacancies are not filled-in expeditiously; and due to this large pendency of cases has become the order of the day.

Finally, since the global free-market consumerism culture is heightened up there is a greater need for spreading consumer education and awareness programme strategies to empower the people to protect and strengthen consumer rights. It will be half-hearted approach if the Government's preoccupation is only to make people aware only through media slogans like *'Jago Grahak Jago'* without adequately spreading awareness education among the business class, under corporate social responsibility, to make them realise that since the backbone of every business is the consumer they are responsible to protect their rights enshrined in the Consumer Protection Act, 1986, If necessary the government must amend the Act to make them follow this code mandatorily. Unfortunately, the corporate social responsibility concept does not highlight this, the most fundamental responsibility that is the consumer rights protection. The term has been conceptualised narrowly as a part of charity and/or philanthropic activity only. It is in this regard that the definition of social responsibility has to be re-defined encompassing consumer right protection issues as fundamental duty to respect in its business charter. It will definitely help them stand in good stead in the global free-market era and bring harmony with the Consumer laws; and only then 21st century India shining can justifiably show the world to follow, as said, what the Father of the Nation, Mahatma Gandhi aptly envisioned: *"A customer is the most important visitor on our premises. He is not dependent on us. We are dependent on him. He is not an interruption in our work he is the purpose of it. We are not doing him a favour by serving him. He is doing us a favour by giving us an opportunity to serve him."* Let the business have some amount of self-respect, mould them to follow best ethical practices as a policy; it will definitely in turn protect and strengthen the consumer rights to take India to a new height. Similarly, the Ministry of Corporate Affairs along with other Ministries that produce goods and services both at the centre and the states has to do a lot of genuine heart-searching in this regard and support the cause of consumers in this global era of free-market scenario and become a role model.

References

1. K. Srinivasan, "A New Era in Consumerism", *The Hindu*, October 31, 1999.
2. Viswanathan, Gomathi, "Consumer Protection in India", http://ezinearticles.com/?Consumer-Protection-In-India&id=1092632. Lewis D. Eigen, A Solution to the Problem of Consumer Contracts that cannot be Understood by Consumers who sign them, Scriptamus, 2009.
4. B. Zutshi, "Consumer Redressal System in India" *Yojana,* Vol. 53, February 2009.
5. Pruthi, R.K. (2006), *NGO in the New Millennium,* Delhi, SAAD Publication.
6. Consumer International, http://www.consumersinternational.org/
7. Majumder, Amita, (1986), "Consumer Expenditure Pattern in India: A Comparison of the Almost Ideal Demand System and the Linear Expenditure System," *Sankhya: The Indian Journal of Statistics,* Series B, Vol. 48, No. 1 (Apr. 1986), pp. 115 -143.
8. Sheetal Kapoor, Legal and Ethical Aspects of Advertising, Seminar Presentation at J.N. University
9. Brinkmann, Johannes, (2004), "Looking at Consumer Behaviour in a Moral Perspective", *Journal of Business Ethics,* Vol. 51, No. 2, Promoting Business Ethics (May, 2004), pp. 129-141.

10. The Consumer Protection Act, 1986 (68 of 1986), 24th December; 1986.
11. Chanda, "Coming Together: Globalisation Means Reconnecting the Human Community", http://yaleglobal.yale.edu/about/essav.jsp
12. Abhilasa Kumari, " Media the Key Driver of Consumer-Macro-Micro Linkages and Policy Dimension. A Case Study of F.M. Radio", ISID Working Paper, 2008/06.
13. Annual Report, 2008-09, Ministry of Consumer Affairs, Food and Public Distribution.
14. K. Srinivasan, "A New Era in Consumerism", *The Hindu*, October 31, 1999.
15. National Consumer Disputes Redressal Commission, New Delhi, January, 2011.

3

Role of Consumer Disputes Redressal System: Issues, Challenges and Opportunities

Prem Lata

Consumer Forums

No one had ever thought or imagined that consumer forums constituted under the Consumer Protection Act shall work so effectively and will run like parallel judicial system to the civil courts in no time. Supreme Court through its landmark judgements brought number of big business houses under the jurisdiction of these forums for redressal of the grievances of consumers. The total scenario was further changed with elaborate amendments made in the Act in 1991, 1993 and 2002 in order to incorporate the new provisions brought through SC judgements during the course. In the first and second amendment itself, medical services, fixed deposit made with industrial financial units, construction companies, government and private insurance companies, telephone, electricity were considered service providers for the purpose of the term defined as service in the Act. Railways, airlines, hotels and restaurants, carrier companies, educational institutes-none was spared from the ambit of consumer forums for the dispute redressal. The credit goes to *Common Cause*, an NGO who filed writ petition before the Apex Court to implement the Act and constitute the forums.

Strengths and Scope of the Consumer Act and Forums

By now we find Consumer Forums equipped with salient features and its specialty is:

1. Court fee just nominal and inexpensive procedure.
2. Presence of advocates not compulsory, matter can be represented through consumer or his representative.
3. Summary procedure as stipulated under Section 13 of the Act provided and Civil Procedure Code or Criminal

Procedure not to be followed strictly. The Principle of Natural Justice kept top of the priority giving ample discretionary powers to the forums.

4. Consumer forum is considered an additional remedy available to him in spite having other Legal Law/Agency in force for redressal of his grievance. In other words, consumer has a choice to accept any remedy among the available choices.
5. Since this is a welfare act, consumer is compensated for the actual loss along with compensation for the mental agony one undergoes in the process. Cost of litigation is also awarded.
6. The orders so issued by these forums are judicial orders and non-compliance of the same are treated as an offence and these forums have first class magistrate's power to get them implemented through Cr.PC provisions. Money can be recovered through recovery procedure in the manner Government revenue is recovered, accused's property can be attached, can be sent to jail for maximum three years and can be fined up to Rs. 10,000/ or can be declared absconding also.
7. In order to avoid misuse of the process of law, Section 26 is incorporated to punish consumers also for filing frivolous complaints.

Apart from the above, Supreme Court explained the law by further widening the scope of Consumer Fora in 2002 in J.J. Murchant case, Supreme Court made it ample clear that Consumer Fora can take evidence, cross evidence through affidavits, can appoint local commissioner, etc. In yet another case of New India Insurance Co. Ltd. vs. Srinivasan decided in 2002 by the Supreme Court, it was held that Consumer Fora need not go into technicalities of CPC or Indian Evidence Act and Cora may go by the summary procedure laid down in the Act itself in Section 13. Had the legislature ever intended or meant to follow CPC, then there was no need to prescribe summery procedure or section thirteen in the Act. In the matter of Kalawati vs. United Vaishya Co-operative Thrift and Credit Societies Ltd case, societies were brought under the purview of Consumer Protection Act. The pleas were taken by co-operative societies referring to the clauses in their Act which bar the courts to interfere in their functioning and their grievance can be settled by the registrar of the society and by no court. Supreme Court rejected their argument stating consumer forums are not courts, hence not barred by their act.

Challenges and Constraints Faced by Fora

The obvious result was a lot of hue and cry over the authority of the forums among big business houses was made. Ever since the Act has come into force, on one hand, the Apex Court went on giving broader description and wider scope to the Act through its various pronouncements, at the same time it also faced numerous problems and several attacks on the authority of these forums from big business houses. Even the Act itself was challenged before the court of law and its legal validity was questioned when a big businessman was ordered to be sent to jail for non-compliance of its order. The questions were raised as to whether Lok Sabha is empowered to pass such an Act by which consumer forums run like parallel courts to/against the civil courts with much more discretionary powers. The matter was finally resolved by the Apex Court in a case of Vishwabharti House Building Co-operative Societies vs. Karnataka State and others decided in 2002 and the Supreme Court held that the Consumer Protection Act is a valid law passed by the Lok Sabha as per the Constitution; it was competent to pass such welfare Act. Further, the forums constituted under this Act are competent to perform their work assigned to them in all respects. These forums can also invoke the provisions of Section 27 of the Act for execution of their order. Consumer became a king after winning this case and of course, the consumer forums are working day in and day out for the consumers.

Laws Interpreted by the Apex Court on Issues Covered under the Consumer Protection Act: Landmark Judgements

There are situations where law is silent and facts of the case demand elaborated meaning to the particular clause. In such a situation many factors are taken into account, circumstances of the case and purpose of the legislature are read together keeping in view the fundamental principle of natural justice. It is a well settled jurisprudence that such interpretations when made by the higher judiciary, at times new dimensions are given under the given circumstances and facts on record. Hence, it will not be out of place to refer to certain such important judgements which made a history and which have become precedence for future cases of similar nature under the similar circumstances. The following cases related to specific areas may be highlighted.

On Housing

1. M.K. Gupta vs. Lucknow Development Authority Civil Appeal No. 6237/1990 Along With Other SLP's decided on 5 Nov. 1993 (SC).
2. Ghaziabad Development Authority vs. Balbir Singh and Others SC, 2004, [CTJ] Page 605.

Issues discussed: Late possession, No possession, Defective dwelling, Area found to be less, Cost escalation, Forfeiture of registration fee in case of cancellation of flat, Approach road dispute etc.

Law laid down: (1) Purchaser is a consumer against board/ construction company for services hired; (2) Erring officer can be penalised with the payment of compensation which is to be paid to the consumer; (3) Order for interest on the amount deposited should be on the basis of facts of the case and not always @ 18 per cent as ordered by National Commission; (4) If order for interest is given, there should not be any further order for compensation as both the things cannot go together; (5) In case where compensation for mental agony is given, there should not be any tax deduction at source as such compensation is not an income.

On Medical Profession

V. Shantha vs. *Indian Medical Association*, Civil Appeal No. 688/ 1993 With SLP (C) No. 6885/95 SC 1995.

Issue discussed: Whether a patient is consumer?

(1) Though Indian Medical Council Act has the provisions to control the medical practitioners and take disciplinary action against erring doctors, consumer courts are additional remedy to the consumer under Consumer Protection Act to get compensated.

(2) Though medical profession is different from other occupations, but commercialisation has already taken place when services are given by payment though it is still a noble profession based on faith and trust.

(3) Though medical profession is technical in nature but it cannot be said that the members of the forum are not capable to deal with such matters. They are equipped with expert opinions on the subject, medical literature and other reports; they are eminent people from the society, judges or retired judges. Three members can be expert of three subjects only and if it is expected of them to know every subject, it will be an impossible situation in all the courts.

When Doctors are Said to be Negligent?

When there is a damage to organ due to negligence, Wrong treatment due to wrong diagnosis; Money receipt or prescription or discharge summary or test reports when not provided; When treatment not chosen as per accepted and established medical norms/as per medical research/available medical literature.

Law laid Down

1. Theory of *res ipsa loquitur* [a thing speaks of itself]- in case any instrument left in the body, a wrong part removed, allopathic treatment given by a homeopathic doctor, etc. amounts to medical negligence.
2. Three steps that are necessary to be observed by the medical practitioners. These are:
   (a) To decide whether s/he has to take up the case or not;
   (b) If taken up the case, s/he is to decide what treatment is to be given; and
   (c) Whether the treatment given as per the diagnosis made.
3. Government Hospital is liable if,
   (a) Payment by insurance company is made; it amounts to payment made by the consumer;
   (b) Five methods available for treatment, one chosen, doctor not negligent;
   (c) Doctor not guarantor;

(d) Error of judgement is different from wrong diagnosis;

(e) Fee/consideration is of three types/categories:

(i) Government hospitals-contribution from the employee's salary deducted;

(ii) Private nursing homes; and

(iii) Charitable but charging from consumers.

Refer: Jacob Mathew Vs. State of Punjab, SC 2005

Law laid down: Act of negligence to be viewed as criminal negligence inviting criminal prosecution would have to be of a gross negligence and must fulfill two tests:

(a) Doctor did not possess the necessary skill required or if possessed the required skill, did not exercise with reasonable competence;

(b) The Act committed ought to be such that no medical professional in ordinary sense would have committed.

(c) Test of Medical negligence in criminal case and under Consumer Protection Act are to be judged on different parameter.

Meaning of commercial purpose/definition of consumer:

In Laxmi Engineering Works Vs. P.S.G. Industrial Institute, 1995 SC 1429

The Issues:

1. Consumer forums are not courts though it enjoys several powers of civil courts and take liberal meaning of consumer.
2. Meaning of commercial purpose defined under sec. 2[l] d of the C.P. Act depends on the facts and circumstances of the case as to purchased goods are for the purpose of using himself for livelihood and self employment or for doing business, selling, manufacturing or trading of the same.

On Education

Suresh Prasad Sinha Vs. Bihar School Examination Board, 2009 (SC) (CP), Page 1057.

Law laid down: Examination boards and universities being statutory bodies falls outside the purview of the Consumer

Protection Act. Board (examination board) is not a 'service provider' and a student who takes an examination is not a 'consumer' and consequently, complaint under the Act (Consumer Protection Act) will not be maintainable against the Board.

Buddhist Mission Dental College and Hospital vs. *Bhupesh Khurana and Others,* (SC) (CP) 373

Law laid down: Misrepresentation by the institute through advertisement giving an impression that the institute had its affiliation with Magadh University, Bodh Gaya and was recognised with Dental Council of India both found incorrect amounting to unfair trade practice and deficiency in service.

Areas Requiring Clarity by Further Amendments

It was considered a big achievement in the amended Act having provided first class magistrates' power to the redressal agencies for the purpose of execution of the orders issued by the Consumer Forums. In this connection, if we see Section Twenty Five of the Act which reads as here under 25[1] where an interim order made under this Act, is not complied with, the District Forums or the State Commissions or National Commission as the case may be, may order the property of the person not complying with such order, to be attached.

25[3]...Consumer Forums or State Commissions or National Commission as the case may be, may issue a certificate to the collector of the district and collector shall proceed to recover the amount in the same manner as arrears of the land.

There are two questions in both the above stated provisions. In Clause 25[1] provision of attachment is against Interim Order and not against final order. This Act awards compensation for the actual losses or for mental agony. Compensation can be decided only in the final order and there is never any interim order for compensation. Interim orders are generally given for restraining disconnection of electricity or telephone, payment of bills in part till final order, restraining any agency to do or omit some act but certainly forums are not passing interim order to seal the property of any business house, manufacturer, insurance company, construction agencies or doctors and clinics merely on the plea that there might be some compensation order against them at the end of proceedings before consumer protection agencies. Had there been some recovery proceedings permitted under the Act, there could have been some assessment of the dues and there could be some interim attachment order but this is not the case here. Yes there are cases against financing companies and agencies wherein amount deposited with them is not returned after maturity and consumer can seek remedy against them for attachment of property but in such cases either respondent approaches CLB or High Court before they make a default or respondent leaves the country without leaving any property behind. Looking into all the above discussion, the words Interim Order need to be replaced by All Orders as it is to be in order to give this provision a practical shape. As a matter of fact this provision has otherwise also very little force in the absence of proper enforcement machinery. More so, it is high time now to have a separate Department for Consumer Affairs with proper infrastructure required to implement this law.

Clause 25[3] talks of Certificate to the collector for recovery but what next after the Certificate is issued? Consumers are now told to contact the collector for recovery of their dues because there is no further provision as to what is the role of Consumer Forums /Commissions after that? Consumers are not at all willing to go to any other agency after they have obtained a long awaited order from the Forum. They are very unhappy if told the role of Consumer Fora is over. There should be a clear provision as to who is responsible for follow-up with revenue department and what should be the stipulated time limit?

Now coming to the other provision which comes in the way of execution of the orders, we find Section 24 of the Act very liberal for the judgement debtor. As per this clause, every order is final if appeal not preferred. That means if appeal is preferred, order cannot be said to be final, hence there cannot be any execution once appeal is preferred. Now JD just files appeal and comes to get stay against execution. Appeal is not admitted as yet, requisite bank guarantee is yet not given, there is no stay granted but consumer cannot get the order complied. Respondent buys time before Forum as well as before Commission stating appeal is preferred. They may not even have the intention to get the appeal admitted. In the mean time they grumble before the Forums for adjournment, if not given and asked to bring stay order, plea is very simple act does not say for stay. This Section needs to be amended by substituting the words appeal preferred with the words stay granted.

Shift in the Attitude of Supreme Court in Recent Cases

In the recent past, Supreme Court has reversed its gears. There is a clear shift in the attitude of Supreme Court which is very visible in the recent landmark judgements pronounced by this Honourable Court in the case of Martin D'Souza in medical negligence matters, making expert opinion compulsory before issuing notice to the doctors, in case of Bihar School Examination Board vs. Suresh Prasad Sinha keeping Examination Boards out of the purview of Consumer Courts in education matters, in case of *General Manager Telecom* vs. *M. Krishnan and others telecom* matters have been withdrawn from the jurisdiction of Consumer Fora.

Reasons for Delay in Disposal of Cases

During the last two-three years, the Ministry of Consumer Affairs has done a lot to make the consumers aware of their rights but at the same time there was a misconception in the minds of consumers that once they have filed the case, they will get relief on the first appearance itself and when it does not happen so, the consumer forums are blamed. The fact of the day is that the Consumer Forums are over burdened with cases not only due to consumer awareness but also due to some practices by the litigating parties during the proceedings which drag the cases and the disposal is delayed just because of small carelessness on the part of both the parties. Clerks of the advocates are managing the whole affair and at times not aware of the case, hence ask for date, reasons given, advocate attending at High Court or another District Court. Appearance by proxy counsel without having any knowledge of the case is another problem. It is observed, some advocates who are at learning stage and are often present in the forum, state while appearing as proxy, that they have got a phone call from such and such advocate requesting to appear on their behalf and interestingly such proxy is not aware of the correct stage of the case and even not aware for whom they have to appear. The result is obvious; proxy is not having file with him and asks for adjournment. The case is delayed by another two to three months. Though a cost is imposed but matter is delayed. At times defence is struck down but it follows another application to set aside the order and in the interest of justice it is heard. Adjournments in execution matters are requested when a plea appeal is being filed but neither they file appeal nor they produce stay order; and in between the situation, they try to bargain with the consumers to drop some of the claimed amount. Every time rejecting the request is not possible. In certain cases, parties insist to hear them at the stage of execution of the order and file applications against the order in spite of having no jurisdiction with the forums to review its own order. There are attempts to frustrate the consumers by delays, adjournments in execution application before the forums. There are yet other situations when expert opinion is required for making prima facie case before notice to medical practitioner, but most of the times, complete papers are not filed by the consumers, either they could not obtained from the treating hospital/doctor or they have misplaced. It is well-settled law by now that the consumer forums are not to follow CPC in strict sense but opposite party tries to file application after application, reply to the application is also expected and then it follows with arguments on the maintainability of the application. Though forums either accept or reject such application then and there, but have to face a lot of agitation, it is simply an attitude of the parties which causes avoidable delay.

Quick Disposal of Cases by Forums

It is going totally unnoticed and nowhere coming on record that the fora are disposing of number of cases on the first date itself when opposite party agrees to redress the grievance. On the basis of mutual consent, the case gets 'disposed of as settled within the parties' or 'withdrawn as settled'. This often happens when both the parties are keen to get the grievance redressed. There is a positive move by the manufacturers; their counsels are given instructions to settle the matter as they receive the notice. Often items are replaced without going into merits. Case against corporate bodies are generally dragged for longer period as no one in the organisation takes lead to settle the matter even if it falls in their interest as they have battery of advocates on their panel to fight out the cases. In some cases consumers are also misguided that they can be compensated with huge amounts and they even refuse to get their goods replaced in the initial stage.

Alternate Dispute Redressal System-Annexed to Court for Helping Redressal Speedily-Possible Ways and Means

There are suggestions extended that some persons having good reputation should be invited from the society to help the consumers in resolving the matters during the proceedings in the consumer forums. It is further suggested to make amendment in the Act by inserting clauses for arbitration in consumer matters so that alternate redressal mechanism can be developed in order to settle the disputes by taking lesser time as it is felt that Consumer Fora are yet not geared up to the tune to dispose off the cases within stipulated time of three months or five months in cases of testing, etc. With the same idea in the mind that the cases should be disposed off in a quick manner, there is also initiative to conduct *Lok Adalats* during the proceedings before The consumer forums, which means deviation from the provisions of Section Thirteen of the Act. For all practical purposes and from the past experience of setting up of family courts for reconciliation attempts and their failure thereof, we can foresee the fate of such attempts in the consumer cases also if tried within the proceedings already going on.

Now let us evaluate the idea in the light of suggested way of conducting *Lok Adalat* on the last working day in the forums by inviting a person of repute to the Fora to assist in arriving to the settlements. First question will be who will decide the person of repute. Even if the power is delegated to someone, what will be the status and strength of such person who is neither a member nor is coming through the provisions of the Act? More so, one Member of the Fora has already been taken a person of repute from the society. It will be just inviting more complications and problems for the Fora who are already over burdened with workload. Redressal process may further get delayed due to confusing status of such *Lok Adalat* which does not match with the provisions of Section 13 of the Consumer Protection Act in any manner. However, separate *Lok Adalat* under the *Lok Adalat* law is a welcome step and proving successful especially in electricity matters.

Regarding proposal to insert more clauses of Arbitration for consumer settlements it may be mentioned that Indian Arbitration and Conciliation Act does not bar consumer related cases to be dealt under that Act which is very much relevant for all types of cases. When a full-fledged Act is already there, suggestions for arbitration clauses to be added shall make it more complicated. In this context, we may refer to the Supreme Court cases on the subject when Apex Court had an occasion to criticise the practice of the commission in appointing arbitrators in pending disputes in Skypak Couriers Ltd. Vs. Tata Chemicals Ltd. 2002(SC) (CP) AIR 2000 SC 2008 and Neeraj Munjal and others Vs. Atul Grover 2005 CTJ 589 (SC) (CP) 2005 Arb. LR. 22 (SC). In Neeraj MunjaTs case the Apex Court on this particular issue of appointment of arbitrator during the proceedings under Consumer Protection Act, held that such appointment is not desired when consumer courts are competent enough to deal with even complicated cases through summary provision. Appointment of arbitrators defeats the purpose of the Act of speedy disposal. Court held as follows:

"Section 22 of the Consumer Protection Act provides that the Commission shall have the power of a court. These powers would include the powers to call for documents and take evidence either by itself or on Commission. However, the final adjudication has to be by the commission. For the purposes of this order, we will presume without laying down any law in this behalf, that Commission may even refer dispute to arbitration/conciliation. However, such reference to arbitrator could only be under the Provisions of Arbitration Act, 1940 or Arbitration and Conciliation Act, 1996. There is no provision in law and we consider it an unhealthy practice for courts/commissions/tribunals to abdicate their duties and functions and to delegate adjudication of disputes before them to third parties. The adjudication can only be by the concerned courts/Commissions/tribunals. For an effective adjudication, the Commission/court must address itself to the evidence, documents, respective case of the parties including submission on their behalf and then give a finding on that bases."

Now coming to the Consumer Protection Act and its provisions which empower the consumer forums to give relief to the consumers, Section 14 of the Act specifies as to what relief can be granted to the consumer after adjudicating the matter on merits:

(a) Cost for Actual Loss

(b) Damages/compensation for mental agony and harassment, etc.

In decided cases by the Apex Court, this has also been held that incidental expenses are not to be paid by way of relief under Section 14 of the Act. Certainly there is no provision of settlement under this section which specifically deals with the reliefs to be granted. More so, there are other provisions in the Act which speak, once the case has been admitted in the forum, the same cannot be transferred to other courts/tribunals or forums unless done so by Commission higher to it and are to be adjudicated by the forum. Under Section 13 of the Act, the Forum has to take preliminary hearing for admission of the case and look into various aspects and technicalities before admission.

Hence, no system is valid or bears strength if contrary to the provision of the existing law. However, settlement by the parties during the proceedings before the courts or outside the courts is always done and settlement is converted into the form of decree or order which becomes non-challengeable once the parties signed to their consent. But for this, no special provisions are to be made, they are being done as a routine matter for years together but since consumer forums are set up for adjudicating the matters, they cannot deny or deviate from their main function and adopt another one without having such provisions in the Act. Setting up of more consumer forums with the increasing cases is the first thing which can be thought of.

After all the discussion above, we feel the urgent need of setting up redressal mechanism for settling the grievances but it can be only outside the court and not within the court proceedings. The moment one enters into the court proceedings, one has to get legal authority by proper appointment under the law. Members or President of the Forums have no authority to delegate any powers to NGO's except for appointing local commissioner which they are otherwise also doing as and when required. There may be a separate institution for mainly and only consumer related cases set up under Arbitration and Conciliation Act, 1996 which can prove very effective and is really the need of the day.

Further, NGO's are yet to contribute and extend their direct help to the consumers for fighting the cases before the forums on consumers behalf as AR which is rarely being done. They could provide them drafting in order to encourage fighting their case on their own. Exchanging number of E-mails to the Customer Care Centers set up by the manufacturers or service providers are proving to be further harassing even when helped by NGOs as the latter also do not possess any legal authority to haul them up for their non-committal attitude. Ultimately cases are coming for redressal with huge bunch of stories in their E-mails to consumer forums for redressal of their grievance. Further, consumers are given an impression that these courts are to compensate them heavily. Once they read in the paper two lakhs or three lakhs awarded in compensation, they hardly understand that it could be the actual loss of the consumer and without knowing the fact of the case, they demand for compensation in lakhs for defective washing machine worth Rs. 10,000 and for defective stitching of a cloth by tailor. It is the NGOs who have to guide the consumer properly that these courts are not meant only to award them huge compensation for petty things. It is high time that NGOs play their vital role in explaining the law and procedure by way of educating and extending practical help, accompany them to the forums, checking their pleadings and explaining the real purpose of law. At this juncture, consumers seems to be aware of the fact that consumer forums are there for invoking their right as consumer but correctness and clarity of concept is lacking and this is being observed at the level of District Consumer Forums.

4

Analysis of Consumer Dispute Redressal System in three States of India

Patrick Von Braunmuehl

Background

The process of development along with the expanding globalisation and liberalisation process has increased the number of consumer related challenges. Consumer protection has earned an important place in the political, economic and social agendas of many nations. In India, the Government has taken many steps including legislative, to protect consumers. The Consumer Protection Act of 1986 has created a unique three-tier redressal system with dedicated consumer courts at the district level and Dispute Redressal Commissions at the state and national level. But consumers are often ignorant of their rights and their collective power as the demand side of the market. They need to be empowered and motivated to exercise their rights.

Study on Consumer Dispute Redressal System in Three States

The present study was undertaken to analyse how the consumer disputes redressal system functions in the three States, Rajasthan, Gujarat and Andhra Pradesh. The study was carried out by Heike Hummelmeier (Germany) and Bharat Jairaj (India) in March 2008.

Consumer Courts (District Fora) in Jaipur, Alwar, Ajmer and Bharathpur in the State of Rajasthan; Vadodara (city and rural area), Ahmedabad (city and rural area), in the State of Gujarat; and six District Fora in Andhra Pradesh (3-Hyderabad, 2- Krishna and 1-Guntur) were visited to know about their status and position in terms of their functioning, etc. Visits to State Consumer Disputes Redressal Commissions in Jaipur and Ahmedabad gave closer insights into the problems of the Redressal system and into possible solutions. Unlike other States, there is relatively less backlog of cases, since Andhra Pradesh has relatively low filing of complaints before District Forums. For instance, the District Forum at Machilipatnam (Krishna District Forum (I)) reports an annual filing of about 80 complaints only. There are some voluntary consumer organisations in Andhra Pradesh, but barring one or two (in particular Consumer Guidance Society, Vijaywada) none file complaints before the District Forums on behalf of consumers. The work procedure, differences and gaps of the consumer Fora were analysed through attendance of court hearings, interviews with members of the courts, members of the staff, lawyers and consumers as well as through hearing expert opinions from consumer and business organisations. To find out whether Alternative methods of Dispute Resolution (ADR) could relieve the pressure on the Fora by taking care of consumer complaints in pre-litigation-state, organisations were visited which already handle consumer complaints by using ADR or could be able to do so. The following is a summary of the study's findings:

Consumer Protection Act, 1986

The Consumer Protection Act (CPA), which was put in effect in 1986 in order to offer better protection of the interests of the consumer, seeks to provide speedy and simple redressal to consumer disputes. The Consumer Protection Act (CPA), which was put in effect in 1986 in order to offer better protection of the interests of the consumer, seeks to provide speedy and simple redressal to consumer disputes. On district, state and national level, quasi-judicial bodies (Consumer Fora, state commission, and national commission) are empowered to give quick release to consumer grievances. The CPA puts an emphasis on the quick disposal of cases and easy access to justice, by stating specified rules for the procedure at the Fora in Section 13 of the Act: The complaint can be filed by the consumer himself. The Fora are obliged to refer a copy of the complaint within twenty-one days from the date of its admission to the opponent, who has to respond within thirty to forty-five days. Every complaint shall be heard as expeditiously as possible and be decided within a 3-months time frame (5 months if analysis is required)[1]. Adjournments should only be granted in exceptional cases. Reasons for the grant have to be put in writing by the forum. The costs of the adjournments shall be burdened upon the party.[2] Interim orders can be issued if necessary. A Consumer Forum is expected to dispose of at least 75 to 100 matters every month.

Challenges for the Implementation of CPA

Analysis of the existing system of consumer redressal showed a number of gaps. The procedure at the courts was slow and complicated according to the persons interviewed. The objective of the Consumer Protection Act is not always met. In very few courts the number of disposals mentioned in the Consumer Protection Act was fulfilled. In a majority of cases the predetermined 90-days time frame stated in the Consumer Protection Act was not met. Quite to the contrary, in all of the courts the procedure from filing the complaint to decision usually took at least one year, sometimes two years and in most of the courts, complaints from 2005 and before is still pending, in some courts, even pendency of cases from 1992 is existent.

It was discovered that the lawyers who represent the parties usually do not make their statements in the given time. They were either unable to do so because of the amount of cases they had taken or they were unwilling to do so due to the fact that quite regularly they get fees for every action they take—even for filing for adjournment. Therefore more often than not the cases are not decided before 30-40 adjournments; at some courts even 70 adjournments had taken place.

Fig. 1: Issues Identified in the District Fora in Rajasthan and Gujarat.

Results

The results showed that, by and large, the entire situation was not satisfying. Although most of the respondents stated that the implementation of the Consumer Fora in the year 1986, has been a great achievement to consumer rights. Consumer complaints could be handled in large numbers since inception under Consumer Protection Act (Table 4.1). However, the study showed that in very few courts the number of disposals mentioned in the Consumer Protection Act is fulfilled. In a majority of cases the predetermined 90 days time frame stated in the Consumer Protection Act is not met. It has been observed that in all of the courts the procedure from filing the complaint to decision usually takes at least one year, sometimes two years. The study showed that in most of the courts, complaints from 2005 and before are still pending, in some courts; even pendency of cases from 1992 is existent.

Table 4.1: Overview of Consumer Complaints since Commencement

Name of Agency	*Cases Filed Since Inception*	*Cases Disposed of Since Inception*	*Cases Pending*	*Percentage of Total Disposal*
National Commission	50656	41576	9080	82.08
State Commision	423160	312044	11116	73.74
District Forum	2450439	2221795	228644	90.67
Total	**2924255**	**2575415**	**348840**	**88.07**

It has been noted that the percentage of consumers who go to court without lawyers is very small; in some of the courts no consumer at all files a complaint without legal assistance by a lawyer. Especially in the rural areas, consumers have to travel long distances, up to 100 km—to come to their court. The Consumer Fora mostly followed more or less the same procedure and suffered under the same problems. There were differences, though the influence of the better organised and stronger consumer organisations in Gujarat was significant. In Rajasthan almost no consumer who files a complaint was represented by a consumer organisation. In Gujarat up to 20 per cent of the cases pending were handled by consumer organisations. In Rajasthan, none of the courts could report about class actions that had been filed by consumer organisations, while a certain number of class actions in Gujarat could be perceived. Andhra Pradesh District Forums have a high majority of representation by lawyers (85-90 per cent). All the Forums visited had lawyers appearing for consumers and opposite parties in virtually all the cases.

However, most of the Fora complained about vacancies at their court and it was significant that in almost all court visited, vacancies were noted (Table 4.2).

Table 4.2: Vacancies in the State Commissions and District Fora[3]

State	*State Commission*		*District Forum*	
	President	*Member*	*President*	*Member*
National Commission	0	1	-	-
Gujarat	0	3	4	14
Rajasthan	0	0	4	25

It has been observed that the influence of the better organised and stronger consumer organisations in Gujarat is significant as compared to Rajasthan. In Rajasthan, almost no consumer who files a complaint is represented by a consumer organisation. In Gujarat, up to 20 per cent of the cases pending are handled by consumer organisations. There is a high rate of disposals in Andhra Pradesh (97 per cent) which is also related to the low filings in the State. The average number of cases filed before District Forums in Andhra Pradesh is about 16-17 cases per month, which is rather low. The following Table 4.3 gives a first impression of the differences and gaps of the District Fora in Rajasthan and Gujarat.

The biggest complaint is one of inordinate delays in Rajasthan and Gujarat. These delays are primarily due to delays in appointments to the District Forums and due to adjournments granted to lawyers. It was observed that Andhra Pradesh District Forums do not suffer on account of excessive delays. Despite

Table 4.3: Facts and Figures Collected by District Fora in Rajasthan and Gujarat

City	*Number of Adjournments*	*Number of Hearings*	*Longest Travelling Distance*	*Decision Without President*	*Oldest Cases Pending*	*In-court Settlement per cent*	*Filling Per Mail*	*Interim Orders*	*Cases Disposed of Per Month*	*Fee*
Ahmedabad (rural)	10–15	N.A.	10 km	yes	2004	10–15	yes	N.A.	50–60	Bank order
Ahmedabad (city)	N.A.	N.A.	N.A.	N.A.	2005	N.A.	yes	yes	N.A.	Bank order
Ajmer	30–40	N.A.	100 km	no	2004	N.A.	No	No	139	Bank or postal
Alwar	N.A.	8-10	50 km	yes	N.A.	1	N.A.	N.A.	60	Postal order
Bharathpur	10–20	2-3	40 km	no	2004	1	N.A.	N.A.	60	Postal order
Jaipur	N.A.	2-4	N.A.	no	N.A.	10–15	N.A.	no	80	Postal bank
Baroda	N.A.	2-3	100 km	yes	1992	10–20		no	100	

complaints of occasional delays in appointments of President and/or Members, and request for adjournments, etc., there is high rate of disposal of cases (97 per cent) in the State.

Andhra Pradesh District Forums have a high majority of representation by lawyers (85-90 per cent). All the Forums visited had lawyers appearing for consumers and opposite parties in virtually all the cases. Adjournment of hearings is also a common practice at the District Forums in Andhra Pradesh.

In Gujarat up to 20 per cent of the cases pending are handled by consumer organisations. Consumer organisations in Gujarat try to cover rural areas as well, while in the rural areas of Rajasthan the impression was given that no NGOs at all exist or at least that they don't work efficiently. Subsequently in Rajasthan none of the courts could report about class actions that have been filed by consumer organisations, while a certain number of class actions in Gujarat can be perceived. There are some voluntary consumer organisations in Andhra Pradesh, but barring one or two (in particular Consumer Guidance Society, Vijaywada) none file complaints before the District Forums on behalf of consumers.

Andhra Pradesh has already introduced a pre-litigation Alternate Consumer Disputes Redressal Cell in the office of the Civil Supplies and Consumer Protection department in Hyderabad. Though the number of complaints filed is low (15-20 per month) consumers bring their complaints to this Cell rather than file it before the District Forums, because of the informal procedure and relative speed of the handling of complaints. Some complaints can get resolved within two weeks, while others may take up to two months. The time period is clearly much less than the District Forum.

Conclusion and Recommendation

Most of the members and judges claim an inadequate infrastructure to be a cause for pendency in the Consumer Fora.[4] Indeed, in those Fora where additional benches have been implemented, pendency is decreasing. But adding benches is not the only way to reduce the pressure and will not resolve the problems that lie within the procedure itself. Instead of looking for remedy from outside, there are other ways to speed up procedures at the Consumer Fora and thus to get cases resolved more quickly and make procedure more consumer friendly. From first insight, there are two approaches:

1. Find ways to speed up the procedures themselves;
2. Find ways to reduce the pressure put upon the forums by reducing the number of cases, finding more efficient ways of dispute resolution.

Possible Improvements of Court Procedures

The courts should be encouraged to implement the regulations of the CPA. The Fora should be obliged to provide data on the number of adjournments given and on the amount of fees granted to evaluate the handling of this aspect of the procedure. Making unnecessary adjournments and forcing unnecessary hearings should be made unattractive for the Lawyers. To ensure this, a compound fee fixed by the Government should be charged depending upon the declared value of the complaint: The contribution of the members could be improved by appointing members with knowledge in the areas of consumer complaints - Banking, electricity, insurance, telecom, educational services. The presidency of retired judges at the Consumer Fora could be reconsidered. Instead of retired judges, young people with a judicial background, who are on the very steps of their career and eager to earn merits by handling cases quickly and in big numbers.

Appeals should be restricted to cases with high amounts at stake and cases that touch difficult judicial questions which need to be decided on a higher level of jurisdiction. The fees for going to appeal should be increased for the manufactures. This will discourage manufactures from unnecessary appeals.

Rolling Fora could be introduced to improve access to justice especially in rural areas and offer their services as non-permanent Consumer Fora on specific dates. The fee for the district forum is very low, but it poses the problem for the consumers that they are not allowed to pay in cash. Abolishing fees completely or giving the possibility of paying in cash would make the access to the forum easier. The courts should be obliged to give proper consumer guidance on how to file a complaint. Court decisions could be made available on the internet.

Adjournments/Rolling Fora

All interviewees—except for lawyers - identified the number of adjournments as the most significant problem to the swift disposal of cases. Unanimously presidents and members of courts as well as Consumer Advice Organisations and FICCI blame this to the involvement of lawyers in the process, either because they are not able to handle the cases or because they want to prolong the process to receive more money.

(a) One solution could be to bar lawyers from the procedure at Consumer Fora. According to the Consumer Protection Act, lawyers are not needed in the process, amendments to restrain lawyers from court completely or to let lawyers into the process only in those cases where the forum advises the consumer to get a lawyer, could be made. Advocates can only be excluded if the system allows consumers to go through the court procedure alone. Consumers can stand for their own rights only if they don't have to travel long distances to court - especially not several times. To make the access to court for the consumer from rural areas possible (and to ease access to court for the urban population) written procedure could be installed, guided by forms. These should be made available by consumer organisations, legal aid centres and local governments like the *panchayats* as well as on internet. The filing of complaints via mail, Fax and maybe even e-mail should be considered. The hearings should be completely given up or be reduced to very rare outstanding cases or depend on the value of the complaint. A small-claims procedure based on written statements should be considered. Definitely not more than one hearing should take place. Admission hearings should be completely banned. The implementation of evening courts could be another step to easier access to Consumer Fora. Consumers who work during daytime could attend court hearings without having to take a day off at work.

(b) On the other hand, all members and presidents stated that advocates help the Forum to find an appropriate decision. Especially in cases which need a judicial decision, the interaction between advocates and judges is considered as helpful. Instead of shutting out the advocates completely, there are other possibilities to quicken the court procedure:

Making unnecessary adjournments and forcing unnecessary hearings should be made unattractive for the lawyers. To ensure this, the fee for Consumer Fora shouldn't be on free negotiation between lawyer and consumer. As in other countries the fee should be fixed by government. This should be a compound fee, covering the whole procedure from filing the complaint to decision. The amount of the fee should depend on the declared value of the complaint. Thus, lawyers will be interested in a swift resolution and stop undertaking unnecessary actions.

(c) Furthermore the courts should be encouraged to implement the regulations of the CPA. Notice should be given to the Fora and bar associations that the provisions in the act from a certain date on will be carried out strictly and that lawyers cannot count on the granting of adjournment's anymore and that the fees will be put upon those who file for adjournment. Additionally, Fora should be obliged to provide data on the number of adjournments given and on the amount of fees granted to evaluate the handling of this aspect of the procedure.

Appeals

A good number of the cases at district level are of small value. Still a majority of up to 80 per cent of the decisions issued by district forum go to appeal, which leads to furthermore delays. According to section 15 CPA, the appeal can be filed by any person aggrieved by an order made by the District Forum within a given time. No further restrictions either to the value or the legal importance of the case are made. These possibilities should be restricted—it is international standard that the stages of appeal are limited to the importance and/or a certain value of the complaint. It doesn't make sense to fight through four levels of jurisdiction if the value of the complaint is insignificant. There may be some cases that touch judicial questions which need to be decided on a higher level of jurisdiction. These cases could be admitted to appeal by decision of the district forum and these cases could also be subject to class action as provided under section 12C CPA. The fee for going to appeal should be increased for the manufacturers: So far, they have to pay 25,000 rupees or 50 per cent of the amount the other party is entitled to by court order whichever is less. This money is placed in deposit. By increasing this amount of money and letting the manufacturers put all of the money they are ordered to pay in deposit (if constitutional problems prohibit this: 75 per cent of the amount), enforcement of orders will be ensured, once the matter is decided upon for good, and it will discourage manufacturers from unnecessary appeals.

The Bench

(a) It should be clarified, that the decision is possible without the president. Although this is stated under Section 22D of the Consumer Protection Act, quite often courts don't work if the president is not in the house. This might be related to the low motivational level of the members. To enhance it, appropriate payment should be granted or at least a certain gratification should be given for each case a member decides.

(b) Since most of the Fora complained about the amount of vacancies, mechanisms should be found to find interested and competent members easily. Many of the cases do not touch judicial questions but deal with certain aspects of Indian economy. By choosing members who have specified knowledge of the main fields of consumer complaints could be a way to make decisions easier and better. A panel of interested and well informed members should be put up so that in case of vacancies the new member can be appointed quickly. These could be named by the chambers of commerce. The contribution of the members could be improved by appointing members with knowledge in the areas of consumer complaints: Banking, electricity, insurance, telecom, educational services.

(c) Computer training for staff and members should be made widely available, so they can use what they have at their hands. In the long run, even a computer based written procedure could be made available that way. This is already standard in European countries. Computer training will enable the staff to give specified statistics as well; this is one of the best ways to find out where and why problems are delaying court procedure.

(d) The presidency of retired judges at the Consumer Fora should be reconsidered. The consumer protection act is meant to be a summary trial, leading to quick results and not as an additional civil court procedure. The retired judges are familiar with court procedure for all of their "legal life"—this is what they know and this is how they have handled all their cases during a considerable time. Thus, they are prone to apply their experiences from the civil court to the procedure of the Fora. A majority of the presidents who were interviewed left the impression that they are not eager to ease the approach of consumers to the Fora or to abandon certain parts of the civil procedure they know. Instead of retired judges, it might be possible to give the presidencies to young people with a judicial background, who are on the very first steps of their career and eager to earn merits by handling cases quickly and in big numbers.

Amendments to Court Regulations/Organisations

(a) The District Fora should be able to set aside their own ex-party decisions. At present, these decisions are only set aside by the appeal court, which produces unnecessary appeals. In those cases, in which a party was prevented to come to court due to calamities like illness, accidents etc., or can claim that notice of the complaint didn't reach the party, the district forum itself should be entitled to lift the ex-party decision.

(b) The fee for the District Forum is very low, but it poses one more problem for the consumer: In none of the Fora they are allowed to pay in cash. Before finding their way to the Fora, they have to undertake one more action - either going to bank for the bank deposit or to the post office for getting a postal order. Abolishing the fee completely or giving the possibility of paying it in cash (by selling out stamps which have to be put on the complaint) would make the access to the forum easier.

(c) The courts should be obliged to give the consumer guidance on how to file a complaint: It should be obligatory that the posters given out by the ministry were hung up in front of the Consumer Fora. Signs should be put up in the Fora to help consumers find their way within court; in front of the courts signboards should clearly indicate where a consumer has to go to file his complaint.

(d) The decisions of the Consumer Fora should be made available on the internet.

Out of Court Solution: Alternative Dispute Resolution (ADR)

Another - and very important way to reduce pressure on Consumer Fora could be the possibility of resolving the dispute between consumer and producer before they go to the Fora. If there were a manner or mechanism to settle matters at a pre-trial stage many matters wouldn't find their way to court. By using alternative dispute resolution techniques like meditation and conciliation and even arbitration, some of the cases could be kept away from courts. This has a tradition in India already[5], as the mediating process at *panchayats* shows (which doesn't deal with consumer affairs though). This tradition is even put in a legal frame by the Arbitration and Conciliation Act of 1996 and put in effect in two civil courts performing in court- mediation in Delhi and as operating experience in other countries shows that ADR offers the parties a way of finding the solution themselves instead of being imposed upon them by an authority, so the contentedness with the outcome is higher[6]. The experiences from other countries show that a large number of cases (up to 60 per cent) can be solved through ADR that can lead to a significant reduction of court cases.

Especially, the introduction of mediation could be a possible approach to speed up procedures at the consumer Fora and to get cases resolved more quickly. GTZ and FICCI have made a joint proposal for the establishment of six court-annexed mediation centers in different States on a pilot basis.

There are several institutions that volunteer the opportunity to find a settlement between consumer and manufacturer: VCOs/ NGOs as well as government organisations offer help on different levels of the dispute and in different ways: Organisations like the National Consumer Helpline give pan-Indian guidance via telephone consultancy without offering help in any written procedure; NGOs like CERC (Consumer education and research centre), VOICE (Voluntary Organisation in Interest of Consumer Education) help or used to help (CUTS - Centre for Consumer Action, Research and Training) the consumer to enforce his rights in written procedure—up to accompanying him to court. Some even file the complaint in his name. Governmental authorities as well offer systems to resolve consumer grievances.

The Department of Consumer Affairs in Gujarat for instance helps consumers to find settlements by forwarding the complaints to the manufacturer. Some of the consumer organisations deal with very large numbers of complaints: VOICE, for example, receives 4000–5000 complaints per year, the Gujarati-Iocated organisation CERC handles up to 100 complaints at the Fora per year and the national consumer helpline deals with about 50,000 calls per annum. Governmental Authorities act on a significantly smaller scale, but still handle several hundred complaints annually. Even mediating panels are available and they report about settlement rates of up to 90 per cent. At FICCI in Delhi, mediation in business-to-business matters is performed in a professional way and with success. In the local *panchayats*, mediation in consumer-to-consumer matters is practiced and they report that "almost always" the parties can come to terms.

The existing mechanisms of mediation, consumer advice and consumer guidance suffer from (mainly) two facts:

(a) The organisations and mechanisms are not in reach for all of the consumers. Only the well-informed consumer will get knowledge of the opportunities he has and only the mobile consumer will be able to come with his complaint to the organisations. Furthermore, the existing court procedure already demands an enormous amount of time and traveling from the consumers. Since most of the consumer organisations and governmental authorities are not situated near the Consumer Fora, the advice given by NGO and/or government adds to the efforts consumer have to undergo and leads to one more effort they have to undertake and to even more time they have to sacrifice for a simple consumer complaint.

(b) No connection between the different organisations exists. In fact, some of them act on the same field of guidance and thus tend to be competitors. Efforts in the field of consumer protection suffer from this fact and could be more effective, if a nation-wide network could be installed.

For the handling of a consumer complaint mediation should be offered free of charge and within the court or during the rolling courts which should go to the rural areas. It is important that consumers are not discouraged by lots of official institutions they have to contact before their complaint is being handled.

The installment of more *Lok Adalat* should be considered, but this will only work if a change in procedure is involved. Cases should be given to the Fora once a solution cannot be found. The *Lok Adalats* should not be entitled to decisions.

Strengthening Cxisting Efforts of the Government/District Forums/State Commission and National Commission

Filling-up Vacancies: The issue of vacancies in the appointment of Presidents and Members came up in virtually every discussion. The backlog of cases in the Forum is directly attributed to the delay in appointing the Presidents and members in time. Though appointments have been made recently to some Forums due to the efforts of the present Secretary to the Government, other vacancies still exist. Given the high number of complaints filed per month, the District Forums have their hands full with new complaints and therefore despite best efforts, the backlog remains. This needs to be addressed by introducing a system that identifies potential vacancies a few months ahead and begin a process of appointment immediately such that the new person takes charge on the day after the earlier person retires or completes his term.

Training/Refresher Courses for Presidents/Members: Several persons interviewed suggest that the appointment of retired District Judges as Presidents with no specific orientation on consumer law, and members with no previous training on consumer rights has severely limited the potential of the District Forums to vitalise the consumer movement. A strong recommendation made by several persons was the need to provide regular training and refresher course-type opportunities to the Presidents and Members of the District Forums at the time of appointment and bi-annually there on.

Need of More Forums for Different Districts: Districts have different populations and different levels of consumer awareness (largely dependent on the penetration by local voluntary consumer organisations) and this also translates to the different numbers of consumer disputes filed before the forums in these districts. More Forums need to be established in districts with a higher rate of consumer complaints. Though Gujarat has made some inroads towards this, more needs to be done.

More Benches, Night Court and Mobile Courts: The options of setting up more Benches, and introducing night district forums and mobile district forum also repeatedly came up as suggestions to reduce backlog and delays. In particular, night district forums may have the advantage of allowing working consumers to attend to their matters and not being required to hand over the complaints to lawyers.

Training for Consumer Protection Officers: There should be frequent training programmes for the Consumer Protection Officer. Gujarat government in 2006 added the responsibility of 'consumer protection' to the existing responsibilities of Officers of the Department of Legal Metrology. This has resulted in the creation of new posts of Director, Consumer Affairs (Controller, Legal Metrology) and District Consumer Protection Officers (Assistant Controllers Legal Metrology). These officers have also begun assisting in complaint resolution though their efforts are limited at this point. It may be useful to also train these officers on consumer law and ADR-techniques, since their office receives consumer complaints from the general public (262 complaints in 2007).

Enforce National Commission Regulations: Adjournments continue to be given "at the drop of a hat" despite the 2005, Regulations issued by the National Consumer Disputes Redressal Commission requiring adjournments to only be provided exceptionally, and only on recording of the reasons for them and imposing costs on the party seeking it. The 2005 Regulations are very detailed on several other aspects—all aimed at making the Forums more accessible and friendly to ordinary consumers. A clear direction from the National Commission seeking compliance of these Regulations will go a long way towards making consumer forums more consumers friendly.

Providing Support to District Forums: Forums made repeated demands for infrastructure and staff support—from simple items such as chairs and tables to competent support staff and even law clerks to help research and write judgments. Forums also complained of inefficient staff, no facilities for word processing and translation etc. These simple support measures will help increase the efficiency of the Forums and speeding up the delivery of justice to consumers.

References

1. Section 13 (3A).
2. The Consumer Protection Regulations, Section 11(3).
3. Data provided by Registar of NCDRC-update on 2.1.2008.
4. Cp: Consumer Affairs, Ram Khanna, Savita Hanspal, Sheetal Kapoor, H.K. Awasthi.
5. Concilation Proceedings under the Indian Arbitration Concilation Act of 1996 and CPC–An Overview, Dr V. Nageswara Rao,www.law commisionofindia.nic.in/adr_confinageswara%20rao10.pdf.
6. Wieviorka in: Die Mediation-ein europaischer Vergleich, S. 16.

5

Consumer Redressal System in India : How are They Efficient?

Sheetal Kapoor

The Consumer Protection Act, 1986, is a socio-economic legislation to protect and promote the interests of consumers in a unified and effective manner. Consumer Protection Act is a weapon in the hands of consumers to fight against the exploitation by the sellers, manufacturers and traders related to defective goods, deficiency in service, restrictive and unfair trade practices. From the time of its inception as on 1st January 2010, the Consumer courts at National, State and District level have together registered 33,30,237 cases and out of which only 29,58,875 cases have been disposed.

But, after 25 years of its implementation it is time to reconsider and rethink whether Consumer Courts have been able to deliver as promised. Are our Consumer Courts able to provide speedy justice to the needy in time? Further whether the members are trained enough to provide justice, needs to be seen. Recently, the working of the adjudicatory bodies has come into sharp criticism by the various stakeholders. The meetings of the Consumer Councils whose main object is to protect the rights of the consumers are not being held regularly and/or as frequently as it is supposed to. Further, the heart-breaking delay in disposal of the cases, non-disposal of cases, lack of manpower and poor infrastructural facilities are many other problems related to Consumer Courts. There have been allegations that the lawyers have taken over the consumer courts and as the consumers are unaware of the legal procedures and processes they hesitate to file complaints in the Consumer Court. The three-tier judiciary is totally dependent on the Ministry of Consumer Affairs for each and every thing including appointment of members and financial support. Further certain judgments given in the recent past by the Supreme Court are having an adverse effect on the consumer. In this paper the author tries to analyse the working of the consumer courts and also provide suggestions, such as adoption of ADR and opening up of more Ombudsman as in banking, insurance and electricity for speedy redressal of consumer complaints.

Consumer Protection Act, 1986

On April 9, 1985, the General Assembly of the United Nations passed a Resolution[1] adopting a set of guidelines for consumer protection and authorised the Secretary General United Nations to persuade the member countries especially the developing ones to adopt policies and laws for better protection of the interests of the consumers. India being one of the signatory to the Resolution enacted the Consumer Protection Act, 1986 (CPA), to fulfill its obligation. The Parliament enacted the legislation in December 1986, which came into force on April 15, 1987. The main objectives of the Act are to provide better protection of the interests of the consumers; purpose to make provision for the establishment of consumer councils and other authorities for the settlement of consumers' disputes. The Consumer Protection Act, 1986 is a benevolent piece of social welfare legislation providing for simple, speedy and less expensive remedy for the redressal of consumer grievances in relation to defective goods and deficient services.

The Act provides effective, people-oriented, broad-based and efficient remedy to consumers against unfair dealings and exploitation in the market. The Act applies to all goods and services whether by private, public or co-operative body unless it is especially exempted by the Central Government by a notification in the Official Gazette[2]. The Consumer Protection Act is an improvement over the other existing laws for consumer protection as it is compensatory in nature, whereas remedies under other laws are basically punitive or preventive in nature, designed to provide relief only in specific situations. The remedy under CPA is in addition to and not in derogation of provisions of any other law for the time being in force.[3] The Act gives statutory recognition to six consumer rights, which are right to safety, right to information, right to choose, right to be heard, right to seek redressal and right to consumer education. The Act postulates establishment of advisory and adjudicatory bodies to safeguard the interests of consumers. The Advisory structure is in the form of Consumer Protection Councils at Centre, State and District levels. These Councils are constituted on public-private partnership basis. The purpose of these bodies is to review the consumer related policies of the government and suggest measures for further improvements.

The Act also provides for quasi-judicial adjudicatory machinery at three levels, i.e., District, State and National levels called District Forum, State Consumer Disputes Redressal Commission and National Consumer Disputes Redressal Commission. At present there are 621 District Forums, 35 State Commissions and apex body the National Commission. The District Forum is presided by a person who is qualified to be District Judge. Besides, President, there are two other members, one member is a woman. The State Commission is presided over by a sitting or retired High Court Judge and the National Commission by a sitting or retired Supreme Court Judge. The pecuniary jurisdiction for these bodies has been prescribed under the Act. The District Forum can adjudicate on matters, where the value of claim is up to rupees twenty lakh, the State Commission where value of claim is more than twenty lakh but up to rupees one crore and the National Commission where the claim is over one crore. These adjudicatory bodies are quasi-judicial bodies and are regulated according to the principles of natural justice. They are required to decide the complaint within a period of three months from the date of notice where no testing is required and within a period of five months where testing is required.

Working of the Consumer Protection Councils[4]

Chapter-II of the Consumer Protection Act initially envisaged the setting up of the Consumer Protection Councils in all the States and at the Centre, namely, the State Consumer Protection Council and the Central Consumer Protection Council.[5] The Consumer Protection (Amendment) Act, 2002 has further provided for establishment of the District Consumer Protection Council in each district. Thus, the Act provides for establishment of Advisory Councils at three levels: National, State and District.

The object of the Councils is to promote and protect the rights of the consumers. The Councils are very important and potent deliberative bodies for the consumers and play an important role in spreading the consumer movement, especially in rural areas. The Councils act as a catalyst for change so that the present market system functions for the welfare of the consumers and for satisfying their needs.

Working of the Councils

Thus, one of the important developments that took place after the third amendments in 2002 in the Consumer Protection Act was that the Consumer Protection Councils at National and State levels must be established without any choice. To this effect Sections 4 and 7 have been amended. In the new construction of these sections the word 'may' is substituted with the word "shall". Thus, it has become mandatory for the governments to establish these consumer protection councils. Further, prior to the 2002 Amendment, there was no provision for number of members of State Council. Now Sec. 7(2)(c) makes provision for maximum 10 members (official or non-official) to be nominated by the Central Government. Section 8A has been inserted to make it mandatory to the State Governments to establish District Consumer Protection Councils in every district to promote and protect the rights of the consumers at the grass root level.

In spite of these amendments there does not appear to have been any significant improvement in the functioning of these Councils. In the last constituted Central Consumer Protection Councils (CCPC) there were over 150 members. Between 2000 and 2006, hardly any meetings of CCPC have taken place. In mid-2006 the Government was considering trimming the body to a smaller size.

The CCPC is a large body and has been frequently filled with persons who may not have any interest in consumer affairs. Its size has made the CCPC unwieldy and the Ministry of Consumer Affairs has tended to avoid holding regular meetings of this body in recent years. Over the 1990's the meetings of the CCPC were held more or less regularly and a number of working groups appointed by it gave important recommendations. These recommendations shaped government policies later on.

Three reasons can be attributed to the lack of effective functioning of these bodies:

1. Lack of Political Commitment: The subject of consumer affairs is being given less attention by political parties. This may be a reflection of the weakness of the consumer movement and lack of public awareness and sensitivity to consumer rights. This is a long term factor and may change only with increase in consumer awareness of the electorate. Politicians may take greater interest in their area if their electorate shows concerns for their consumer rights.

2. Quality of Non-official Appointees: Apart from officials of wide variety of public agencies, a large number of non-officials are appointed by government. These appointments are made by ministers-in-charge of Consumer Affairs in States. It has been frequently observed that a number of persons are appointed based on political patronage or the non-deserving ones are getting such appointments. The quality of these nominations also has an adverse impact on the effective functioning of these bodies.

3. Lack of Formal Systems for Effective Functioning: The functioning of these bodies is left to the executive discretion of the ministers and civil servants in charge of these ministries. There are hardly any mandatory requirements which can guide the ministries concerned to organise the work that these Councils can render useful advice to government on a wide variety of subjects on contemporary consumer affairs.

Total Number of Cases Disposed by Consumer Forums since Inception: A study of Table 5.1 depicts that 62,302 cases were registered since inception up to 15th January 2010, with the National Commission out of which 87.7 per cent cases were disposed of, while 12.3 per cent were still pending with the National Commission. In case of State Commission 4,92777 cases were registered since inception up to January 2010, and 77.76 per cent cases were disposed off. A staggering number of 27,75,140 cases were registered throughout the District Consumer Forums in the country and performance of District Consumer Forums was better as 90.84 per cent cases were disposed off. This indicates that consumer redressal system is now being, utilised at the district levels, which is a positive sign of generating awareness to seek redressals.

Table 5.1: Total Number of Cases Disposed by Consumer Forums Since Inception (Update on 15-1-2010)

Sl.No.	Name of Agency	Cases Filed Since Inception	Cases Disposed of Since Inception	Cases Pending	Percentage of Total Disposal
1.	National Commision	62320	54654	7666	87.70
2.	State Commision	492777	383166	109611	77.76
3.	District Forums	2775140	2521055	254085	90.84
	Total	**3330237**	**2958875**	**371362**	**88.85**

A Statewise analysis indicates (Tables 5.2 and 5.3) shows significant variations in the number of cases registered and per cent cases disposed by the State and District Consumer Forums. The total number of cases registered up to January 2010 with various State Commissions was higher for Uttar Pradesh followed by, Maharashtra, Rajasthan, Haryana and Delhi. Thus, it signifies consumer awareness is associated with consumer movement as in case with Rajasthan, Kerala, Himachal Pradesh, Uttarakhand and Delhi where literacy rates are higher.

Per cent cases disposed off both by the State District Consumer Forums also depicts regional variations. States with poor disposal system were Uttar Pradesh (41.07 per cent disposal), Assam (58.93 per cent), Haryana (66.79 per cent), Bihar (72.69 per cent), Jharkhand (74.15 per cent), at the State Commission level.

Table 5.2: Statement of Cases Filed/Disposed of / Pending in the National Commission and State Commissions (Update on 14.1.2010)

Sl.No	Name of State	Cases Filed Since Inception	Cases Disposed of Since Inception	Cases Pending	Percentage of Disposal	As on 14.1.10
	National Commission	62320	5464	7666	87.70	14.1.10
1.	Andhra Pradesh	24594	21382	3212	86.94	31.10.2009
2.	A & N Islands	42	38	4	90.48	31.1.2008
3.	Arunachal Pradesh	52	47	5	90.38	31.10.2009
4.	Assam	2284	1346	938	58.93	30.11.2009
5.	Bihar	13319	9681	3638	72.69	31.10.2009

6.	Chandigarh	10465	9577	888	91.51	30.11.2009
7.	Chattisgarh	5865	5245	620	89.43	30.11.2009
8.	Daman, Diu and DNH	29	29	0	100	30.09.2008
9.	Delhi	30183	29044	1139	96.23	31.12.2009
10.	Goa	2103	1987	116	94.48	30.11.2009
11.	Gujarat	31949	26699	5250	83.57	30.11.2009
12.	Haryana	37246	24876	12370	66.79	30.11.2009
13.	Himachal Pradesh	6494	5872	622	90.42	30.11.2009
14.	Jammu	5776	5050	726	87.43	30.11.2009
15.	Jharkhand	4097	3038	1059	74.15	31.07.2009
16.	Karnataka	31947	29799	2148	93.28	31.12.2009
17.	Kerala	22515	20385	2130	90.54	30.11.2009
18.	Lakshadweep	16	15	1	93.75	31.10.2009
19.	Madhya Pradesh	33915	30451	3464	89.79	30.11.2009
20.	Maharashtra	48540	30715	17825	63.28	31.10.2009
21.	Manipur	139	96	43	69.06	30.09.2008
22.	Meghalaya	238	152	86	63.87	30.06.2009
23.	Mizoram	162	149	13	91.98	30.11.2009
24.	Nagaland	94	64	30	68.09	31.12.2006
25.	Odisha	18968	11734	7234	61.86	31.10.2009
26.	Puducherry	886	836	50	94.36	30.11.2009
27.	Punjab	23088	17763	5325	76.94	30.11.2009
28.	Rajasthan	42206	39049	3157	92.52	30.11.2009
29.	Sikkim	35	31	4	88.57	30.09.2009
30.	Tamil Nadu	20784	17894	2890	86.1	31.10.2009
31.	Tripura	1179	1160	19	98.39	30.11.2009
32.	Uttar Pradesh	56649	23263	33386	41.07	30.11.2009
33.	Uttarakhand	3645	2945	700	80.8	30.11.2009
34.	West Bengal	13273	12754	519	96.09	31.08.2009
	Total	**492777**	**383166**	**109611**	**77.76**	

Table 5.3 shows the statement of cases filed/disposed in various District Forums since inception (update as on 14-1-2010). Performance of District Forums was better across the states except for Daman and Diu (with 79.84 per cent of disposal of cases), Nagaland (with 83.33 per cent disposal of cases) and Uttar Pradesh (with 83.33 per cent). If we see the average percentage of disposal

of cases by the District Forums since their inception we find that 90.84 per cent of cases have been disposed, which is a positive sign.

Table 5.3: Statement of Cases Filed/Disposed of/Pending in District Fora (Update on 14.1.2010)

Sl. No.	*Name of State*	*Cases field Since Inception*	*Cases Disposed of Since Inception*	*Cases Pending*	*Percentage of Disposal*	*As on 14.1.10*
1.	Andhra Pradesh	176653	172153	4500	97.45	31.10.2009
2.	A & N Islands	330	301	29	91.21	31.3.2006
3.	Arunachal Pradesh	300	265	35	88.33	31.10.2009
4.	Assam	13084	11730	1354	89.65	30.6.2009
5.	Bihar	75919	65056	10863	85.69	31.10.2009
6.	Chandigarh	39536	38520	1016	97.43	30.11.2009
7.	Chattisgarh	29805	27273	2532	91.5	30.11.2009
8.	Daman & Diu & DNH	129	103	26	79.84	30.9.2008
9.	Delhi	204398	189858	14540	92.89	30.9.2009
10.	Goa	5856	5272	584	90.03	30.11.2009
11.	Gujarat	147102	124987	22115	84.97	30.11.2009
12.	Haryana	187157	168177	18980	89.86	30.11.2009
13.	Himachal Pradesh	50331	47520	2811	94.41	31.12.2009
14.	Jammu	20792	18855	1937	90.68	31.12.2007
15.	Jharkhand	30455	28105	2350	92.28	31.7.2009
16.	Karnataka	126892	122256	4636	96.35	31.12.2009
17.	Kerala	163073	154859	8214	94.96	30.11.2009
18.	Lakshadweep	58	55	3	94.83	31.10.2009
19.	Madhya Pradesh	146084	133775	12309	91.57	30.11.2009
20.	Maharashtra	222376	204371	18005	91.9	31.10.2009
21.	Manipur	1037	1012	25	97.59	30.9.2008
22.	Meghalaya	322	308	14	95.65	31.3.2007
23.	Mizoram	2065	2011	54	97.38	31.12.2006
24.	Nagaland	246	205	41	83.33	30.6.2006

25.	Orissa	79856	74996	4860	93.91	31.10.2009
26.	Puducherry	2646	2470	176	93.35	30.11.2009
27.	Punjab	124787	119452	5335	95.72	30.11.2009
28.	Rajasthan	239011	219885	19126	92	30.11.2009
29.	Sikkim	249	231	18	92.77	30.9.2009
30.	Tamil Nadu	91321	82795	8526	90.66	31.10.2009
31.	Tripura	2015	1807	208	89.68	30.9.2008
32.	Uttar Pradesh	487126	405559	81567	83.26	30.11.2009
33.	Uttarakhand	31035	28991	2044	93.41	30.11.2009
34.	West Bengal	73094	67842	5252	92.81	31.8.2009
	Total	**2775140**	**2521055**	**254085**	**90.84**	

Justice Delayed is Justice Denied

Unlike the civil courts, the consumer courts are quasi-judicial authorities that have to follow simple, summary procedure for quick disposal of complaints. The Presidents and Members of the District Forum constitute the backbone of the Forum. They play a major role in enhancing the faith of the consumers in the redressal mechanism. Table 5.4 shows the information regarding whether State Commissions or District Forums are functional in every state or not. It is a big relief to note that in 2010 the State Commissions are functioning in all the States. Further analysis of the Table 5.4 shows that out of 621 district forums only 594 are functional. Delays in appointments affect the speedy adjudication of consumer complaints.

Table 5.4: Information Regarding Functional/Non-functional (State Commissions/ District Forums)
(Update on 14.1.2010)

Sl. No.	*States*	*Whether SC Functional or Non-functional*	*No. of District Fora*	*Functional*	*Non-functional*	*As on 14.1.2010*
1.	Andhra Pradesh	Yes	29	29	0	30.9.2009
2.	A & N Islands	Yes	1	1	0	31.3.2006
3.	Arunachal Pradesh	Yes	16	13	3	30.9.2009
4.	Assam	Yes	23	23	0	30.9.2009

5.	BiharYes	38	36	2	30.09.2009	
6.	Chandigarh	Yes	2	2	0	30.9.2009
7.	Chattisgarh	Yes	16	16	0	30.9.2009
8.	Daman & Diu & DNH	Yes	2	2	0	30.6.2008
9.	Dadra & Nagar Haveli	Yes	1	1	0	30.9.2008
10.	Delhi	Yes	10	10	0	30.6.2009
11.	Goa	Yes	2	2	0	30.9.2009
12.	Gujarat	Yes	30	30	0	30.9.2009
13.	Haryana	Yes	19	19	0	30.9.2009
14.	Himachal Pradesh	Yes	12	11	1	31.12.2009
15.	Jammu	Yes	2	2	0	31.3.2009
16.	Jharkhand	Yes	22	22	0	30.6.2009
17.	Karnataka	Yes	30	30	0	31.12.2009
18.	Kerala	Yes	14	14	0	30.6.2009
19.	Lakshadweep	Yes	1	1	0	30.9.2009
20.	Madhya Pradesh	Yes	48	47	1	30.9.2009
21.	Maharashtra	Yes	40	40	0	30.9.2009
22.	Manipur	Yes	9	9	0	31.12.2008
23.	Meghalaya	Yes	7	7	0	30.6.2009
24.	Mizoram	Yes	8	8	0	30.9.2009
25.	Nagaland	Yes	8	8	0	31.12.2008
26.	Odisha	Yes	31	31	0	30.9.2009
27.	Puducherry	Yes	1	1	0	30.9.2009
28.	Punjab	Yes	20	19	1	30.9.2009
29.	Rajasthan	Yes	33	30	3	30.9.2009
30.	Sikkim	Yes	4	4	0	30.6.2009
31.	Tamil Nadu	Yes	30	15	15	30.6.2009
32.	Tripura	Yes	4	4	0	30.9.2009
33.	Uttar Pradesh	Yes	74	74	0	30.9.2009
34.	Uttarakhand	Yes	13	13	0	30.11.2009
35.	West Bengal	Yes	21	20	1	31.8.2009
	Total	**621**	**594**	**27**		

Table 5.5 shows that as on 14.1.2010, there were three vacancies of the President and 16 vacancies of members of the State

Commission lying vacant. In case of District Forums there were 65 posts of Presidents and 200 members of the District Forum lying vacant. For law to be effective there should be no posts in the District Forums and State Commission lying vacant otherwise consumers would loose faith in the system.

Table 5.5: Information Regarding Vacancy Position in the State Commissions and District Forums (Update on 14.1.2010)

Sl.	*States*	*States Commision*		*District Forum*		*As on*
No.		*President*	*Member*	*President*	*Member*	*14.1.2010*
	National Commission	**0**	**0**			30.9.2009
1.	Andhra Pradesh	0	0	6	23	30.9.2009
2.	A & N Islands	0	0	0	0	31.3.2006
3.	Arunachal Pradesh	0	0	0	14	31.10.2009
4.	Assam	1	0	1	2	30.11.2009
5.	Bihar	0	0	1	16	31.10.2009
6.	Chandigarh	0	0	0	0	30.11.2009
7.	Chattisgarh	0	0	0	2	30.9.2009
8.	Daman & Diu & DNH	0	0	0	0	30.9.2008
9.	Delhi	0	1	0	1	31.12.2009
10.	Goa	0	0	2	1	30.11.2009
11.	Gujarat	0	2	5	23	30.11.2009
12.	Haryana	0	2	2	10	30.11.2009
13.	Himachal Pradesh	0	0	0	8	31.12.2009
14.	Jammu	0	0	0	0	31.3.2009
15.	Jharkhand	0	0	2	4	30.6.2009
16.	Karnataka	0	0	2	2	31.12.2009
17.	Kerala	0	0	0	1	30.6.2009
18.	Lakshadweep	0	1	0	0	31.10.2009
19.	Madhya Pradesh	0	1	0	32	30.11.2009
20.	Maharashtra	0	4	6	10	30.9.2009
21.	Manipur	1	0	0	1	31.12.2008
22.	Meghalaya	0	0	0	0	30.6.2009
23.	Mizoram	1	0	0	0	30.9.2009
24.	Nagaland	0	0	0	0	31.12.2008
25.	Odisha	0	0	3	3	31.10.2009
26.	Puducherry	0	1	1	0	30.9.2009
27.	Punjab	0	2	3	1	30.11.2009
28.	Rajasthan	0	1	7	9	30.11.2009

29.	Sikkim	0	0	0	0	30.6.2009
30.	Tamil Nadu	0	1	0	12	31.10.2009
31.	Tripura	0	0	0	0	30.9.2009
32.	Uttar Pradesh	0	0	18	16	30.11.2009
33.	Uttarakhand	0	0	1	7	30.11.2009
34.	West Bengal	0	0	5	2	31.8.2009
	Total	**3**	**16**	**65**	**200**	

In order to ensure expeditious disposal of complaints, Section 13 (3A) of the Consumer Protection Act provides for disposal of cases within 90 days where no analysis or lab testing of the products is required. Where testing of products is required the disposal of case can be done in 150 days. But what happens in reality is that cases are allowed to run for many years and this clause is often breached. For example, adjournments, according to the CPA amendment in 2002, should not be allowed except in exceptional circumstances, and if given the court should record the reasons for it in writing and justify it.

Certain Judgements Having Adverse Effect on Consumers

On 1st September, 2009, Supreme Court passed certain judgement that Consumer courts have no jurisdiction to try telecom disputes. Any dispute of the consumer against its service provider related to inflated bills, value-added services, etc., cannot be taken to consumer courts. The Supreme Court in its judgement has said that from now onward such disputes would be resolved through arbitration provided under Section 7B of the Indian Telegraph Act, 1885. As the Telegraph Act is a special law, its provisions would prevail over a general law, such as the Consumer Protection Act, 1986.

In another landmark judgement on 13th November, 1995, by the Supreme Court in *Indian Medical Association* vs. *V.P. Shantha* case it said that though medical practitioners belong to the medical profession, and are subject to the disciplinary control of the Medical Council of India and/or State Medical Councils constituted under the provisions of the Indian Medical Council Act but this would not exclude the services rendered by them from the ambit of the Consumer Protection Act. But in 2005 in Jacob Mathew's case the Supreme Court said that every error of judgement is not a case of medical negligence. Doctors can adopt one of the several accepted courses of treatment.

The Monopoly and Restricted Trade Policy Act had the powers to take *suo motu* action in the case of misleading advertisements whereas the Consumer Protection Act does not have such powers. Only if a consumer or industry complaints to the Consumer Courts or to ASCI then the action can be taken. By the time the action is taken by these bodies to either withdraw or modify the offending advertisement, the advertisement has already passed and/or conveyed the said false message to the consumers. Therefore, it is time to make some amendment in the Act and to give powers to the consumer courts for *suo motu* action so that they can take up cases of false advertisements on their own.

Suggestions to Make the System More Consumer-friendly

1. Since 2007, the consumer courts have been overburdened with cases and the buyer-seller contract is tilted in favour of the seller. Further, of late, the procedures have become so expensive and time-consuming that it is time to reform the existing system and redesign the same. The possible incorporation of Alternative Dispute Redressal (ADR) mechanism may be helpful. Thus, by amendment of the CPA it may be suitably introduced to give relief to the aggrieved consumers since this system includes Arbitration, Conciliation, Mediation and Negotiation.
2. Consumer courts are mostly made to function with staff deputed from other departments who may not have any skills and experience in judicial practices. Therefore, it is necessary to provide intensive training to the members of the Consumer Forums before recruiting or putting them on the specific job. The present practice is to provide training after assuming charge as members may be discontinued to make it more functional and effective.
3. All members of consumer fora should shed civil court personality and demehour. Their judgements should be pro-consumer.
4. There should be proper coordination among the President and Members of the Fora, so that the cases are decided in

time without any adjournments unless required under special circumstances.

5. The President of the National Commission should be empowered to take up *suo motu* action in consideration of the damages affecting a sizable number of population, e.g., misleading advertisements on the children.
6. Ombudsman has been created in various sectors such as insurance, banking and electricity. There is a need to create more Ombudsmen for free and fast redressal of consumer complaints in fast developing sectors such as, advertising, real estate, tourism.
7. Inability of the companies to sort the complaints internally on their own forces the consumers to go to Consumer courts. There should be an audit by an independent agency regarding consumer complaints and the data should be freely available on the websites of companies.
8. Voluntary Consumer Organisations should be encouraged to come forward in settling consumer disputes. Many VCOs are involved in comparative testing of various products and services but the consumers do not know about it.
9. More Mediation centers such as National Consumer Helpline, Core Centres should be opened for dissemination of information to the consumers. The National Consumer Helpline, a project started by the Ministry on March 15th 2005, attends consumer grievances from all over India. It has a toll-free number 1800-11-4000 which can be dialed from BSNL/MTNL lines, between Monday to Saturday from 9:30 am to 5.30 pm. It provides information and advice about alternate dispute resolution methods in a wide range of products and services.
10. It is time to have further Amendment in the Consumer Protection Act, 1986, for quick and speedy redressal of consumer cases.

Thus, Consumer Courts can only be said to be efficient if they are able to meet the expectations of the consumers. For this it is required that the procedures should be made as simple as possible and the judgements should be pro-consumer so that the plight of the common man should be heard within stipulated time.

References

1. *General Assembly Resolution*, 39/85.
2. *Consumer Protection Act*, 1986 Section 1(4).
3. *Ibid.*, Section 3.
4. Ram Khanna, Sheetal Kapoor, *et al: Consumer Affairs* (Universities Press, 2007).
5. *The Consumer Protection Act*, 1986, Bare Act.

6

Consumer is God, Forum is to Protect: Advocate's Experience of Consumer Fora

Biraja Mahapatra

The consumer is God. He is not to be bullied and he must get for what he has paid for; it is his/her right to get value-for-money. It is s/he who brings more customers. This concept has been a *mantra* for the businessmen for their success. Customer's satisfaction is the biggest infrastructure to build an empire of business.

Now things have not altogether changed. The trade and business have expanded phenomenally. The international trade and commerce have given a fillip to the ever-expanding market throwing a wide variety of products in the most alluring way. There are also a large number of business houses, which do a lot of research as to what the consumer needs. Businessmen have to compete in order to survive. Multinationals have already made a dent in the country. Now, the choices before the consumers are manifold.

But then manufacturing defects continue to worry the consumers. Many a time services rendered by them or by their employees remain far from being satisfactory. Many unscrupulous businessmen try to make a fast buck by duping the consumers. Dishonesty in the business is a rule for such businessmen who think, they can get away from the clutches of law. The consumers, most of whom are easily bullied, think what to do?

Now, a time has come to throw the weeds out. Spread of adulterated and substandard items has to be checked. Standards have to be maintained so far as the quality, quantity and purity are concerned. We have a host of laws like the Code of Civil Procedure 1908, Indian Contract Act, 1872, Sales of Goods Act, 1930, Indian Penal Code, 1860, Standards of Weights and Measures Act, 1976, and the Motor Vehicles Act, Prevention of Food Adulteration Act and Monopolies and Restrictive Trade Practices Act to take care of the consumers. But these proved inadequate keeping in view the changing nature of business.

Keeping all these in view, the government came out with the Consumer Protection Act on December 24, 1986, and Consumer Protection Rules in April 1987. The aim was to provide better protection to the interest of the consumers. The new law aimed at "providing better protection of interest of the consumer. During the last few years preceding the enactment there was, in this country, a marked awareness among the consumer of goods that they were not getting for their money's worth and were being exploited by both traders and manufacturers of consumer goods. The need for a consumer redressal forum was, therefore, increasingly felt. Understandably, therefore, legislation was introduced and enacted with considerable enthusiasm and fanfare as a path breaking benevolent legislation intended to protect the consumer from exploitation by unscrupulous manufacturers and traders of consumer goods. A three-tier forum comprising District Forum, State Commission and the National Commission came to be envisaged under the act for redressal of grievances of the consumers," a Supreme Court bench comprising justice AM. Ahmadi and Justice K. J. Reddy had observed in a judgement in the case of Common Cause Vs. Union of India case in 1993.

The new law was enacted a year after the United Nations had passed a resolution prescribing guidelines under which the government could make laws for better protection of the interest of the consumers. Such laws were necessary, more in the developing countries to protect the consumers from hazards to their health and safety and make them available speedier and cheaper redress. Consumerism has been a movement in which the trader and the consumer find each other as adversaries. Till last two decades, in many developed and developing countries, powerful consumer organisations have come into existence and such organisations have been instrumental in dealing with consumer protection laws and in expansion of the horizon of such laws. In our country the legislation is of recent origin and its efficacy has not been critically evaluated which has to be done on the basis of experience. This has been observed by a Supreme Court bench comprising Justice S. Sagir Ahmad and Justice G.B. Patnaik in a judgement in the case of Spring Meadows Hospital and another Vs. Harjol Alhuwalia in 1998. It is needless to say that we need more consumer organisations to spread out and increase the awareness among people particularly at the village level to make this movement a success.

The Act creates a framework for speedy disposal of consumer disputes and an attempt has been made to remove the existing evils of the ordinary court system. The Act gives a comprehensive definition of consumer, who is the principal beneficiary of the legislation but at the same time in view of the comprehensive definition of the term consumer even a member of the family cannot be denied the status of a consumer under the Act and in an action by any such member of the family for any deficiency of service, it will not be open for a trader to take stand that there is no privity of contract, the bench of Justice Ahmad and Justice Patnaik had said.

The bench had said "the Consumer Protection Act confers jurisdiction on the Commission in respect of matters where either there is defect in goods or there is deficiency in service or there has been an unfair and restrictive trade practice or in the matter of charging of excessive price. The Act being a beneficial legislation intended to confer some speedier remedy on a consumer being exploited by unscrupulous traders, the provision thereof should receive a liberal construction."

According to the new law, a consumer is he "who buys any goods for a consideration which has been paid or promised or partly paid and partly promised or under any system of deferred payment and includes any user of such goods other than the person who buys such goods for consideration paid or promised or partly paid or partly promised or under any system of deferred payment, when such use is made with the approval of such person, but does not include a person who obtains such goods for resale or for any commercial purpose or ..."hires or avails of any services for a consideration, which has been paid or promised or partly paid and partly promised or under any system of deferred payment and includes any beneficiary of such services other than the person who hires or avails of the services for consideration paid or promised or under any system of deferred payment, when such services are availed of with the approval of the first mentioned person".

Consumer Forums and Some Experience

There is a departure from the long drawn proceedings in the civil court with the establishment of the Consumer Forums. As expected, these forums are doing an excellent work as far as the speedy disposal is concerned on record. To achieve the purpose, quasi-judicial machinery is set up at each District (583), State (35) and National Level.

Sl. No.	Name of Agency	Cases Filed Since Inception	Cases Disposed of Since Inception	Cases Pending	Percentage of Total Disposal	Remark
1.	National Commission	62320	54654	7666	87.70	
2.	State Commssion	492777	383166	109611	77.76	
3.	District Forums	2775140	2521055	254085	90.84	
	Total	**3330237**	**2958875**	**371362**	**88.85**	

The table above may paint a rosy picture about the quick disposal of cases but it is my personal feeling that the institution has been serving as a rehabilitation department for many retired judges and members. In fact, it could have been more efficient, had it been filled up with young and energetic talents from across the country. In Delhi, most district forum judges do not sit before 11.30 am. Most judges never come prepared with the contents of the case. It is just a time pass for some members. This is one observation and I think it has to be addressed. If this is the state of affairs in the capital, what happens in the rest of the country-one can easily imagine.

I have seen from my experience, that cases of 1994, have still been admitted without there being any rhyme or reason.

I have seen many a time whims of the judges take precedence over their wisdom. A reputed real estate company cheated an aspirant property buyer after taking the entire money from him and deliberately delayed handing over possession of the property. When the buyer went to the consumer court, the counsel for the real estate company straightaway offered 25 per cent interest on the money deposited. The court readily agreed to it and rather put pressure on the buyer to accept the money back. Now, let us examine what the consumer court did, the real estate company had taken the money and invested it in buying the property. The company delayed and did not want to allot the land as its price sky-rocketed in the market and the cost went up by 40 to 50 times than the market price when the company had bought the plot to allot in the name of the buyer. According to me, the court became a spokesperson of the real estate company.

I have seen in one district forum to my dismay, that a member was giving dates, another members hearing cases in which pleading were to be completed and the Presiding Judge was hearing arguments. A lawyer in me did protest but then I was advised not to object as I should not annoy a judge.

Throwing some advertisements in newspapers will not do. It is to be understood that efficient working of the institution will encourage and educate the consumers to take recourse to law and the number has to increase. We need not be happy that the pending cases are not increasing. We should be disappointed that more and more people should repose their faith in the institution and more and more cases should pour in and that is not happening. Litigants are also consumers of law in the Consumer Courts as well. But common men really do not distinguish between a Civil Court and a Consumer Court.

The Supreme Court had in a judgement in the case of *Charan Singh* vs. *Healing Touch Hospital* warned "the consumer forums must take expeditious steps to deal with the complaints filed before them and not keep them pending for years. It would defeat the object of the Act, if summary trials are not disposed of expeditiously by the forums at the District, State or National levels. Steps in this regard are required to be taken in the right earnest."

The greatest object of getting justice at the earliest can only be achieved if it is cheaply available to the poor and within the time that has already prescribed in the law itself. That continues to be a dream. For achieving such an object, judges, lawyers and the litigants and more importantly the other officials of the institution have a role to play. If a case is really decided before the consumer forum within the prescribed period of three months after issuance of notice, it would be a great achievement and followed by the other institutions. But we have miles to go to achieve such an objective even if we are on the right track. After all the legislative intent for enacting the legislation is to provide a speedy summary trial, to settle the claim of the complainant at the earliest.

Consumer Court is a good vehicle to reach out justice to the people but what we need is good and skilled drivers—it means we need justice oriented trained young judges who can deliver more in terms of the demand of the time.

7

Position of District Consumer Courts in India: From a Consumer Perspective

Savita Hanspal

The separation of ownership and management of business brought in a revolution for the consumers. It ensured availability of products and services beyond physical boundaries, thereby adding and/or making variety at comparatively affordable and/or competitive prices. At the same time, the distancing of producers and consumers has raised many issues influencing the satisfaction of consumers with the goods and services marketed. One such issue is how the consumer approaches the business to help him in case of grievances on purchasing and/or consumption. But since the business organisations are becoming huge, organised and powerful, it does not really matter to them whether a single consumer has any complaint. While in popular parlance business they say the customer is the king, but they do not always walk the talk.

While we, the concerned consumers, agree that the consumers not only needs some protection, but also requires that his grievances are properly addressed as per law of the land. When his communication with the manufacturer or marketer fails, he needs to take a legal recourse for redressal of grievances. In a huge country like India, the normal courts are already clogged with suits and thus, a consumer may have to wait for decades before he gets an opportunity to be heard and, in the meanwhile, it may happen that the business may go out of business leaving behind a trail of casualties.

In order to provide speedy, inexpensive and simple redressal of consumer grievances, Chapter III of the Consumer Protection Act, 1986, makes provision for the establishment of remedial agencies for settlement of consumers' disputes and related matters. The Act provides a three-tier system set up at the district, state and national level, consisting of:

1. A Consumer Disputes Redressal Forum also known as the "District Forum", set up at the district level to entertain complaints up to the value of Rupees twenty lakhs.
2. A Consumer Disputes Redressal Commission also known as the "State Commission", set up at the state level to entertain complaints of value ranging from rupees twenty lakhs to one crore as well as appeals against the orders passed by district courts.
3. A National Consumer Disputes Redressal Commission also known as the "National Commission", set up to address issues that cannot be handled by the District and State Commissions or those involving a value above rupees one crore.

While the National Commission is set up by the Central Government, the State Commissions and District Forums are set up by the respective State Governments. In Laxmi Engineering Works vs. PSG Industrial Institute (AIR 1995 SC, 1428), the Supreme Court observed that the quasi-judicial bodies created by the Act known as District Forums, State Commissions and the National Commission are not courts though invested with some of the powers of a civil court. They are quasi-judicial tribunals brought into existence to render inexpensive and speedy remedies to consumers. These Forums/Commissions were not supposed to supplant but supplement the existing judicial system. The idea was to provide additional forum providing an inexpensive and speedy resolution of disputes arising between consumers and suppliers of goods and services.

Procedure and Regulations for Consumers in the District Fora

Consumer Protection (Second Amendment) Rules, 2006, and the Consumer Protection Regulations 2005, lay down the procedures and the structural facilities that must be followed by the District Fora to provide the consumers with a trouble-free experience in getting their grievances redressed. The purpose was to make the consumer feel comfortable and prevent him from getting nervous or overawed by the ambience of a regular court. Some of the provisions are explained below :

Particulars in Filing a Complaint

To make it convenient for the consumers to file a complaint in the District Forum, it has been specified that it may be filed on plain paper containing the following particulars:

(a) The name, description and the address of the complainant.

(b) The name, description and address of the opposite party or parties.

(c) The facts relating to the complaint including when and where it arose.

(d) Documents, if any, in support of the allegations contained in the complaint.

(e) The relief sought by the complainant.

The complaint should be duly signed by the complainant himself or his authorised agent. The Forum provides reasonable opportunity of hearing to both the parties to present their case.

Fee for Filing Complaints before District Forum

Rule 9A[1] specifies the prescribed fee for filing a complaint before the District Fora. Every complaint filed under Section 12(1), section 17 (1) and section 21 (a)(i) of the Act shall be accompanied by the prescribed fee in the form of crossed Demand Draft drawn on a nationalised bank or through a crossed Indian Postal Order drawn in favour of the Registrar of the State Commission and payable at the respective place where the State Commission or the National Commission is situated. The following Table 7.1 indicates the fee to be paid based on the total values of the complaint a consumer files.

Table 7.1: Complaint Filing Fee

Sl. No.	*Total value of goods or services and the claimed*	*Amount of fee payable (in Rs)*
	District Forum	
1.	Upto one lakh rupees–For complaints who are under the Below Poverty Line holding *Antyodaya Anna Yojana* Cards	Nil
2.	Upto one lakh rupees–For complaints other than *Antyodaya Anna Yojana* card holders.	100
3.	Above one lakh and upto five lakh rupees	200

4.	Above five lakh and upto ten lakh rupees	400
5.	Above ten lakh and upto twenty lakh rupees	500
	State Commission	
6.	Above twenty lakh and upto fifty lakh rupees	2000
7.	Above fifty lakh and upto one crore rupees	4000
	National Commission	
8.	Above one crore rupees	5000

The complainants under the Below Poverty Line shall be entitled for the exemption of payment of fee only on production of an attested copy of the *Antyodaya Anna Yojana* cards.

Admission of a Complaint/Pre-admission Hearing

After filing the complaint, it is revised by either the staff or a forum member or president. Then, a first hearing, called admission hearing, takes place, with the complainant only in order to decide whether the complaint can be admitted at all or not under the Consumer Protection Act, 1986.

Despite providing consumers an option of filing postal complaints, the Forums "prefer" that the consumer files the complaints in person. Forums state that if the consumer comes in person, then they could be advised on the flaws in the complaints and they could immediately correct them. Once it is admitted the complaint is then communicated to the defendant who should be provided with an opportunity to present its side of the story before a decision is taken.

The admissibility of complaint is decided within 21 days from the date from which the complaint was received. Once the complaint is admitted by the Forum, a copy of the same is sent within 21 days from the date of admission to the opposite party to provide his version of the case within a period of 30 days or extended period not exceeding 15 days. The District Forum can get the quality of a product sample tested, if required for verification within a period of 45 days.

Further, the Regulations require that every complaint, appeal, or revision petition shall be numbered by the Registrar after it is filed. If there is any defect in the filing of the complaint, appeal or revision petition, the particulars of such defects shall be recorded and the party or his agents shall be informed of the defects by asking them to remove them within 15 days time period. In case the party disputes the correctness of the defects so detected, the matter shall be placed before the Consumer Forum for appropriate orders. The Regulations also specify that after the expiry of the time given, the matter shall, irrespective of the fact as to whether the defects have been removed or not, be placed before the Consumer Forum for appropriate orders. The days allowed for removing the objections raised by the Registrar but not removed within the time allowed for the purpose, shall not be excluded for counting the period of limitation.

If a Complainant Fails to Appear?

Where the complainant fails to appear on the date of hearing the District Forum may either dismiss the complaint for default or decide it on merits. The dispute in the forums is settled primarily on the evidence presented by the parties.

Time-limit for Decision

The Consumer Protection Act[2] provides that where no analysis or testing of commodities is required to be done by the laboratory, the complaint shall be decided within a period of three months from the date of receipt of notice by the opposite party. If it requires analysis or testing of commodities, the period for giving final order is five months.

Adjournments

In order to avoid delay in disposal of the complaints, the District Forum shall not ordinarily grant adjournment unless sufficient cause is shown to the forum. If adjournment is granted, the District Forum shall record the reasons for grant of adjournment and also award costs. The forum may, if it appears necessary, also pass suitable interim order. The Districts Forums are vested with powers of civil forums under the Code of Civil Procedure, 1908, for conducting the proceedings before them. The proceeding of the District Forum cannot be called in question in any forums on the ground that the principles of natural justice have not been complied with.

Composition of the District Forum

A District Forum is composed of President and two members (with one woman member mandatoriy). The President is a person who has been or is qualified to be a District Judge. The minimum qualification for a member is graduation. The law also stipulates that two other members of the District Forum shall be persons of ability, integrity and standing, and should have adequate knowledge or experience of, or have shown capacity in dealing with, problems relating to economics, law, commerce, accountancy, industry, public affairs or administration.

Every member of the District Forum shall hold office for a term of five years or up to the age of 65 years, whichever is earlier, and shall be eligible for reappointment. Every appointment to the District Forum is made by the State Government on the recommendation of a selection committee consisting of :

(i) The President of the State Commission who is the Chairman;

(ii) Secretary, Law Department of the State is a Member; and

(iii) Secretary, Department of Consumer Affairs in the State is a Member.

The salary or honorarium and other allowances payable to, and the other terms and conditions of service of the members of the District Forum shall be such as may be prescribed by the State Government.

The District Fora: Some Ground Realities

The District Consumer Fora are the first contact point for consumers who have claims up to Rs. 20 lakhs. This paper describes some qualitative aspects that contribute to the working of the District Consumer Fora and influence the consumers' experience in availing of these facilities. These observations were made during the authors' visits to consumer courts (District Fora) in Jaipur, Alwar, Ajmer and Bharatpur (Rajasthan), Delhi and Ahmedabad.

Number of District Fora

There are a total of 600 plus District Fora[3] in the country. The State governments generally establish more than one District Forum in a State. The following Table 7.2 provides the number of District Forums established in certain States of India.

Table 7.2 Number of District Consumer Courts in Selected States

No. of District Fora	*States*
1–2	Andaman & Nicobar, Goa, J & K
10	Delhi
17–20	Punjab, Haryana
22–26	West Bengal, Gujarat
29–33	Andhra Pradesh, TN, Rajasthan, Karnataka, Odisha
37–45	Bihar, Maharashtra, MP
70	UP

The Table 7.2 shows that the number of District Fora varies with the size of the state but even so, these numbers clearly indicate that they are not adequate to cater to the number of consumers in the state. Interviews with the members of some District Fora revealed that consumers in certain cases have to travel up to 100 kilometres to reach them. Travelling such a distance surely involves spending some amount of money as well as a lot of time and effort to even try to reach the nearest justice delivery point. This may not be a little area of concern because the story does not end with one visit to get speedy and inexpensive justice from the temple of justice. The consumer is required to travel as many times as the hearings are scheduled for one reason or the other, which is a difficult proposition for consumers living in far flung areas and especially for consumers who are living below the poverty line and the like.

It may not be out of place to mention that with the technological developments, it may be more convenient to arrange mobile courts to reach these areas and schedule the hearings from consumers living in that area on a particular day after giving an advance notice to the concerned consumers. This may require some distance travelling by the goods and service providers but at the same time, the inconvenience of such a travel may also act as a deterrent for them; and by this they may forced to think to behave more responsibly towards the consumers in the market.

Locating the Forum

A visit to several District Fora revealed that it was indeed a task to locate the former as there were no signboards indicating the directions to locate them. Though people in the immediate vicinity were aware of the existence of these courts, but general people living say within 2–5 kilometers were not at all aware of where one could find them. The Forum itself was barely visible; several people had to be asked before they could be located. Not even a signboard outside the building indicated where consumers could find "their" Court. Almost none of the Fora provided signboards inside the building, to ensure that a consumer could find his way within the premises.

It is important that all shopping areas carry boards prominently displaying the name, address, and telephone number of the nearest District Fora along with a map displaying the location. It may also be possible to have a kiosk that accepts complaints on predesigned forms like RTI Application Form with the facility of issuing e-receipts of the complaints on the pattern of electronic deposit of cheques presently done by banks. Such boxes could be then emptied periodically and the complaints may be sent to National Consumer Helpline or State Helpline. Any charges for filing complaints may be accepted when the consumer is invited for a hearing. This would at least reduce the burden of travelling to file a complaint and also provide information and data to the Helplines on the nature of complaints received against specific manufacturers and service providers including retailers.

Structure and Upkeep

The Consumer Fora are situated in shabby and rundown buildings. The premises badly needs upkeep. It appears the premises have not been cleaned for days and the walls are not whitewashed for years, and/or somehow roughly touched/whitewashed; there is dust and dirt and cobwebs hanging from the ceilings and windows. The windows are broken or in a state of disrepair. There is insufficient light in the corridors and rooms. Such presentation shows that the functions performed by the Fora are not important to receive resource allocations so as to ensure professional and respectable appearance.

Equipment and Furniture

The Consumer Protection Rules[4] also specify that a Consumer Forum being not a regular court, shall have the arrangements so as to depict it distinct from a usual court. In the hall in which the

Consumer Forum shall hear the parties, the dais may not be kept more than 30 cm. in height than the place earmarked for the parties to occupy. At the dais of the hall, the President and the members of the Consumer Forum shall use the same type of chairs at the same level and these chairs need not have high backs.

The District Fora Situation

On reaching inside the Forum, there was even no sign to know how and where the consumers could go to file a complaint; neither a specific desk for the receiver of complaints was earmarked nor a specific room allocated for complainants was visible. There was no waiting area where people could sit and wait or sit and write out their complaints.

The courtrooms were in a bad condition, rundown furniture was available only, and not one chair matched the other. The ambience was thus, not at all professional and bespoke of neglect and disregard, especially in Fora other than Delhi. Files covered with dust were bulging out of cupboards in some of the offices, including Delhi giving the premises a very untidy look and disorganised appearance.

In all of the courts visited, computers were available but in many the machinery was standing on tables covered with cloth or plastic sheets serving more as showpieces. When asked about whether the computers were used and for what purpose, it was found that they were not used because "the Ministry didn't send a computer operator". In such a circumstance, a better upkeep of the buildings and office space is essential. The visitors should understand that important business of redressing consumer grievances is conducted within the premises. The organisation of computer training programme is essentially required for all. If that is not possible, a younger computer literate assistant must be made available to the judges and members of the Fora.

Presence of Lawyers

The Consumer Protection Act, 1986, did not foresee participation of lawyers in large numbers as it was expected that the consumers would be able to present their story themselves. The visits to the Fora revealed that lawyers were present in great numbers because very few consumers are able to handle proceedings without the help of the lawyers. Moreover, the product and service providers engage lawyers whose technical expertise and language manipulation cannot be matched by consumers who may not know the appropriate use of language/ words that may convey as well as serve their interest unlike the defendant's lawyers. Since none of the cases is decided without hearing and adjournments and in some of the courts not even written statements sent by mail are accepted, the handling of the complaint by a consumer without lawyer is virtually not possible; out of sheer practical reasons. The Opposite Party lawyers generally seek more adjournments than lawyers for consumer complainants, because the former seems to be "busier". No consumer, whether from urban or rural areas will be able to travel to court as often as it is required. In such a scenario, it is important to regulate the conduct of lawyers.

Member Sharing

The visit also revealed that there was delay in appointing Presidents and Members. In Vadodara (Gujarat) Court, for example, only one member was "shared" by two Presidents. This lead to the situation that the member worked three days a week for the Forum of one President and three days for the other. This meant that while one President worked, the other President could not finish any case as one of the members was not available even though two Presidents were available and paid. Practically, only one Forum at a time was working. It is, thus, important that appointments be made on time to ensure that another person is available from the day the former's terms comes to an end. Where the duration of appointment requires an extension, such extension should be made before the expiry of the previous appointment. Where it is not clear that the appointment of the existing member would be extended, a new Member from a previously selected pool/panel of members should be immediately asked to take over till further decision/order. This would ensure that the precious time is not lost in the process, and the work of the Forum is not unduly disrupted.

The motivational level of the members is found to be at low ebb. All members and Presidents felt that they were definitely under-paid. Moreover, as said earlier, the ambience of the office, the furniture and facilities provided, have a large impact on the morale of all the people working there.

No President No Action

The Consumer Protection Act provides that the courts could decide with two members only in case the President was not present. It was also revealed in some Fora during the interviews that if the President of the Forum was not present, no decision could be taken. This leads to a widespread but unfortunate practice: the Fora neither decide nor do hearings when the President is not in. They were unaware of the provisions of the Act and/or the subsequent changes that took place in the procedures. This results in unnecessary but avoidable delays in many of the complaints.

Number of Adjournments

The provisions require that proceedings before a Consumer Forum shall be conducted as expeditiously as possible. The Regulations specify that the Consumer Forum shall record the reasons for any adjournment made by it and that the cost of adjournment, if asked by the opposite party or parties, shall be not less than five hundred rupees per adjournment and/or could be more depending upon the value and nature of the complaint as may be decided by the Consumer Forum. The complainant, appellant or petitioner, as the case may be, may also be burdened with cost unless sufficient cause is shown for seeking adjournment. The cost imposed may be given to the other party or parties to defray his or their expenses or be deposited in the Consumer Legal Aid Account to be maintained by the respective Consumer Forum, as the Consumer Forum may order. If any adjournment is granted without awarding cost, the order sheet shall mention the reasons thereof. All orders adjourning the matter shall be signed by the President and members constituting the Bench and not by the Court Master or Bench Clerk. Non-availability of a lawyer who is representing the party shall not be a ground for seeking adjournment of the matter unless absence is beyond the control of the lawyer such as his sudden illness or bereavement in the family.

The visit revealed that delays in providing judgements also resulted on account of adjournments which ranged from 10 to 40 in many cases defeating the provisions and intent of delivering speedy justice/redressal. It would substantially improve the situation in case the reasons for seeking adjournments by lawyers could be made open to the public. Such information would guide them whether lawyers have sufficient time to take up their cases. It would also enhance efficiency as the lawyers would not want to be shown/identified as a person responsible for delaying justice delivery.

Fee for Filing a Complaint

The fee for filing a complaint in bank order or postal order puts another task on the shoulders of the consumer. In many places it is time-consuming to get a draft/postal order made; and it may require some travel especially in rural areas to make a DD. The fee, therefore, may be allowed and/or collected through cash/credit cards at the point of filing a complaint or at the time of hearing. This would save the consumers from the hassle of getting drafts/postal orders made.

Role of Members in Consumer Fora

The survey also revealed that mostly the President dominates the proceedings at the Forum. The members merely act as spectators; it seems their roles are at best "ornamental" and/or "ineffective". In the District Forums we visited, this seemed apparent. In fact, during our investigation no Member spoke during the proceedings; neither to each other, nor to the President or the parties in the case. In fact, in some District Forums, the Members did not even receive their set of case papers and/or were sharing the set of papers provided to the President. Their interactions with vulnerable consumers as well as consumers in general were not very polite and/or encouraging. Consumers were made to feel guilty and worthless as they chose to complain and were demoralised by lawyers of opposite parties as well.

Conclusions and Recommendations

Thus, while we are overtly concerned with reducing the backlog of cases, it is equally important to take a look at the qualitative aspects of justice delivery and the experience of the complainants at the Fora. We might have the best of laws and regulations but unless the experiences of consumers at the delivery point are improved to instill a positive mindset and become confidence-inspiring, we can't be very sure that the aggrieved people/consumer-victims would like to take advantage of the existing District Fora. Negative experiences would result in loss of consumer faith and confidence in the institution; and it negates the good intentions of the policy makers. Further, the complaint making should be on a re-designed form which should be able to capture consumer demographics, that is, data on-age, income, educational background, occupation, area of residence, etc. Such data is important both for research as well as further policy making.

More information is required at the level of the judgement. Along with the summary of cases filed and disposed off —a summary of the cases that were not permitted to be filed or the complaints not entertained with reasons must also be displayed. Summary of reasons for adjournment should also be provided in the Case-narrative on the net. This would provide a good database for research and designing the consumer guidance while filing the complaints.

Courts and the staff including members and the President need to be trained to become consumer-friendly to different segments of population like, women, rural, urban, and disabled; and they need to adopt a more humane-face and approach differently in dealing with the consumer-victims. It may be said that whether the District Fora look like Courts or not, the mere fact is that there are lawyers in the Fora and presence of Judges/ Presidents that instills a sense of awe and fear in the minds of common people. Personal losses, loss of money and respect drive away the complainants and it also encourages unfair trade practices as consumer voice is not found to be against them.

Summer internship courses on Consumer Affairs with appropriate modules may be accepted to help train the members of the Fora irrespective of status and positions. This would empower them practically. Some other interested people whether consumer activists or the like may also be allowed to undergo internship programmes so that they could be recruited as members in future either on a part-time/whole-time basis.

References

1. The Consumer Protection (Second Amendment) Rules, 2006.
2. Consumer Protection Act, 1986.
3. www.ncdrc.nic.in
4. http://ncdrc.nic.in/Regulations2005.html.

8

Consumer Disputes Redressal Mechanism: A Case Study of District Forum of Jharkhand

Sapna Chadah
Pankaj Singh

Introduction

Consumer protection, though as old as consumer exploitation, has assumed greater importance and relevance. Now there exist laws and policies which focus on consumer protection and welfare. In India various Acts intended to protect the consumers, directly or indirectly, against different forms of exploitation were enacted from time to time. However, except for the Monopolies and Restrictive Trade Practices (MRTP) Act, 1969, all the other Acts were mainly punitive and preventive in nature. In spite of these Acts the consumers did not have any effective mechanism or institutional arrangements for the speedy redressal of their grievances and also the lack of effective popular movement isolated the consumer and his plight only increased. Seeing the pressure mounting from various consumer protection groups and the consumers themselves, the Parliament enacted the Consumer Protection Act in 1986.

The enactment of the Consumer Protection Act in 1986, was a milestone in the history of consumer movement in the country. Before this, most of the legislations to protect the consumers were punitive in nature and did not provide for a holistic protection to the consumers in a cost-effective and time-bound manner. There were no institutional mechanisms available to the consumers which would redress their grievances in a simple and expeditious manner unlike the civil courts which took a lot of time and money to decide a case. The Consumer Protection Act, 1986 is a benevolent piece of social welfare legislation. The Act seeks to provide for better protection of the consumers and stipulates the establishment of authorities for the settlement of consumer disputes. The Act applies to all products and services whether provided by public, private or cooperative body. The remedy provided under the Consumer Protection Act to the consumer is in addition to and not in derogation of the provisions of any other law for the time being in force.

The Act enumerates six rights of the consumers and provides provisions for speedy and simple redress to consumer disputes for which quasi-judicial machinery is sought to be set up at the district, state and the national level. The quasi-judicial bodies are to observe the principles of natural justice and have been empowered to give relief of a specific nature and to award, wherever appropriate, compensation to consumers. Penalties for non-compliance of the orders given by the quasi-judicial bodies have also been provided.

District Consumer Disputes Redressal Mechanism

The Act empowers the state government to establish a consumer disputes redressal agency known as District Forum in each district. The state government, if it deems fit can establish more than one District Forum in a district. The Consumer Forum is an alternative forum, less formal and more consumer-friendly for providing, speedy and inexpensive justice. Cases are decided on the basis of justice, equity and good conscience, and Principles of Natural Justice are required to be adhered to. The rigours of the technicalities of civil law have no place. Some provisions of the civil law have been incorporated in the Consumer Protection Act which provides guidelines for conducting the proceedings and to receive evidence on affidavits. Strict rules of evidence and procedure do not come in the way of the working of the Consumer Forums. Material which has probative value and can pass the test of a reasonable man is accepted.

Each District Forum shall consist of a President, who is, or has been, or is qualified to be a District Judge and two other members, one of whom shall be a woman. The person to be a member should not be less than thirty five years of age, possess a bachelor's degree from a recognised university and be a person of ability, integrity and standing, and have adequate knowledge and experience of at least ten years in dealing with problems relating to economics, law, commerce, accountancy, industry, public affairs or administration. Every appointment to the District Forum shall be made by the State Government on the recommendation of a Selection Committee consisting of the President of the State Commission as Chairman, Secretary, Law Department of the State as Member and Secretary in-charge of the Department dealing with Consumer Affairs in the State as Member. Every member at the District Forum shall hold office for a term of five years or up to the age of sixty five whichever is earlier.

8.1: Status of District Consumer Forum in India

Functional	617 (98.4)
Non-functional	10 (1.6)
Total No. of District Consumer Forums in India	627

Source: Report of National Consumer Dispute Redressal Commission, 2010.

The District Forum has the jurisdiction to entertain complaints where the value of the goods or services and the compensation, if any, claimed does not exceed rupees twenty lakhs. A complaint shall be instituted in a District Forum within the local limits of whose jurisdiction (a) the opposite party or each of the opposite parties, where there are more than one, at the time of the institution of the complaint, actually and voluntarily resides or carries on business or has a branch office or personally works for a gain, or (b) any of the opposite parties, where there are more than one, at the time of the institution of the complaint, actually and voluntarily resides or carries on business or has a branch office or personally works for gain, provided that in such case either the permission of the District Forum is given, or the opposite parties who do not reside or carry on business or have a branch office or personally work for gain , as the case may be, acquiesce in such institution, or (c) the cause of action, wholly or in part arises.

Every complaint shall be heard as expeditiously as possible and endeavour shall be made to decide the complaint within a period of three months from the date of receipt of notice by opposite party where the complaint does not require analysis or testing of commodities and within five months, if it requires analysis or testing of commodities. No adjournment shall be ordinarily granted by the District Forum unless sufficient cause is shown and the reasons for grant of adjournment have been recorded in writing by the Forum. Further, the District Forum shall make such orders as to the costs occasioned by the adjournment as may be provided in the regulations under the Act.

If after conducting the proceedings, the District Forum is satisfied that the goods complained against suffer from any of the defects specified in the complaint or that any of the allegations contained in the complaint about the services are proved, it shall issue an order to the opposite party directing him to do one or more of the following things; (i) to remove the defects, (ii) to replace the goods with new goods of similar description, (iii) to return to the complainant the price or the charges paid by the complainant, (iv) to pay such amount as may be awarded as compensation to the consumer, (v) to remove the defects or deficiencies in the services in question,(vi) to discontinue the unfair trade practice or restrictive trade practice, (vii) not to offer the hazardous goods for sale, (viii) to withdraw the hazardous goods from being offered for sale, (ix) to cease manufacture of hazardous goods, (x) to pay such sum as may be determined by it, if it is of the opinion that loss or injury has been suffered by a large number of consumers who are not identifiable conveniently. Provided that the minimum amount of sum so payable shall not be less than five per cent of the value of such defective goods sold or services provided to such consumers. The Forum can also direct to issue corrective advertisement to neutralise the effect of misleading advertisements at the cost of the opposite party responsible for issuing such misleading advertisements. It can also impose adequate costs to the parties.

The Act provides that every proceeding of the District Forum shall be carried out by the President and at least one Member sitting together. Every order made by the District Forum shall be signed by its President and a Member or Members who conducted the proceedings. It is, further, provided that where the proceeding is conducted by the President and one Member and they differ on any point or points, they shall state the point or points on which they differ and refer the same to the other

Member for hearing on such point or points and the opinion of the majority shall be the order of the District Forum. The State Commission shall have administrative control over all the District Forums within its jurisdiction.

8.2: Position Vacant in the State and District Forums

Redressal Agency	*Post*	*No. of Vacancy*
State Commission	President	3
	Members	19
District Forum	President	56
	Members	228

Source: Report of National Consumer Dispute Redressal Commission, 2010.

Section 25 of the Act provides that, where an interim order made under this Act is not complied with, the District Forum may order the property of the person, not complying with such order to be attached. In case any amount is due from any person under an order made by the District Forum the person entitled to the amount may make an application to the District Forum and the District Forum may issue a certificate for the said amount to the Collector of the district and the Collector shall proceed to recover the amount in the same manner as arrears of land revenue. As per Section 27 of the Act, in case a trader or a person against whom a complaint is made or the complainant fails or omits to comply with any order made by the District Forum, such a trader or person shall be punishable with imprisonment for a term which shall not be less than one month but may extend to three years, or with fine which shall not be less than two thousands rupees but which may extend to ten thousand rupees or with both. Thus, in the legislative scheme of consumer protection, the District Forum is the most important redressal mechanism as the faith and confidence of the consumers in these adjudicatory bodies will depend to a large extent on the functioning of these forums. They are the first contact point for the consumers, where they seek redress to their grievances. The consumer forum provides the way to the consumers to get speedy and inexpensive justice against the producers and the service providers.

However, the working of the District Forums has come into sharp criticism by various stakeholders as the delay in disposal of the cases, being the most important criticism. There have also been allegations that the lawyers have taken over the consumer courts and as the consumer is unaware of the legal procedures and processes, he hesitates to file a complaint in the consumer court. During various interactions the point is stressed that the consumer courts are people's court and the interest of the consumers is supreme.

8.3: Total Number of Consumer Complaints Filed/ Disposed since Inception under Consumer Protection Law

Redressal Agency	*Cases Filed Since Inception*	*Cases Disposed of Since Inception*	*Cases Pending*	*Percentage of Total Disposal*
National Commission	65849	57626	8223	87.5
State Commission	515527	407143	108384	79.0
District Forums	2875132	2622983	252149	91.2
Total	**3456508**	**3087752**	**368756**	**89.3**

Source: Report of National Consumer Dispute Redressal Commission, 2010.

The Study

The Consumer Protection Act was enacted by the Parliament in 1986 for better protection of the consumers. The state of Jharkhand came into existence in 2000, and the State Consumer Disputes Redressal Commission came into existence in December 2001. Up to March 2002 for periods ranging between sixteen months and thirty six months, the posts of the Presidents and the Members remained vacant. During the period no Consumer Protection Councils were established at the State level and the district level. However, in Jharkhand since inception (upto 31.1.2009), only 29,544 cases were filed in the District Forums out of which 27,283 cases have been disposed of and 2,261 cases are pending. The disposal of cases stands to 92.35 per cent.

The Presidents and Members of the District Forum play a major role in enhancing the faith of the consumers in the redressal mechanism. There have been various studies highlighting the reasons for non-disposal of cases, the lack of manpower and infrastructural facilities. However, there is no study which focuses on the perception of the Presidents and the Members of the District Forums towards the Consumer Protection Act and the working of the Forums. This study essentially fills that gap. It looks at various aspects with which the Presidents and Members of the Forum have to deal with. The study is an attempt to examine the implementation of the Consumer Protection Act in the State of Jharkhand and also to assess the effectiveness of the District Forums in disposal of the cases and the problems faced by them.

Objectives of the Study

1. To evaluate the implementation of the Consumer Protection Act in the State of Jharkhand.
2. To critically examine the perception of the Presidents and Members of the District Forums towards the Consumer Protection Act.
3. To identify the nature of problems being faced by the Presidents and Members of the District Forums in discharging their functions.
4. To recommend suggestions for improving the working of the District Forums.

Methodology and Data Collection

Jharkhand is divided into twenty two districts and each district has a District Forum for redressal of consumer's grievances. Out of these, only twenty one District Forums are functional as per data available up to March 2009. In these twenty-one Forums there are six vacancies, two of Presidents and four of Members of the District Forums. In the State there are a total of fifty-seven Presidents and Members of the District Forums. The Data was collected through a structured questionnaire, which was administered to a sample size of 35 persons which included seven Presidents and twenty-eight Members. Apart from the questionnaire, discussions were also held with them regarding the working of the District Forums and the problems faced by them. Discussions were also held with the President of the SCDRC to ascertain his views on the working of the District Forums. Various reports and other published material were also scanned. The data so collected was tabulated and is presented in a report form. Table 8.1 indicates the number of Presidents and the Members of the sample size and the coverage of the District Forums.

Table 8.4: Sample Size, Position and Coverage of the Respondents

District	*President*	*Members*	*Total*
Ranchi	0	2	2
Lohardagga	0	1	1
Gumla	1	1	2
Simdega	1	1	2
Palamu	0	1	1
Latehar	0	1	1
Garhwa	0	1	1
West Singhbhum	0	1	1
Saraikela	0	1	1
East Singhbhum	1	1	2
Dumka	1	1	2
Jamtara	0	2	2
Sahebganj	0	2	2
Godda	0	2	2
Hazaribagh	0	1	1
Chatra	1	2	3
Koderma	1	0	1
Giridih	1	2	3
Dhanbad	0	2	2
Bokaro	0	1	1
Deoghar	0	2	2
Total	**7**	**28**	**35**

Perception of the Presidents and Members of the District Forums

1. **Profile of the Respondents:** The sample size consists of 35 respondents, which includes Seven Presidents and 28 Members. Out of the total respondents, 34 per cent of the respondents are women and 66 per cent are males. As far as the age of the respondents is concerned 49 per cent are above 60 years of age because of the appointment of retired District Judges as Presidents of the Forums. 20 per cent of the respondents are less than 40 years of age. 20 per cent are between the age group of 40–50 years and 11 per cent belong to the age category of 50–60 years.

2. **Educational Qualification of the Respondents:** About 57.14 per cent of them are law graduates, 22.86 per cent are graduates, 5.71 per cent have done LLM, 5.71 have BSc degree, 5.71 per cent possess MA and 2.86 per cent M.Com degrees respectively. An overall look at the educational qualification reveals that most of the respondents are well qualified.
3. **Previous Occupation of the Respondents:** Only 25 per cent of the respondents are from the judicial services, 20 per cent are from government service, 11 per cent are lawyers, 17 per cent belong to the private sector, nine per cent are social workers and six per cent are housewives. The District Forums have a mix of people from various professional backgrounds. This has brought in people with varied experience and backgrounds thereby enlarging the scope of the consumer movement.
4. **Knowledge of Consumer Protection Legislations and other Procedures:** Only 11.40 per cent of the respondents felt that to discharge their functions effectively it was not essential to know all the consumer protection legislations and the procedures. But they agreed that one should have a thorough understanding of the Consumer Protection Act. Majority of them (88.60 per cent), accepted that to effectively discharge their functions it is imperative that one should have a thorough knowledge and understanding of the provisions of various laws and the procedures to be followed. Only 14 per cent agreed that not knowing other consumer protection laws created difficulty in passing an order, while 86 per cent said that it did not create any such difficulty.
5. **Understanding of Law:** Of the total respondents, 62.86 per cent are law graduates and 37.14 per cent do not posses law degree but have degrees from other disciplines. Only 5.71 per cent of the respondents who did not posses law degree agreed that they experienced problems in discharging their functions. About 51.43 per cent said that they did not experience any difficulty in discharging their duties due to lack of a law degree. What is more interesting is that 42.86 per cent of the respondents did not answer this question.

About 95.45 per cent of the respondents with a law degree did not have any difficulty in passing a legal order; while on the other hand, about 30.77 per cent of those not having a law degree had difficulties in passing a legal order.

6. **Functioning of the District Forum:** About 91.43 per cent of the respondents agreed that the functioning of the District Forums was good and only 8.57 per cent said it was satisfactory. About 94.29 per cent agreed that the sittings of the District Forums were held regularly and the Members were punctual. As regards the working relationship between the Members of the District Forums, about 77.14 per cent said that the relationship was very cordial and they functioned like a team. However, only 22.85 per cent felt that the relationship was cordial but there were problems especially between the President and the Members.

7. **Major Obstaose Faced by the District Forums:** Only 72 per cent of them said that they lacked the required manpower and as such they were not able to function effectively. Only 58 per cent felt that the problem was due to lack of laboratory testing facilities. It took a long period to get the report after the tests are done. Lack of funds was another major problem faced by 48 per cent of the respondents. Only 45 per cent felt that in spite of Central Government providing the fund, infrastructure remains a problem. Nearly 40 per cent of the respondents felt that after filing the complaint the parties do not take the required interest which creates a lot of problem. About 22 per cent said that when a member retires his position is not filled up in time and due to the non-filling of vacant posts delay in disposal of complaints takes place.

8. **Need to Amend the Consumer Protection Act:** About 37.14 per cent of the respondents agreed that there was a need to amend the Act to provide more teeth to the Consumer Redressal Agencies.

9. **Fee Structure for Filing a Complaint:** Only 65.71 per cent of the respondents are of the view that the prescribed fee is reasonable and any hike in fee will deter the consumer from coming to the consumer forums to file a complaint. only 34.29 per cent of them felt that it is unreasonable. Most of

them felt that no fee should be prescribed for value of goods or services and the compensation claimed up to one lakh rupees.

10. **Level of Awareness among Consumers about Consumer Rights:** According to the respondents only 20 per cent of the consumers are aware about their rights and 28.57 per cent are aware to some extent and 51.42 per cent of the consumers are not at all aware about their rights and the Consumer Protection Act. A total of 68.6 per cent of the respondents felt that the consumers do not approach the District Forums as they are ignorant about their rights and the existence of any redressal mechanism. Only 54.72 per cent don't have much idea about the Consumer Protection Act, 22.9 per cent are afraid of the technicalities involved in approaching a consumer court, 17.1 per cent don't want to assert their rights, 17.1 per cent don't have much faith in the long procedures and only 8.6 per cent preferred mutual settlement to filing a complaint in the consumer forums.

11. **Involvement of NGOs in Filing of Complaints:** Only 68.57 per cent of the respondents are of the view that the NGOs must be involved in filing a complaint while 22.86 per cent did not favour the involvement of the NGOs in filing a complaint.

12. **Representation by Advocates in the District Forums:** Nearly 66 per cent of the respondents agree that the advocates should represent the parties in the District Forums, while 31.43 per cent felt that the advocates should be kept away from the consumer courts. The Members felt that there are a number of legal issues that the consumers are unable to understand and hence the cases take longer time to settle.

13. **Difficulty in Execution of the Orders of the District Forum:** A total of 37.12 per cent agreed that there is a problem of non- execution of the orders of the Consumer Forums.

14. **Efforts to Settle Cases through Mediation or Mutual Consent:** Majority of the respondents (91.42 per cent) are of the view that large number of complaints being filed in the District Forums could be solved through mediation or mutual understanding if there is a structured system available to the consumers before coming to the District Forums.

15. **Capacity Building Programmes:** A total of 71 per cent of the respondents have attended a training programme and 29 per cent have not attended any training programme. However, among those who have attended a training programme, 74.29 per cent found the programme to be very useful and 22.86 per cent benefited to some extent.
16. **Computer Literacy:** Nearly 74 per cent of the respondents are not computer literate. Only 2.65 per cent of the respondents are computer literate and 24 per cent are computer literate to some extent.
17. **Consumer Awareness Programmes:** Nearly 70 per cent of the respondents agreed that the responsibility for organising consumer awareness programmes should be with the District Forums for which the Central/State Government should give adequate funds. 18 per cent preferred the District Administration and 15.60 per cent felt that it should be the responsibility of the State Government.

Findings and Suggestions

1. The District Forums are functioning well, the sittings of the Forums are held regularly and the members are punctual. The delay in the disposal of the cases is because of other reasons and not due to the absence of the members. Most of them agreed that the work environment was very cordial and they functioned as a team.
2. The District Forums have been facing a number of problems, like lack of manpower, funds, infrastructure, lab testing of products, non-cooperation by the parties, etc. The computers have been acquired and installed but due to lack of manpower it is not of much help. The record rooms are not up to the mark and there is not much space to store the records. Computerisation of the records is the need of the hour. The members do not have any financial power which caused lot of delay. Even adequate stationary is not available in some of the District Forums. Moreover, the working condition of the employees also needs to be improved.
3. Most of them are satisfied with the major provisions of the Consumer Protection Act. However, some feel that there is

a need to amend the Act to give more teeth to the consumer courts. As far as the fee structure is concerned the majority of the respondents felt that it is reasonable.

4. Major impediment in the implementation of the Act is lack of awareness among the consumers. Due to this the consumers do not approach the consumer courts for redressal of their grievances. Efforts must be made to educate the consumers about their rights and also create awareness about the benefits of the Consumer Protection Act. The District Forums can play a major role at the District level in organising suitable awareness programmes for the consumers. At present the funds for awareness programmes are at the disposal of the District Administration and not the District Forum. Due to the lack of awareness about their rights and also the procedures under the Act, the consumers hesitate to approach the consumer forums in case of a complaint.

5. Majority of the respondents felt that the NGOs should play a proactive role and help the consumers in filing of the complaints. Involvement of NGOs in filing-in of the complaints will streamline the process and help in quick disposal of complaints. The consumers are not aware of the procedures of filing-in a complaint and the documents they are required to submit, the NGOs could themselves file the complaint on behalf of the consumers. This will avoid delay in disposal of cases.

6. The procedures to be followed by the consumer courts are very simple but with the involvement of the advocates the process has become very technical and legal. Even though the Act does not envisage the involvement of advocate yet (based on their experience), a majority of the respondents are of the view that the advocates should represent the cases. As the manufacturers and service providers are hiring the services of advocates, the consumer is at a loss as he lacks the required knowledge of the legal procedures. Moreover, there are a number of technical issues involved, which only the advocates know.

7. Execution of the orders of the District Forums is a major problem. The District Administration and particularly the police do not cooperate. No policeman is attached to the District Forums for execution of the orders of the Forum. As a result, large number of execution cases are pending mainly due to non-execution of warrant of arrest or attachment order by the police authorities. This is sending a wrong signal among the consumers. The Act needs to be amended and appropriate measures are required to be taken to ensure that execution of the orders of the forum is done in a time bound manner, otherwise the consumer will lose faith in the consumer courts.
8. The members are in favour of ADR before the complaint is filed in the District Forum. There should be some mechanism, at the level of the producer/service provider so that the grievances of the consumers can be addressed by mutual settlement failing which the consumer can file a complaint in the District Forum. Majority of them agreed that they do give an opportunity to the parties to settle their dispute through mediation or mutual consent. The Government of West Bengal has appointed District Consumer Welfare Officer who plays the role of a mediator. This system can also be introduced in other states provided a separate Department of Consumer Affairs is created as in the case of West Bengal.
9. As the scope of the consumer courts and the nature of complaints being filed are increasing, it is important that efforts are made to build the capacity of the members. Training has to be more systematic. Users' manuals in the local languages should be prepared for the use of the members of the District Forums. It would be better if induction training programmes are organised for the members of the District Forums. The recommendation of the Shenoy Committee set up by the NCDRC should be accepted by the State Governments and funds be made available to organise such induction training programmes.

10. Though the scheme of computerisation and computer networking of consumer forums was launched, but the working of the District Forums has not improved to a large extent. The District Forums are not able to take the full benefit of computerisation and computer networking. Adequate staff needs to be sanctioned for manning the computers. The members and other staff of the Forums should be imparted training in computer literacy and the operation of the software.

9

Unfair Trade Practices and Consumer Exploitations in India: How Can These be Eliminated?

B. Vaidyanathan

It is a fact that the Consumer Disputes Redressal Mechanism has failed considerably to meet the general expectations of the common man and consumer activists. This is more so when one considers the avowed objectives of the Consumer Protection Act, which aims to provide speedy redressal of consumer grievances, in an inexpensive manner. Major reasons for this malady are:

- Lack of understanding of this Social Welfare Legislation among those who administer the Act;
- Certain shortcomings in the Act and the associated rules;
- Non-existence of suitably devised Alternate Dispute Redressal (ADR) System; and
- The deteriorating governmental initiative to consult the stake holders, for a meaningful strengthening of the Disputes Redressal System.

Our experience over the past two decades, clearly indicate the need for:

- A separate Consumer Jurisprudence;
- A well devised ADR System and to incorporate the work done therein to decide punitive damages;
- Sufficient reward for NGOs, which take well meaning initiatives, as provided under Sec. 14(hb), against Unfair Trade Practices, affecting large number of consumers; and
- A proactive role by the government for strengthening the quasi-judicial bodies formed under the CP Act. All these help in realising Consumer is the King!

Introduction

It was at the initiative of the United Nations in 1985, that has resulted in the promulgation of the Consumer Rights Protection Act, 1986, in our country. The objectives of the said benevolent Act are indeed laudable. All the pamphlets and publicity that heralded the launch of the Act literally promised a great deal for the gullible consumers in this country. It was indeed an Act for time bound, simple and speedy redressal of consumer grievances without spending a paise, as the cases were supposed to be processed without any court fee and consumers could appear in the consumer courts in person or through a Voluntary Consumer Association (VCA), without having to hire and/or approach a qualified lawyer. The consumer courts were supposed to function without the frills of the civil court procedures. The expectations of the *aam aadmi* and even the knowledgeable consumers went sky high. Overnight innumerable number of Voluntary Consumer Associations sprang up across the country as though there was a big bounty on offer.

Secondly, after the initial inertia, the District Forums and State Commissions started functioning in many of the states from 1990, thanks to the initiative taken by Sri H.D. Shourie, the founder an NGO called Common Cause, who approached the Supreme Court highlighting the indifference of the government. But unfortunately this initial euphoria of the common man turned into despair within a decade of the enactment of this most benevolent and historic Act. In fact, the people, who had hitherto never approached a court, approached the District Forums as recommended by the consumer activists and the government. But to their horror they found that the Fora are manned by indifferent presiding members who are steeped in cumbersome and inefficient civil court procedures hardly equipped to redress the grievances of the litigants in a time-bound manner. Adjournments were being given without much concern for the hapless consumer-litigant. Even after all the painstaking efforts, what the consumer got was just peanuts, as the consumer Fora were found to be quite conservative while awarding cost and compensation. As a result of all these, overwhelming majority of consumers have become so de-spirited and disillusioned that they think twice to approach the consumer courts unless the stakes are very high and/or a compromise is possible. By and large, the situation is somewhat similar to what happens in the civil courts. We also notice that an increasing number of commercial and industrial organisations are utilising the Consumer Courts for settling their Insurance and other disputes.

An Anatomy of the Malady

Several factors contributed to this state of affairs:

1. Poor quality of the presiding officers/members, especially the non-judicial members, mainly due to:
   (a) Very low compensation, in comparison to the high level of competency expected for adjudicating the disputes;
   (b) Appointing retired judicial officers, who lack the motivation or zeal for undertaking such assignments;
   (c) Political interference in the appointments; and
   (d) Appointing practicing lawyers as presiding officer of the Forum.
2. Inefficient and corrupt staff manning the fora;
3. Non-allocation of sufficient funds and inappropriate administrative controls;
4. The hangover of the civil court procedures and practices; and
5. Lack of commitment on the part of the government.

An Approach for Eliminating Unfair Trade Practices

The Laws and Rules alone cannot deliver the results. It is the people (consumers), who can make the difference. Unless we make the quasi-judicial system, formed under the Consumer Rights Protection Act, 1986, more effective and efficient, consumers will never feel encouraged to approach them. So, the crux of the problem is that an average consumer should feel enthused and confident to approach a consumer court, when he encounters an Unfair Trade Practices. Towards achieving a Consumer-oriented Redressal System, we have to address the following issues:

1. A jurisprudence for consumer protection;
2. Changes needed in the CP Act and Rules;

3. Alternate Disputes Redressal System and its integration into the Consumer Justice System; and
4. Orientation of Governmental Actions.

(a) Is there a Need for Separate Consumer Protection Jurisprudence?

The unjustifiable delays in disposing of consumer disputes for years, improper interpretation of the consumer laws, lack of empathy for the sufferings of the consumer, a paltry relief in terms of compensation and cost and even dismissal of the complaint petitions on flimsy grounds, etc., are all quite common grievances among the consumer-litigants, who approach the consumer courts with lot of hope. All these clearly indicate that there is a total lack of understanding of the CP Act among those who administer it. In this context it will be quite appropriate to seriously consider the need for an appropriate consumer protection jurisprudence and implementation of the same, fitting the objectives of the Consumer Rights Protection Act, 1986. Herein we should clarify that this jurisprudence or interpretation and administration of the law, befitting the spirit of the landmark Consumer Protection Act must take into consideration the following. For example:

(i) The Act provides for deciding the case *ex parte* (sec. 13(2)(b)(ii)) when the opposite party fails to turn up even after service of notice, based on evidences. This provision needs to be carried out ruthlessly if the consumers are to be dispensed justice within the stipulated timeframe. This will also enhance the image of the consumer courts that these bodies mean business and they cannot be taken lightly. Further, such *ex parte* orders should not be allowed to be questioned in the appellate bodies (higher Commissions), unless such an appeal is made on a question of law. Our past experience reveals that the consumer courts are, in general, reluctant to pass *ex parte* orders and the opposite party is invariably given ample opportunity to respond, putting the consumer-litigant to avoidable hardship.

(ii) When the consumer litigant files a case in the District Forum, the Act provides for either dismissing the complaint for default or deciding it on merits (sec. 13(2)(c)). Since, in several cases the consumer-litigant is approaching the Forum for a small quantum of relief and they are also finding it difficult to attend the proceedings, the Consumer Courts, unless it is unavoidable, they should, in a consumer friendly manner, decide the matter (case) on merit, even if the petitioner fails to appear. It is generally found that the Forums prefer to dismiss the case, when the consumer-litigant is not present. In our own case, *Consumer Protection Council, Rourkela Vs Lohia Machines Ltd., OP No. 30 of 1990, NCDRC,* though the author himself was attending the case, spread over half a dozen sittings, representing the Council, and on behalf of over 1500 consumers, on the fateful last date of hearing, due to very heavy delay of one of the prestigious trains, could reach the Commission only by 4 PM. Though the concerned official in the NCDRC appreciated the problem and the same was communicated to the then President of the NCDRC, that did not reflect in the final order. All our efforts went in vain; there was no mention about Council's extra-ordinary efforts and the computer generated data sheets, which could be a model for any NGO interested to approach consumer courts, for public at large; and the Council was not awarded any cost, though the other complainant received Rs. 15,000.

(iii) Similarly there is confusion regarding applicability of the Consumer Protection Act to the services provided by certain service providers like telecom. Though instances of such nature have already been discussed and have been ruled that the Act will be applicable irrespective of Departmental Tribunals being made available for redressal of grievances. Another major area of concern is regarding the execution of the Orders.

Hence, in the interest of enhancing the effectiveness of the Consumer Rights Protection Act and safeguarding the consumers, all the relevant issues of the said Act which require a different spirited approach than that dictated by conventional jurisprudence should be studied in detail and the necessary changes can be made and notified.

(b) Need for Certain Changes in the CP Act and Rules

To make the consumer disputes redressal machineries more efficient, certain changes have to be made as follows:

(i) Eligibility criterion of the President of the District Forum (sec. 10(l)(a));

(ii) Salary and allowances payable to the members of the State Commission (sec. 16(2));

(iii) Sitting of Circuit Benches, in different notified cities (sec. 22C);

(iv) Fee for making complaints before District Forum (sec. 9A of CP Rules);

(v) Credit of the fine into the Consumer Welfare Fund (sec. 10A(1) of CP Rules); and

(vi) Limiting the appearance of lawyers.

(i) Eligibility Criterion to Become a President of District Forum

As per Sec. 10(1)(a) of the Act, any person who is qualified to be a district judge can be made the President of a District Forum. As per this provision, a lawyer with an experience of 10 years in the Bar can be appointed as the President of a District Forum. There are two issues which are likely to have an adverse impact on such appointments. Since the President of a District Forum is a tenure post/job and the remunerations are also meager, it is likely that only those without good practice will opt for such an appointment. Further, such an appointee as the President of a Forum, after completion of his term, is likely to go for practice, unless he is reappointed for a similar assignment. In such an eventuality, the President who is to adjudicate disputes based on arguments of the lawyers with whom he has to work again as a fellow-advocate is not likely to remain unaffected mentally/emotionally, while he is considering their arguments as the presiding officer. So, one of the prerequisites of a neutral presiding officer of the Forum is getting compromised.

Justice Balakrishna Eradi, Founder President of NCDRC, while addressing a Consumer Rights Protection Seminar at Puri, Odisha succinctly observed that practicing lawyers should not be appointed as the President of a District Forum, for the above explained considerations and reasons. But unfortunately, in Odisha and other States such appointments are being made even today. Hence Sec. 10(l)(a) of the C.P. Act should be amended that reads: *"a person who is, or has been a District Judge, appointed by the State Government, who shall be its President."*

(ii) Salary and Allowances of Members of State Commissions

As per Sec. 16(2) of the Act, salary and allowances payable to the members of the State Commission shall be as prescribed by the State Government. While in case of the President, who happens to be from the High Court, s/he continues to get the benefits of a High Court judge, whose compensation is decided by the Central Government, with the approval of the Parliament, as they belong to the higher judiciary, whereas the non-judicial members get their salary and other allowances, as prescribed by the State Government. But the package offered by the State governments are quite low, even in comparison to other state government officials, not to talk of the remuneration of a High Court judges.

That is why it is suggested that the salary and allowances of the Members of the State Commission should be prescribed by the Central Government. Such a step will help in eliminating the anomalies in respect of different State Commissions and it can be expected that the salaries as prescribed by the Central Government will be consistent with those of the National Commission. It is also pertinent to note that the presiding members of the State Commissions, who are supposed to be doing the same job in different states, but are not paid uniformly, which in itself is an anomaly. Though the suggested change could entail an additional burden on the exchequer of the State governments but it will help motivating the competent persons to come forward and offer their services for such positions. Thus, accordingly it is suggested that Sec. 16(2) may be amended that reads: *"as may be prescribed by the Central Government."*

(iii) Sitting of Circuit Benches

Though a provision has been made for constituting the Circuit Benches in 11 cities other than New Delhi by the National

Commission (under Sec. 22C), it is noticed that such circuit benches are holding their hearings only in a few of those 11 cities every year. This means that the same city will get an opportunity once in several years, for hosting the Circuit Bench. In a consumer-friendly way, the circuit benches should function in all the cities, in at least those already notified, at least once in a year, unless it is found that there are not enough cases to hold a sitting in a particular city at least for a week.

Accordingly Sec. 22C needs to be amended by inserting a clause at the end: ".....from time to time. Such a sitting of the National Commission in major cities shall be done at least once in a year, unless the number of cases to be disposed do not justify holding a sitting in the city for at least 5 days."

(iv) Withdrawal of Fee for Complaints up to Rs 1 Lakh

Filing of a case in the consumer court and processing it has remained un-remunerative. Since our interest is to encourage aggrieved consumers to fight for their rights, it will be quite appropriate if the charges for all the cases up to Rs. one lakh are waived off. It is in this context that necessary changes are required to be made in the Table sec. 9A, of CP Rules.

(v) Benefits of Fine Awarded Should be Given to the VCA/ Litigant

The Consumer Rights Protection Act has the noble objective of eradicating the unfair trade practices prevalent in the market. Such an objective will be best served, if and only if, there are strong deterrents against such misadventures by the marketers. Secondly, though the Act has made provision for filing complaints by an individual consumer or a group of consumers, who are affected by a common issue say, defective good or deficient service (under Sec. 2(l)(b)(iv)) and has empowered the District Forum (under Sec. 14(hb)) to award a minimum of five per cent of the value of such defective goods sold or deficient services provided, Consumer Rights Protection Rule 10A(1) requires the money so awarded to be credited to the Consumer Welfare Fund. Is it not a fact that the incidences of unfair trade practices have become quite rampant and are spreading unchecked in spite of the awareness that is being created among the general public?

Is it also not an accepted fact that the resources of the government machineries are overstretched and in many cases they may not even have the necessary wherewithal to identify and take up such cases affecting a huge population?

Is it also not true that overwhelming majority of the individuals do not have the technical competence or abilities or the legal expertise or the required information to comprehend such highly organised unfair trade practices and how to proceed against them? It is in this context that the role of Voluntary Consumer Associations (VCAs) will have to be seen and understood. At least some of them will be able to develop the competencies and/or expertise to unravel the unfair trade practices of organized business organisations and also to fight against such cases. But, even in such instances, if such an enterprise and initiative of a VCA is not getting compensated sufficiently, all the wishful thinking of those who enacted the Act will remain only a dream and the said Consumer Rights Protection Act as nothing but a paper tiger.

Though provisions do exist for awarding punitive damages (under Sec. 14(d)), and for adequate cost to the parties (under Sec. 14(i)), but seldom the compensation and cost awarded by the Consumer Courts have been found inspiring.

It is a bitter truth that an overwhelming majority of the VCAs are struggling to survive as the financial resources they are able to muster through voluntary contributions are quite meager and adequate to come forward to rescue the affected consumers. It is because of this ground reality that the ones which are able to make a meaningful existence are the ones which receive support from international funding agencies, or from individual patrons and well wishers, as in the case of our organisation, Consumer Protection Council, and from the government to a lesser extent.

It is in this context that the Consumer Rights Protection Rule 10A(1) has to be viewed. This rule shall have to be amended so as to allow the fine imposed under Sec. 14(hb) to be credited to the VCA or the individual or the group of consumers, and to be utilised in a manner like, for example, to create a Trust and utilise the amount for Consumer Protection activities only as prescribed by the National Commission. This policy is bound to spur all those who identify and are able to take up the matter legally, to proceed against such Unfair Trade Practices. After all, prosecuting of such cases involve quite a good amount of research, time and other resources. Once such initiatives are assured that they would be rewarded once their work delivers the result, in terms of exposing the Unfair Trade Practices and bring relief to a huge number of consumers, there are bound to be more takers for such initiatives. It is my strong view that an award of one incentive of this nature can help to mobilise the VCAs as well as the general public in an effective manner to fight the ever growing market injustices. Can there be any better deterrent than this?

(vi) Limiting the Appearance of Lawyers

A broad consensus has to emerge that to enable effective functioning of consumer courts, appearance of lawyers should be minimised. It is widely felt by the consumer rights groups that the appearance of the lawyers for all cases were not desirable and that they should appear only in cases involving finer questions of law and as desired by the Forum. Somehow this amendment did not come through during the last amendments, introduced in 2002. In the interest of making the consumer courts consumer-friendly, this change will have to be introduced to encourage the aggrieved consumers approach in right earnest the consumer courts to take the market injustice head on.

(c) Alternate Disputes Redressal (ADR) Systems

Alternate Disputes Redressal Systems are in place in many of the well-managed companies. In a way, some VCAs have also been taking up such initiatives. As a matter of fact, in our organisation, Consumer Protection Council, Rourkela, we started taking up individual complaints since 1987. Having handled thousands of complaints, we always feel and give the first opportunity to the opposite party to intervene and sort out the matter of disputes. This we find as an effective and efficient way of redressing consumer grievances. We venture to approach the consumer courts when we fail to elicit the appropriate response from the opposite party and we find the merits of the case warrant such legal action. That is why our success rate in consumer courts (District Forum, State Commission and National Commission) have been very high (more than 90 per cent), of the fifty and odd cases that we pursued.

To make the ADR initiatives more meaningful and relevant, the initiatives of the VCA need to be embedded in the Act. For example, if the defendant/opposite party is not amenable to reason when systematic approaches were made by the VCA or the concerned individual, the consumer courts will have to give weightage while deciding on the punitive damages, compensation and cost. Such approach is likely to give more weightage and teeth to VCA-initiated ADR and this, in turn, can substantially reduce the consumers with grievances to approach the consumer courts in the country. In this context, the procedure to be followed by the ADR systems can be appropriately prescribed and/or standardised format may be incorporated through the amendment of the Consumer Rights Protection Act, Rules and Regulations.

(d) Orientation of Governmental Actions

The governments, both at the centre and the states, have an important role to play for the effective and efficient performance of the quasi-judicial bodies formed to protect the consumers under the Consumer Rights Protection Act, 1986. It is in this context, we have to consider amendment of Sec. 4, 5, 6, 7 and 8 of the said Consumer Rights Protection Act. When the Consumer Rights Protection Act, 1986 came into being, one of the important noticeable activities of the Central Government had been the constitution of the Central Consumer Protection Council (CCPC). For less than a decade or so, the said Council met regularly, at least thrice in a year and gave a good opportunity for interaction and exchange of ideas. Sri A.K. Antony, who was the then Minister for Food, Civil Supplies and Consumer Affairs, gave sufficient attention to this activity. It was at his initiative that the then Prime Minister, Sri P.V. Narasimha Rao, attended one of the CCPC meetings. These consultations, in fact, kept up the momentum on consumer rights protection initiatives as all the stakeholders namely, the State Ministers, officials of the Union and State governments, President of the NCDRC and the Voluntary Consumer Associations assembled in one place. It is rather because of such an opportunity, this author had highlighted the plight of the Rourkela residents who had to travel to Sundargarh, a place 100 km away for attending the District Forum, since the District Forum for Rourkela was to be located in the District Headquarters at Sundargarh. Since more than 90 per cent of the cases of the District Forum used to be from Rourkela, the responsive Minister of the State and the pro-active Secretary of the Odisha Government, hearing my appeal in the CCPC meeting, where they were also present, took immediate steps for constituting a District Forum at Rourkela. This only shows how an active involvement and/ or action on the part of a Minister can invigorate the VCA initiatives.

Unfortunately, the Union government's initiative in the last decade or so has been either totally lacking or half-hearted. However, there was some initiative when Sri Wajahat Habibullah was heading the Department of Consumer Affairs. The government has to be pro-active in taking initiative of providing the real momentum while safeguarding the consumer rights other than giving only media-based advertisements, *"Jago Grahak Jago"*. Sloganeering can hardly make any real difference to the aggrieved consumers.

Conclusion

It is a fact that the Consumer Disputes Redressal Mechanism has failed considerably to meet the general expectations of the common man and the consumer activists as well. This is more so when one considers the avowed objectives of the Consumer Rights Protection Act, 1986 which aims to provide simple and speedy redressal of consumer grievances, in an inexpensive manner for the consumers of this country. We may highlight the major reasons for this malady as follows:

- Lack of understanding of this Social Welfare legislation among those who administer the Act;
- Certain shortcomings in the Act and the associated Rules;
- Non-existence of suitably devised Alternate Dispute Redressal (ADR) System which is to be made an integral part of the Consumer Justice System; and
- The deteriorating and/or half-hearted governmental initiative to consult the stakeholders and to meaningfully

involving them to strengthen the Disputes Redressal System for the benefit of consumers.

Our experiences over the past two decades clearly indicate that there is need for the following:

- A separate Consumer Jurisprudence;
- Making necessary amendments to the Act and the Rules; some of these have already been suggested above. For example, sufficient reward for NGOs, which take well-meaning initiatives as provided under Sec. 14(hb), against the Unfair Trade Practices that affect large number of consumers;
- An appropriately well-devised ADR System incorporating the policy of punitive damages; and
- A pro-active role by the government for strengthening the quasi-judicial bodies formed under the Consumer Rights Protection Act, 1986 may go long way in realising the statement: "Consumer is the King"!

10

Role of Mediation in Settling Consumer Disputes: An Experimental Case of West Bengal

P.K. Agrawal

People, in general, are afraid of going before the Courts whatsoever simple procedure or inexpensive procedure may be like the procedure before the District Fora, State Commission or the National Commission. It is increasingly felt that there is a hiatus between the Judge and the petitioner. Secondly, in spite of liberty to appear in person, the petitioner appears only through the Advocate. He is not able and/or encouraged to say his prayer directly before the Consumer Forum or Commission. Therefore, there is always a gap and the consumer as the petitioner is not happy about it. Moreover, by and large, advocates believe and love procedures. It is in this regard, the mediation can overcome this difference to a large extent. And this is most appropriate in India because court cases are mired in procedural and technical niceties, and this is one of the reasons that delay the adjudication in time. There are about three crore cases pending in various courts of the country for years.

It is now a well-established fact that there is no problem in adopting mediation as a tool to solve consumer disputes, though mediation has not been mentioned specifically in the Consumer Protection Act, 1986. The word used in the Act is settlement of disputes and not the suit or case. Section 89 of Civil Procedure Code after an amendment in it which became effective w.e.f. 1.7.2002, provides that every Presiding Officer of the Court should try to settle the dispute between the parties by way of reconciliation, mediation or arbitration before the regular case is taken up for hearing by the Presiding Officer. Thus, Section 89 is the *magna carta* or breathing device for the Indian Judicial System. According to Section 13(2)(a) of the Consumer Protection Act, 1986, District Consumer Dispute Redressal Forum will try to settle each dispute. That is why Advocates are not mandatory to appear before Forum or Commission. The Code of Civil Procedure is the "ground norm" for India as far as civil disputes are concerned. Therefore, it becomes our pious obligation to use mediation as a tool to settle consumer disputes, which are basically civil in nature. The Arbitration Conciliation Act, 1996 deals with the arbitration and conciliation. The Lok Adalats are also there to settle the disputes amicably under the Legal Services Authority Act, 1987. The mediation is to fill in the gaps especially in petty matters where the Acts of 1996 and 1987 are not invoked. To make the provision of Section 89 of CPC successful, it is essential that there is one officer present in every Court who can act as Mediator and amicably settle the disputes between the parties since the District Forums and Commission are overburdened with increasing number of cases, disputes or consumer matters, and they don't have time to settle the consumer disputes before them speedily. Secondly, their normal procedure will not permit such huge deviation.

Procedure

In West Bengal, mediation is now a regular institution or mechanism to settle consumer disputes under the Consumer Affairs Department and it is done through the Directorate of Consumer Affairs and Fair Business Practices. There are officers deputed in every Forum and the State Commission who will take up the mediation at the instruction of the Presiding Officer of the Forum or the State Commission or at the behest of any of the party. The procedure is kept simple, on receipt of the petition the designated Consumer Welfare Officer gives notice to the other party inviting him on the date fixed to the mediation table for settlement of dispute amicably.

On the date fixed, the designated official conducts preliminary hearing and decides to call both parties on a convenient date to arrive at a settlement. On the fixed date and time, he sits in a free and open atmosphere so that parties can negotiate without preconceived notions or their rigid stands.

Firstly, he sits in a room which is free from disturbances. He starts the mediation after their preliminary introduction. Then the Petitioner presents his case with detailed facts.

Mediator elaborates the facts which opposite party may not be aware of. The opposite party gives his reply. Then the mediator chalks out points for discussion. He briefly outlines the points of consideration of the consensus. Then he clarifies the stand of every party as per the provisions of the Consumer Protection Act, 1986. Afterwards, he allows elaborate discussion on points settled, i.e., examination, cross-examination, arguments and counter arguments all together.

The parties may be emotionally surcharged at this stage. In that situation, he takes the assistance of an outsider including some psychologist, if possible. He sits with each party separately. Then, he arranges their joint meeting. After their consent, a joint draft is prepared and is discussed again and weighed in the light of the relevant provisions of the Consumer Protection Act, Rules and Regulations. When it is agreed upon and signed by both the parties in his presence, it is referred for implementation.

Performance

About 3500 disputes have been settled in West Bengal out of about 5000 disputes filed with various mediation officers or otherwise in the State till 2009. Brief account of a few cases successfully solved through mediation process is given below to get a better picture how properly-guided mediation can attain success in solving many consumer disputes under the Consumer Protection Act, 1986.

For example, in the case of Sri Ashish Siddhanta and Smt. Sujata Siddhanta Vs. M/s Dulichand Motors Pvt. Ltd., it was found that the complainants paid a sum of Rs. 8,54,000/- only to the opposite party for purchase of a "Tavere Captain B-4" car. The opposite party made a commitment of delivery of the car within one month from the date of payment. But, such commitment turned to be a mere "paper-promise". The complainants contacted the opposite party time and again either over phone or through e-mail. Each time, the opposite party fixed a new date-line of delivery but failed to comply. The whole process killed at least 90 days. Aggrieved by this inaction, Sri Siddhanta lodged a complaint with the Directorate of Consumer Affairs and Fair Business Practices. On receipt of the complaint, the Directorate HQ found that the complaint centered on alleged inordinate delay and deviation from commitment for delivery of the car. The dispute was over apparent 'deficiency in service' and 'unfair trade practices' as defined under Sections 2 (l)(g), 2(1)(o) and 2(1)(r) respectively of the Consumer Protection Act, 1986 (as amended). In order to resolve the dispute through the process of mediation, the Directorate HQ arranged for tripartite meeting on 2009. Since ice was not broken in the first tripartite meeting, the second tripartite meeting was convened on 2009, wherein the opposite party admitted their fault and assured of delivery of the car within 10 days period. Finally, the opposite party delivered that car to the complainants on 6.8.2009. The Directorate HQ took less than one month in resolving the dispute. Thus, practically such a big issue was settled amicably through mediation process within a month; which would have taken years through the Forum and Appellate Fora.

Similarly, there was a dispute before the Directorate CA and FB between Smt. Kajal Banerjee and M/s. Ishika Jewellers. The facts of the dispute are: Smt. Kajal Banerjee purchased a finger-ring stated to be made of gold from the opposite party at a cost of Rs. 4,250. As Smt. Banerjee has been a long-time customer known to the opposite party, she believed the opposite party and never doubted the quality of goods sold to her by the opposite party. But, her faith on the opposite party received a severe blow when she had given the ring for remodeling to another Jeweler of her locality. To her utter surprise, she came to know now that the ring she bought from the 'long-time trusted party' was not made of gold at all; it was a ring made of material other than gold with golden colour coat. Smt. Banerjee brought the matter to the notice of the opposite party with the request to refund the amount incurred on such purchase. The opposite party not only denied the allegations, but used humiliating words to the complainant as alleged.

Finding no other way, she lodged the complaint with the Directorate of CA and FBP. The Directorate observed that the complaint centered on alleged misrepresentation, sale of fake goods and refusal to refund amount incurred on such purchase. Apparently, the dispute was a glaring example of 'unfair trade practice' as defined under section 2(1)(r) of the Consumer Protection Act, 1986 (as amended). In order to resolve the dispute through the process of mediation, the Directorate arranged for tripartite meetings on 2.9.10 and 6.10.10. The opposite party did not turn up at the tripartite meeting held on 2.9.10. In the tripartite meeting held on 6.10.10, the opposite party ultimately admitted that the ring was not made of gold but took a plea that they just sold it as a dealer but did not make it. It was clearly pointed out to the opposite party that as the ring in dispute was sold by them, the onus should always be with them. It was amicably resolved that the opposite party would refund the amount of Rs. 4250 incurred on account of cost of the ring, and Rs. 5,7507 as compensation for causing harassment and mental agony, together totaling an amount of Rs. 10,000 only was settled in the presence of the Mediating Officer. And the opposite party agreed to it and paid the amount to the complainant on 7.6.2010.

It is another case of settlement through mediation between Sri Soumitro Basu and Country Vacations (A unit of Country Club Ltd.). Sri Soumitra Bose had a card of Country vacations against a payment of Rs. 25,000. By virtue of having that card he was entitled to have accommodation for three nights and some other facilities free of cost at some resorts under the opposite party, the list of which was provided to the complainant. As alleged, the complainant booked one of such resorts for three nights and the booking was confirmed. He, then, booked Railway tickets to and fro also. But, just before starting his journey when he contacted the opposite party for other details of the resort, he was told that the resort was since closed. The complainant had to cancel Railway tickets and suffer financial loss. He noticed it also that the resort was closed before the card was issued to him. The complainant being fully dissatisfied with the opposite party, requested them to refund the amount incurred on the card and railway ticket but the OP refused to make such payment. Aggrieved Sri Basu then lodged complaint with the Directorate of Consumer Affairs and Fair Business Practices. Since the dispute was, prime facie, over "deficiency" in 'service' as defined under Sections 2(1)(g) and 2(1)(o) of the Consumer Protection Act, 1986 (as amended) for not providing the complainant with the information of closure of the resort in time and 'unfair trade practice' as defined under Section 2(1)(r) of the Act *ibid* for misrepresenting him about existence of the resort at the time of issuance of the card to him, the Department Head Quanter tried to resolve the dispute through the process of mediation in tripartite meetings. In the tripartite meeting held on 5.4.2010 the opposite party could not but admit their faults and assured of refunding the amount incurred on the card and cancellation of Railway Tickets. It was resolved that such refund would be made to the complainant by the opposite party in presence of the Mediating Officer on 26.4.2010. Accordingly, an amount of Rs. 25,000 on account of card and Rs. 640 on account of charges for cancellation of Railway Tickets, totaling an amount of Rs. 25,640 was refunded to the complainant on 26.4.2010. Thus, Sri Bose got peace of mind and his faith in the administration and quasi-judicial forum got strengthened because his complaint could be solved without further trouble to him in going to the Advocate and Forum. This is what the citizens expect from the State run machinery, whether it is administration, judicial or quasi judicial Fora. They want justice on their doorstep without more wastage of their time, energy and money. In fact, the citizens or consumers expect settlement of their genuine disputes on telephone or through video-conferencing.

In an epoch making complaint, Dr. Asit Baran Chakrabarty brought a dispute against Bharat Sanchar Nigam Ltd., being a Deputy Secretary in the Department of Consumer Affairs. Dr Chakrabarty had a post-paid Mobile phone connection with BSNL, on account of which he paid consumption bills regularly within the due date. On 30.3.2010, out-going facilities in connection with his mobile phone was disconnected. Dr. Chakrabarty contacted Customer-Care Cell of BSNL and he was informed that out-going facility in respect of his mobile phone no. was disconnected as had not paid the bill for January 2010 and the incoming facility would also be disconnected within an hour in case of non-payment of outstanding amount right then. Dr. Chakrabarty tried to convince them that the amount of the bill had already been paid but the customer care cell of BSNL did not pay any heed to his words. Aggrieved Dr Chakrabarty, then, lodged the complaint with the Directorate of Consumer Affairs and Fair Business Practices, H.Q. on 30.3.10 by FAX. Scrutinising the complaint and photocopies of the money-receipts, it was apparent to the Mediating Officer of the Directorate that the bill in dispute was paid in full within the due date. The matter was taken up immediately over telephone with A.O. (T.R.) of BSNL. The A.O. (T.R.) requested to send copy of money receipt of the bill in dispute to him. It was sent immediately to him by FAX. At about an hour after, the A.O. (T.R.) informed over telephone that bill in dispute was really paid up and admitting the fault on their part assured of restoring outgoing facilities within next 24 hours. On 31.3.2010 Dr. Chakrabarty, the complainant informed in writing that outgoing facility of his mobile phone connection was restored that very morning. Thus, government servants working in the Consumer Affairs Department are not barred to bring their complaints through this mechanism. In fact, the mediation process is applicable to all without any discrimination. As it is a conciliatory matter of settlement, no allegation or liability is later attracted or incurred to anybody.

The process is going on successfully. This is the most successful wing of the Consumer Affairs Department. Many letters of appreciation are received by the Department for the services rendered by the Mediation Officers with the State. If any of the party does not agree, he is free to go to the Forum in regular course. To be successful mediator, the mediator has to put himself into the shoes of both parties. He should have sufficient knowledge of consumer laws and procedure to bind parties. For this purpose training is required for officers in the government set up so that they can forget their government hat of power and work for amicable settlement in a free and relaxed manner.. However, some of the list of cases given in Annexure covering most of the rural districts in West Bengal show that the mediation process is applicable to all cases from the smallest one to the highest valued dispute. However, the governments or local self governments have to set up necessary infrastructure for mediation including appointment of willing and trained Mediators. For example, in West Bengal, the mediators are posted in each district unit of Consumer Affairs Department in each Forum, in the State Commission and at the Directorate level. Department of Consumer Affairs also tries to settle cases of complaints regarding advertisements and bad quality of goods or services especially against companies or government or semi-government organisations, provided the issue covers general public interest. If "there is a will, there is a way". The Consumer Affairs

Department absorbed the surplus declared staff and officers of Entry Tax Directorate, Government of West Bengal. Thus, the mediation in West Bengal is going on without further burdening the government exchequer.

In USA and in Europe, most of the consumer disputes are settled by way of mediation by NGOs, VCOs or the Advice Centers. They charge fees also and are functioning very successfully. In India, it will take some time. It is feared that NGOs may not become another power-centre in the process and may misuse their power.

Conclusion

Times are not far when mediation will be accepted as a legitimate tool in India in the field of resolution of consumer disputes and will be implemented with free help, patronage and support of the Central and State Governments. Already the Government of Delhi has initiated action in this regard. It is expected that it will find specific mention in the rules under the Consumer Protection Act, 1986. The mediation as a process is well recognised in law of the land now and many High Courts including Calcutta High Court have laid down detailed guidelines on how the process can be initiated and implemented. Times are not far when the mediation process will be accepted as normal phenomenon in India especially in Consumer Disputes cases filed in Fora. Detailed accounts of some of the settled cases in West Bengal mediation are as follows:

Some of the Case Settled in West Bengal Through Mediation are as Follows

Sl. No.	*Name of District*	*Name of Petitioner*	*Opposite Party*	*Date of Complaint*	*Brief about the Complaint in brief*	*Date of Disposal*	*Terms of Settlement*	*Remarks if any*
1.	Bankura	Tarak-nath Datta	M/s Jyoti Sales Corpn., Lal Basar, Bankura	26.07.2006	Compensati on for sale of defective fridge for Rs. 9,750	11.10.2006	New Godrej Fridge was given in Exchange	Time taken 2½ months only
2.	Bankura	Dr. Kavya Shree Jana	M/s Singhal Trading and Co., Savarkar Sarani, Bankura	21.03.2007	Compensati on for defective mobile set of Rs. 12,100.	04.09.2007	New Mobile set was arranged in place of the old one	Settled in 5 ½ months

3.	Bankura	Sh. Manmath Mahato	Dr. Jitendra Nath Banerjee, Bankura Seva Niketan, Nursing Home, Bankura	18.07.2007	Compensation for defective family planning operation	09.08.2007	Dr. Banerjee paid Rs. 61,000 for lapse in treatment,	In only 20 days compensation was piad
4.	Uttar Dinajpur	Smt. Manju Bhattacharjee	Post Master, Hemtabad Post Office	04.06.2007	There was a recurring deposit in the name of her husband for Rs. 6,400	14.06.2007	Smt. Bhattacharjee got the money back	In 10 days the matter was settled
5.	Jalpaiguri	Sh. P.K. Biswas	Sh. Prakash Ch. Karmakar Prop. Trinath Jewellery Home, Surya Colony, Siliguri	23.07.2007	The ring was made of lower quality of gold.	13.08.2007	The opposite party paid Rs. 1000 as compensation	In only 20 days Compansation was paid
6.	Birbhum	Smt. Renu Dey	1 Sub Post Master, Karidhya	03.05.2007	Rs. 8072 not deposited in Account No.1026042	01.06.2007	Rs. 8072 got deposited in account	Post Master accepted the claim
7.	Birbhume	Sh. Arun Bhandari	M/s Bajaj Auto Finance Ltd., Durgapur	11.12.2006	Additional instalment demanded while settling the account of Rs. 2,342.	01.02.2007	Additional instalment was returned	1½ months
8.	Birbhum	Sh.Kamini Mohan	Unit Trust of India, Kolkata	21.03.2007	After the period of Ulip-71 was over on 04.07.2005, the money was not returned	04.04.2007	Rs. 87,221 was returned to the Petitioner	In 13 days huge sum was retunre
9.	Malda	Sh. Dilip Kumar Bhowmik	State Bank of India, Malda	06.03.2007	Interest on FDR of Rs.4,75,590 was not given for 8 months.	23.04.2007	Rs. 20,776 got deposited in the account of the Petitioner	Bank agreed for giving interest

10.	Malda	Sh. Abdul Latif, Bhduhia, Malda	Malda Medical Centre, Malda	-	He admitted his wife for removal of stone but the stone remained.	13.12.2006	The Nursing Home agreed to remove stone without any further expenditure	In diagno-stic and nursing cases, Act applies fully.
11.	Malda	Sh. Manoj Saha	WB SEB, Gazole, Malda	-	Inspite of deposit of Rs. 1,00,354, connection was not given.	20.12.2006	The reconnecti on was given	Through interve-ntion of mediat-ion
12.	Coochb ehar	Smt. Nupur Rai	M/s Tolaram Dolly Chand COBR Cooch beher	-	Defective Chair was sold for Rs.2,200	-	Rs. 2200 was refunded	Within 6 days matter was settled
13.	Dakhin Dinajpur	Sh. Nripendra Nath Rai	Branch Manager, LIC Balurghat husband	17.01.2007	No money was given . after the death of her	.06.2007	The grievance was redressed.	LIC accept ed media-tion
14.	Purulia	Sh. Jeevan Kumar Deb Village Mungaldah	Post Office	-	Rs. 10000 NSCs were lost but copies were not given	-	The Complain ant got back money after maturity	The Compl ainant got back money after maturity
15.	Kolkata	Sh. Anoop Kumar Bal	Promoter	-	The plot was not registered in the name of the physically handicapped person inspite of full payment	-	The plot got registered. *	
16.	Kolkata	Shri Tarani Gangopa-dhyay Begurihati	The Diagnostic Laboratory	-	The test of blood was faulty	24.11.2007	Rs. 1 lakh compensa tion was paid by the Laboratory	This is a rare success example.
17.	Kolkata	Smt. Dwipanna Mazumdar, Grove	The Hospital	-	The hospital did not adjust Rs.2000/-	-	In spite of no proof, the hospital	On visit of mediat or the

		Lane, Kolkata-26			advance given		gave adjustment of Rs. 2000	problem was solved
18.	Bardhman	Sh. Paritosh Mandal	R&R Automobile G.T. Road, Bardhman	-	Inspite of demand draft of Rs. 70,000 tractor was not given	-	Rs. 95,000 was returned alongwith interest.	Two three meetings were taken by Mediator
19.	Uttar Dinajpur	Smt. Swapna Kundu Raiganj	Sahara India Financial Corporation	29.06.2009	The company didn't return even the principal due to irregular payment of instalments	10.07.2009	Rs. 9,444 were returned	Media-tion, prevail-ed on NBFC
20.	Uttar Dinajpur	Sh. Lantoo Barman Rainganj	State Bank of India, Hemtabad	22.09.2008	Papers for Collateral Security of Rs. 50,000 were lost in Bank.	29.09.2008	All papers were returned within 7 days to the Petitioner by the Bank.	Bank acted on advise of mediat or

References

1. Justice Kapoor, J.D.: Commentary on "Arbitration and Conciliation Act", Universal Law Publishing Co. Pvt. Ltd. CFF-IA- Dilkush Industrial Estate, G.T. Karnal Road, Delhi-110033, Year 2009, Total Pages 1466.
2. Rao, Rajya Lakshmi Rao: *Consumer is King*, Universal Law Publishing Co, 2008, Total Pages 355.
3. *Annual Report 2006-07* : National Consumer Helpline, 1800-11-4000.
4. Cases discussed: Directorate of Consumer Affairs, Fair Business Practices, Govt. of WB, 8B- Neli Sengupta Sarani, 6th and 8th Floor, Kolkata-700087, E-mail-cafbpwb@vsnl.net
5. Cases in Annexe: Tri-monthly journal "*Upbhokta Samachar*" (in Bengali) 2nd edition of 2003, pages 6-8, Department of Consumer Affairs, Govt. of WB, 11 A—Mirza Ghalib Street, Kolkata-700087, 4th edition of 2009 (pages 13–18).

11

Consumer Welfare and Protection in India: Present Scenario

Meenu Agrawal

Consumer Welfare

Today everyone is a consumer in one way or the other; therefore directly or indirectly consumer welfare is central to all of us. It is true even in the case of a child when s/he purchases a chocolate or attending a school by paying a consideration, s/he is a consumer or is when someone gets a TV repaired, opens a bank account or takes a life insurance policy, s/he becomes a consumer of services. Consumer welfare ensures that without any unfair or dishonest practices on a consideration a consumer is provided with appropriate services by the service-provider. It is the government that should ensure the welfare of consumer is respected. Keeping this in mind, the Government of India has started mass media campaign for consumers with a slogan "*Jago Grahak Jago*". In fact, accepting the responsibility, the government has framed and enacted various Acts and Rules. A separate Department of Consumer Affairs was created at the Centre by the Government of India. The State Governments have also created many such departments. The ultimate aim of all exercises is to ensure consumer welfare. No country, be it capitalistic or socialistic, can afford to ignore consumer welfare.

The Consumer Protection Act, 1986 defines consumer as any person who buys any goods and/or hires services. Thus the concept of "Consumer Welfare" essentially includes the promotion and protection of consumer rights. Consumers throughout the world, in general, and Indian consumers, in particular, are more or less disorganised. The consumer in current Mall-culture has become a mere helpless entity whose interests are often ignored by the sellers, service providers and/ or businessmen. In addition, the consumer also faces the difficulty of trying to determine the quality what is good or bad or right or wrong for him. The Consumer movement is a socio-economic movement which seeks to unite and protect the rights of the consumers in relation to the goods purchased and services availed of.

Similarly, the basic objective of Consumer Policy of the State Government is to ensure that goods and services are available to consumers at prices and quality as per the law of the land. Keeping in mind the complexity of the market place, ever-changing technology and the impact of globalisation, consumers need to be protected. Unfair trade practices need to be identified and regulated in order to prevent exploitation of gullible consumers and enable them to reach higher states of well-being.

The Government of India has provided financial support for various special schemes and institutions such as Consumer Clubs, District Consumer Information Centers, Mass awareness campaigns, training programmes, State Consumer Disputes Redressal Commission, District Consumer Fora, etc. New schemes such as establishment of some State-level consumer helpline were proposed in the 11th Five Year Plan period.

History of Consumer Protection

Consumer protection, as it is known today, has its roots and consumer protection movement is not a new concept in India. It is as old as trade and commerce itself. Kautilya, the great thinker and author of the well known ancient text of "*Arthashastra*" had written considerably on this and has referred to protection of consumers in this book. There are many references to the protection of consumer interests against exploitation by trade and industry as well as underweight and adulteration. He understood the need for punishment for many of these offences. The problems we are facing today, also existed many centuries back in India.

A seller sells a commodity to a buyer, and the buyer finds the product is short of standard as claimed by the sellers. Some would say it is a coincidence, but is it true? In the absence of definite statistics, the instinct of a consumer living in a capitalist society would lead me to wonder if the seller did not intentionally do something that led to dissatisfaction of the consumer ! The concept of consumerism, as it stands today, finds its origin in the late 19th and early 20th centuries' marketplace in the United States. The United States Congress made history in 1872, when it enacted-the first of its kind—The Consumer Protection Law, and The Mail Fraud Law, which made mail order fraud a punishable offence. Rudimentary at its best, and lacking teeth to curb anything but false advertising, this law nevertheless failed to prevent unsafe, unhealthy and dangerous products from reaching the hands of trusting consumers.

Other landmark acts in the consumer protection movement were the establishment of the Federal Trade Commission (FTC) in 1914 and the establishment of the Food and Drug Administration (FDA) in 1931. This was closely followed by the Food, Drug and Cosmetics Act of 1938, which enabled the FDA to test new drugs before they reached the consumers. In the mid-twentieth century, the two stalwarts in the consumer protection movement were Ralph Nader and President John F. Kennedy. Ralph Nader of USA is known as father of consumer movement. In a historic speech in 1962, Kennedy was the first to define basic consumer rights as they are used today at the global level. Another milestone in the consumer protection movement came with the publication of Ralph Nader's book *Unsafe at any Speed* in 1967. Leading to the enactment of The National Traffic and Motor Vehicle Safety Act in 1966, this book was the first attempt by a common citizen to exercise his consumer rights against the big corporate sharks.

Kennedy introduced the Consumer Bill of Rights in 1962 in the US Congress. This was closely followed by several other bills/legislations such as The Cigarette Labeling Act (1965), the Fair Packaging and Labeling Act (1966), and the Wholesome Meat Act (1967) and the establishment of the Consumer Product Safety Commission (CPSC) in 1972. India, too, could not be far behind in the changing global scenario. Indian political leaders soon realised that they could not hold on any longer protecting their business patrons against public outcries of corporate fraud, deceit and callousness. So the Government of India passed the Consumer Protection Act in December of the year 1986. If reviewed independently, the Consumer Protection Act, 1986 is fraught with the shortcomings which the consumer legislations of developed economies suffered from about 25-50 years ago.

Consumers Rights

As a consumer, one enjoys special rights. Consumers in the advanced countries are obviously better aware of their Rights than in developing countries like India. On March 15, 1962, the then US President John F. Kennedy made a historic speech about consumer rights as he introduced "The Consumer Bill of Rights" in the US Congress. 24th December is celebrated as the "National Consumer Day" in India and 15th March is celebrated as the "World Consumer Rights Day". Kennedy strongly believed that it is vital for 'United States' national interest to ensure the welfare of its consumers, as at the fundamental level it is the consumer who drives the economy. He formulated four rights for consumers:

- Right to Safety
- Right to Choose
- Right to Information
- Right to be Heard

Later on, the Informational Organisation of Consumers' Union (IOCU) added four more rights. These were:

- The Right to Redressal
- The Right to Education
- The Right to Healthy Environment
- The Right to Needs

The Consumer Protection Act, 1986 of India recognises six rights of the consumers:

- Right to Safety
- Right to Choose
- Right to Information
- Right to be Heard
- Right to Seek Redressal
- Right to Consumer Education

Recognition of the rights of consumers is essential. Though the consumers get commodities from the shopkeepers in exchange of their hard earned money, there is no certainty that they will get the commodities as they qualitatively desire them to be.

A consumer giving high price for the commodity, expects satisfaction everyway in return. But if the commodity purchased does not meet his expectations or does not satisfy him, his interest ought to be protected. It is said that the consumer gets goods and services of less than half the original worth of the money he pays. The industries and the producer firms should see to it that the rights of the consumers are well protected. There is now growing awareness among the consumers and they want their rights to be recognised and accepted by the producers. However, no sincere efforts have yet been made by the business houses to recognise and evaluate the rights of the consumers. The producers, whose goods are purchased by consumers and distribution or selling agencies, whose services are hired by consumers should protect the interest of consumers and recognise their rights in the right earnest.

It is hoped that the awareness of the existence of these rights will inspire the consumers to build a strong association or society of them in the entire country. This movement will hopefully ensure welfare of the consumers. The Government has accorded high priority to the programme of consumer protection. The Department of Consumer Affairs, being a nodal Department in the field of consumer protection, has initiated a number of steps to promote responsive consumer movement in the country. Such measures include the use of media for promoting consumer awareness and encouraging consumers' involvement through efforts of governmental and non-governmental organisations and others. It is a fact that the ignorance of consumers is solely responsible for their exploitation. The consumers should know their rights and must exercise them.

How to know about the Rights

An example: For the layman in his daily life, there is practically no difference between the words 'consumer' and 'customer'. But in fact, the two words do not mean the same thing. Consumers are just one sub group of customers. An example showing the difference between a consumer and a customer:

If a restaurant purchases a dining table for customers to have their food on, then the restaurant is only a customer not a consumer. But if one goes and buys a dining table for family purpose, then he is a consumer.

This example explains that only when one buys a product purely for his own consumption does he become a consumer. But if one buys a product solely for any commercial purpose, then he is a customer, and not a consumer.

The word 'Consumer' is well defined in The Consumer Protection Act, 1986 and according to this law, the consumer is not only a person who uses the product for merely domestic or personal use, but also one who uses the commodity to earn his daily livelihood. Needless to mention, Consumer Protection Act 1986 provides protection only to consumers. Buying a product for commercial purposes is a business transaction, since there is no intention to consume the product for personal use.

Some Examples about the Rights of Consumers

A consumer goes into a shop, and wants to buy a product with a maximum retail price (MRP) of Rs 80. However, just as the consumer is about to pay he realises that the seller wants to charge Rs. 85. The consumer refuses to buy the product and walks out without buying the product. In this condition, can such a consumer seek protection as per the provisions of Consumer Protection Act, 1986? The answer is a "Yes". As a consumer, it is one's right not to be charged more than the MRP.

To take another example, a consumer reads an advertisement in the newspaper claiming a Music System has specific features. The consumer goes to the dealer to purchase the Music System. When the consumer discusses with the dealer about the system, he discovers that it does not have all the features that were advertised. The consumer does not purchase the Music System. Can this consumer seek protection as per the provisions of Consumer Protection act? Again the obvious answer is a "Yes"'. Because the Consumer Protection Act, 1986 guarantees to the consumer right not to be misinformed about any features of a product.

Please note, however, that in the first example cited above it will be difficult for the consumer to win the case. This is so because since he refused to purchase the product, it would be well nigh impossible for him to establish that the shopkeeper attempted to charge Rs. 85 for the product. But in the second case, he stands a good chance of winning the case if he has a certified copy of the newspaper advertisement about the features of the product and any product literature at the dealer's store that shows the lack of availability of any feature(s).

How can the consumer win the second case? If he has not purchased the Music System, it is hard to prove damages. Still he could seek to get punitive damages against the Company for trying to defraud readers, he being one of them. However, this is not something to bet on. One's relief as a consumer lies in the form of a request to the Consumer Court to order the Company to correct the advertisement, or to withdraw the product with such claims. One is very likely to win the former relief; the latter would again be uncertain.

Consumer Protection Act, 1986

The Consumer Protection Act (CPA) was the nicest gift our government has given to consumers. Consumers now finally have a voice and a forum to air their grievances. Using Consumer Courts, many citizens have been able to retrieve their money from sloppy builders, dishonest shopkeepers, shoddy sellers of all kinds, and even from Governmental organisations such as the railways, state-run companies, and so forth. But on the flip side, a consumer may have to suffer loss also if he fails to abide by the important rules while filing a case in Consumer Forums. The most important thing for a consumer is to always keep in mind, in order to be able to initiate judicial proceedings against any producer or seller, as the case may be, is that he should get a bill for whatever he buys, for the obvious reason that if he does not have a bill to prove that he has bought something, it will be nearly impossible for him to prove his case at the Consumer Forum, not to add the fact that the court may not, so much as, even entertain the matter if the consumer fails to produce the necessary bills.

The Consumer Protection Act, 1986 came into effect first on December 24, 1986, after being passed by the Indian Parliament, and after being signed by the President of India. The Act has undergone three amendments, in the years 1983, 1991, and 2002.

Consumer Protection Councils

The Act provides the Central and State Governments with the power to create Consumer Protection Councils at the Central, State and District levels to promote consumer welfare. The Consumer Protection Councils have very little statutory powers and as such any direct benefit one can get as a consumer from these councils is practically very little.

Consumer Disputes Redressal Agencies

The Act also provides for the establishment of Consumer Courts. The Central Government is responsible for the establishment and maintenance of the National Consumer Disputes Redressal Commission at New Delhi. The State Governments are responsible for the establishment and maintenance of the State Consumer Disputes Redressal Commissions at the State level and District Consumer Disputes Redressal Forums at the District level. The statutory powers and jurisdiction of the three Commissions are summarised as under:

Table-11.1

Amount of Compensation	*Court*	*Qualifications of President*	*Other Members*
Up to Rs 20 Lakh	District Consumer Disputes Redressal Forum	Must be qualified to be a District Judge.	Two other members one must be a woman.
Rs 20 Lakh to Rs 1 crore	State Consumer Disputes Redressal Commission	Must be a person who is or has been a judge of a High Court.	At least two other members.
High than Rs 1 crore	National Consumer Disputes Redressal Commission	Must be a person who is or has been a Judge of the Supreme Court.	At least four other members.

Some other important provisions of the Act also deserve mention. A complaint can be filed free of cost before the District Forum, the State Commission or the National Commission; the Complainant or any of his/her authorised agent/person can present the Complaint in person. It is not obligatory to engage a lawyer. Even a Consumer Organisation can be authorised to represent the case. The Complaint can also be sent by post to the appropriate Forum/Commission, as the case may be. One cannot file a Complaint in a Consumer Court if a period of two years has elapsed from the date of the cause of action (such as payment of a bill or the incident that started the dispute with the company).

The Act is applicable in all states in India except in Jammu and Kashmir. The Act makes provisions to include both tangible goods and intangible services purchased from a trader or hired from a service provider. The Act can apply to any consumer who uses the product for non-commercial activities, the only exception being the use of it to earn his livelihood. In other words, the Act excludes commercial customers fully, but includes individual domestic customers, groups of domestic customers, societies and not-for-profit organisations.

This Act has completed more than 20 years but the common consumers as well as producers are not yet aware of the Act and its provisions, this is in spite of governmental efforts to create awareness at state as well as centre levels. It requires an active role of educational institutions, voluntary organisations and NGOs to make people aware to their rights and responsibilities. It is astonishing to see that in spite of U.N. recognition and encouragement from developed nations, consumers in India still do not get their due. It is high time that we woke up and realised the consumer rights.

The need of the hour therefore, is to highlight consumer protection and consumer welfare by educating the common consumers, giving special emphasis on rural consumers, who are generally more susceptible to exploitation, so that they become aware of different schemes and reap maximum benefits. This will safeguard the common consumers of the country and thereby add to their welfare.

The rural consumers are easy to be exploited, owing to their ignorance and illiteracy. They are more or less ignorant about the market conditions. The producers and sellers usually take undue advantage of this position. Thus, these consumers need protection as their rights are adversely affected in the market. In promoting consumer education the shift from 'buyer beware' to 'seller beware' has increased the role of the government. It is in this that the education of consumers plays an important role in safeguarding their rights and welfare. However, the Government of India has made its best efforts to educate and to make aware the consumers to safeguard their interests and welfare.

The governments at the Centre and the States continue their efforts to enforce the intent of the Act and make Consumer Courts more effective. Government efforts are also directed at the creation of consumer awareness through various agencies. The welfare of consumers now remains in their own hands. Hence alert consumers, aware of their rights and responsibilities, can not only protect themselves but can also make consumer sovereignty a reality.

Some Suggestions for Protection of Consumers

- To create suitable administrative and legal mechanisms, which would be within the easy-reach of consumers;
- To involve and motivate various sections of society such as consumer organisations, women and youth to participate in the movement;
- To generate awareness among consumers about their rights and responsibilities;
- To motivate consumers to assert their rights by education and not to compromise on quality and standards of goods and services and seek redressal in Consumer Courts, wherever required;
- To publish product specific booklets, pamphlets, cassettes, CDs, documentary films and other mass communication methods to promote consumer protection in English and Regional languages;
- To launch campaign programmes for potential customers in rural and urban areas;
- To promote, seminars, workshops and group discussions, these will provide a good platform for threadbare discussion of the issues;
- To establish healthy relations with educational institutions such as Universities, Colleges, Intermediate and High schools to emphasise the need for improving consumer education in the curriculum;

- To bring together the consumers, traders and policy makers to exchange information of mutual interest for better coordination. Bring together NGOs and consumer activists operating in different areas and to equip them with the necessary information and knowledge to enable them to act as nodal agents of change in rural areas;
- To coordinate with programmes organised by Central and State Governments, State Legal Aid Authorities, Academic institutes, National and International Consumer Organisations;
- To make the process of consumer litigation time-bound so that consumers get justice quickly. The consumer groups may fight legal battle on behalf of individual sufferer; and
- Consumer movement should be launched in the rural areas to educate the customers and consumers in connection with prices, packages, laws for their protection.

While concluding it may be pointed out what the President of India, Shrimati Pratibha Devisingh Patil, said at the plenary meeting of the committee on "Consumer Policy" on 27th May, 2009 in New Delhi:

"Standards (BIS) play a key role in consumer protection. Moreover, there is also a need to encourage the implementation of standards concerning consumer safety. For building confidence more meaningful participation by consumer organisations is required for developing standards both at the national and international levels. In an interlinked world, it is equally important to expeditiously conclude mutual recognition agreements of standards between countries to promote international trade and to enable faster movement of goods. A common set of accepted standards will avoid unnecessary trade disputes and will be a guide to exporters for supplying standard goods overseas. A legal system and a strong dispute redressal mechanism must also be in place. This can make consumer protection effective and meaningful, nationally and internationally."

12

Consumer Law in India and How a Dream House became A Nightmare

Atulesh Kumar

Indian Ancient Consumer Laws

Consumer Rights and their protection are not a new concept for India. Since time immemorial it is one of the prominent socio-economic problems faced by people in India. Consumer rights issues and problems have deep roots in the ancient Indian Jurisprudence. Historically, Consumer rights consideration dates back to the Vedic age (5000 BC-2500 BC). The Vedic age was a glorious period of cultural evolution of Indian civilisation. Matters relating to civil rights and criminal offences are elaborately discussed and found place in the Vedas. Four broad types of relevant Criminal Offences related to consumer issues were prominent in the ancient period in India.

(a) Adulteration of food-stuff;

(b) Charging of excess prices;

(c) Fabrication of weights and measures;

(d) Sale of forbidden goods and articles, etc.

For all these offences statutory measures and punishments were recommended from time to time. Some of the prominent texts of the ancient time were:

(i) **Manusmriti (800 BC–600 BC):** *Manusmriti* explains that it is obligatory on the part of the king to fix the rates for the purchase and sale of all marketable goods having duly considered from where they have originated, their destination, transport charges, value of goods, incidental expenses and margin of profit. The fixation of prices by the king was to be made public. If the merchants conspired to raise the prices of the commodities at their own will, they were punished and/or severely dealt with. The *Manusmriti* provided that all weights and measures must be duly marked by the king and should be re-examined every six months.

(ii) **Kautilya's Arthashastra (400 BC–300 BC):** *Kautilya* wrote the *Arthashastra* in an, elegant style. He dealt with administrative law, civil and constitutional law, criminal law and international law. According to the *Arthashastra,* a superintendent of weight and measures was to be appointed to maintain control over fabrication of weights and measures. Constant watch and periodical checking was indispensable.

(iii) **Yajnavalikasmriti (300 AD–100 BC):** It has a very systematic account and is considered to be an authority in the realm of Hindu law as well as of *Vyavahara* (behaviour) and personal rights of a man. *Yajnavalikasmriti* also deals with the issue of excessive price charging by the traders: Demanding a higher price was made punishable.

(iv) **Naradasmriti (100 AD–200 AD):** It has clearly delineated the channels of civil and criminal law.

(v) **Brihaspatismriti (200 AD–400 AD):** It gives an elaborate description of civil and criminal law. It mentions the offences very clearly and also mentions the punishment and penalty to be imposed on the violations of the law. Manufacturing of inferior quality or spurious gold and gems was also punishable according to *Brihaspatismriti.* Manufactureas of duplicate articles were also punished severally.

(vi) **Katyayanasmriti (300 AD–600 AD):** It deals extensively with the substantial and procedural law as well as with the rules of evidence. In those days cheating of any kind, be it selling counterfeit gold or adulterated commodities or unclean meat was regarded as a crime and the culprit was severally punished. The *Manusmriti* and *Yajnavalikasmriti* advocated for the punishments. Adulteration of grains, fat, medicine, perfumes, salt, sugar attracted severe penalty.

(vii) **Agni Purana** also mentions about merchants dealing fraudulently in respect of quality or price of the commodity. Such merchants were punished and their goods were confiscated by the state.

Modern Consumer Law

The Consumer Protection Act, 1986 is a unique/path-setting legislation. Neither the USA nor the Western countries have set up separate courts for redressal of the grievances of the Consumer. Our Act encompasses wide range of subjects which do not come under the purview of Consumer Disputes in USA or Western countries. For instance, medical negligence or insurance claims in western countries are not considered to be consumer disputes.

A Consumer Forum is required to follow the principles of natural justice and is not bound by the strict rules of procedure as contained in the Code of Civil Procedure, 1908 which leads to enormous delay in deciding the matter. When a Consumer Forum is not bound by the strict rules of procedures why should it take time to decide a matter?

The objective of the Act is to ensure better protection to the consumers and thus provide for the establishment of Consumer Fora for the settlement of Consumer Disputes and for matters connected therewith.

Why Consumer Protection Act was enacted by the Government of India? The Consumer Protection Act, 1986 was enacted to provide for better protection of the interest of consumers and for settlement of their disputes. The main object of the Act is to promote and protect the rights of Consumers such as:-

(a) the right to be protected against marketing of goods which are hazardous to life and property;

(b) the right to be informed about the quality, quantity, potency, purity, standard and price of goods to protect the Consumer against unfair trade practices;

(c) the right to be assured, wherever possible, access to an authority of goods at competitive prices;

(d) the right to be heard and to be assured that consumers interest will receive due consideration at appropriate forums;

(e) the right to seek redressal against unfair trade practice or unscrupulous explanation of consumers, and

(f) the right to consumer education.

To provide speedy and simple redressal to consumer disputes, quasi-judicial machinery has been set up at District, State and Central level. These quasi-judicial bodies will observe the principle of natural justice and have been empowered to give relief of a specific nature and to award appropriate compensation to consumers. This paper especially deal with the problems related to housing rights of the consumer.

Consumer Laws and Housing Rights

One of the most important objectives of the state is to provide living accommodation to the people. To realise this goal, the State Governments have set up Housing Development Boards. They are engaged in serving the public in the matter of providing housing by acquisition of land, development of sites, construction of houses thereon and allotment of plots/houses to the public. The Housing Development Board is engaged in rendering services for consideration to the public and therefore those who are allotted plots/houses from Board are clearly consumers falling within the definition of Sec. 2(1)(d) of the Consumer Protection Act, 1986. The consumer forum is empowered with the jurisdiction to grant appropriate relief to any of the harassed consumer who approaches the forum.

However, the performance of these housing boards has been highly unsatisfactory both in terms of facility and constructions. We often find the construction is to be sub-standard and there is inordinate delay in allotment of flats and/or sometimes possession of flats is not handed over in a reasonable time period. There may be failure to provide amenities, demanding more money from one person or the other, delay in giving possession of constructed house/flat despite price being fully paid, failure of housing boards and/or housing societies to execute conveyance deed, ineligible persons included in allotment of flat by draw, etc. are the ever-growing problems that are causing concerns to the stakeholders/bonafide members.

In such a situation, we may say that the dream house of the bonafide member becomes a real nightmare. We all are aware that food, clothes and shelter are the three basic necessities of every human being and these are also a part of human rights. For example, to procure a house/flat in a metropolis/city for a middle class family is nothing but a dream project and it is considered as a life time achievement if one gets it by investing even his life's savings and hard earned money. Thus, ultimately at the end of the day when he is not able to get possession of the flat where he invested money then he starts suffering every way mentally and financially. But his suffering does not stop here; when he goes to Courts for redressal of his problems when he files a case before consumer court and could not get relief due to various reasons or get relief after a long period of time he further suffers. I strongly believe this is the main concern for all of us to think afresh how we should help reduce if not eliminated the problems of the suffering consumers and bring smile to them. Thus, there is a serious need to discuss this issue, debate and find out the solutions for it.

As said, the Housing Development Board and/or Housing Societies render service as defined under sec. 2(i)(o) of the Consumer Protection Act, 1986. The Supreme Court in Lucknow Development Authority Vs. M.K. Gupta (1994) 1 SCC 243/AIR 1994 SC 787 has held that if a builder of a house uses sub-standard material in construction of a building or makes false or misleading representation about the conditions of the house or delay in delivery of house then it is a denial of the facility or benefit of which a consumer is entitled to claim adequate compensation under the Consumer Protection Act.

The delay by the Housing Development Board and/or Housing Societies in execution of the conveyance deed on payment of transfer fee has been held to be deficiency in Service under the Act (Gujarat Rural Housing Board Vs. Suryakantaben Ramcharan Adhikari (1992) 1 CPR 117 (Guj. CDRC).

The benevolent Consumer Protection Act, 1986 has still not achieved the requisite satisfactory results by the Consumer Fora set up under the said Act. Of course, we also know that these fora do also suffer from several constraints. In other words, various issues and challenges have different connotations. If I may say so the word issues and challenges are for both advocates and for Consumer Fora and word opportunities is for consumers, and therefore, being a practicing advocate I perceive that the main issues are:

1. Time-bound Disposal of the Cases: District Forum has to decide the cases in three months from the date of receipt of notice by the opposite party and appeal by the State Commission and National Commission within 90 days from the date of admission.

But what we normally see is that District Forum takes on an average three years or so to decide a case and State Commission and National Commission takes another three years. So where is the time-bound disposal/speedy justice as stipulated in the Consumer Protection Act, 1986?

2. Pendency of Cases: It is very difficult to accept the argument that since there are a large number of cases pending in the consumer forums so it takes lot of time to decide the cases. In my considered opinion it is not true, because the consumer courts deal specifically only with consumer matters unlike the normal courts like District Court, High Court and Supreme Court which deal with various types of matters. Thus, the Consumer Fora cannot say that they are unable to decide the cases as per the time limit prescribed in the statute.

I have gone through some practical experience in the Consumer Fora and based on this I can vouch that they are very prone to give very long date and in such a situation certainly the pendency would increase. The Consumer Fora should give very short date as far as possible so that the Consumer can get speedier justice.

3. Competency of Members: Experience makes me believe that there is an absolute need for appointment of more competent, efficient and pro-consumer members in Consumer Fora to facilitate the redressal of consumer disputes speedily. Moreover, persons who are well versed in Consumer jurisprudence should be appointed as members of Consumer Fora only then consumer-friendly justice may be delivered without fail.

4. Appointment of Presidents and Members: As in normal course we invariably find that the Presiding officers of District Fora, State Commission and National Commission are the retired judges of District Courts, High Courts and Supreme Courts respectively. I am of the opinion that when these 'Judges' are not officially fit to decide cases in respective courts due to their age and they are 'retired', how come they are found fit to be appointed as 'Judges/Presidents' to sit for another five years without much knowledge and expertise in specific area of law, that is, 'consumer jurisprudence' to deal with consumer disputes in these Consumer Fora. It is high time that we immediately change this practice and relieve the aggrieved consumers whose cases are habitually found to be understood and dealt in civil procedures framework where technicalities become more important including the help of lawyers. One of the suggestions would be to appoint sitting judges, who are sensitive and well-versed in consumer jurisprudence, on deputation as Presiding Officers in these Fora so that they could perform their specialised role as per Consumer Protection Act. Moreover, they would be more sincere and accountable since they have to get back after their tenure in consumer fora to the respective Courts, High or Supreme Courts. Because the present system of appointment has certain inherent weaknesses the appointed Presidents may feel that since they have already retired, they have not to be efficient, sincere or accountable and they just have to sit for another five-years term which came to them as bonus in their lifetime.

5. Competence of Lawyer: Sometimes Consumer suffers due to lack of competency and/or efficiency of a lawyer in consumer jurisprudence and they try to follow the technicalities more since the Presidents are also habituated in this frame of mind. Although the consumers are not required as per Consumer Protection Act, 1986 to appear before Consumer Fora through their lawyers but we invariably find that they represent either the consumers or the opposite parties and usually become more prone to follow the technicalities of civil law procedures. I believe since the consumers are the sufferers they are definitely more competent to narrate their problems and positions. Therefore, both the complainants and defendants must be encouraged to appear and argue their respective cases for summary adjudication.

6. Unawareness of Consumer Laws by the Parties/ Consumers: The other major problem is unawareness of Consumer Laws by the consumers as well as the traders. Although the Consumer awareness is gradually generating momentum in India, still large section of our population is not aware of the working and procedure of consumer courts. There is a high need to educate the people in this regard.

7. Delicate/Complex Procedure: As said, normally the consumer Fora are not to stick/attach to the intricacies of Civil Procedure Code because the Consumer Protection Act underlines that the procedures followed should be simple and there is no need for adherence to the strict rules like in other courts. So I am unable to understand that why the Consumer Fora do stick to complex procedures; and this is one of the reasons for delay in the justice delivery of cases.

We are aware that the Presiding Officers face several challenges to deal with consumer cases which also need urgent attention from the policy-makers and practitioners of consumer laws. Moreover, the issues highlighted above need also sensitivities of the people and stakeholders to tackle the ever growing challenges faced by consumer-victims of the market and service provides. They must not be discouraged and forced to think/feel as victims as the delivery of justice is delayed in the Consumer Fora. Under this circumstance, they would feel as double victim. Rather than involving in blame game we need to understand these challenges to find an opportunity to think fresh about the remedies to these challenges before the Consumer Courts. So, there is great burden on the shoulder of advocates and Consumer Fora to meet these challenges well within time-frame so that the faith of the Common citizen/consumer's are not lost and the justice delivery system is not bogged down.

Conclusion

We all are consumers in one form or the other in this market-driven society. In the present socio-economic scenario, we find that consumer is increasingly becoming victim to many unfair and trade unethical practices adopted in the market places. The Consumer is very often cheated in the quality, quantity and price of goods or services. The traders must know that markets exist because of consumers but it is a very sorry state of affairs when the so-called 'king of the market' becomes the victim of it.

The Consumer Policy is no longer can be viewed solely at the national level. Since the world economy has become so interdependent that the National Consumer Protection policies have now acquired international dimensions. Today, number of countries all over the world have laws to regulate and control unfair and deceptive trade practices and to provide adequate protection to the consumers. As a developing country, India's biggest problem is that still a large section of the population is living below poverty line. The consumers are ignorant of their rights and in India consumer justice is a part of social and economic justice as enunciated in the Constitution of India. Following the Constitutional mandate, a number of legislations have been enacted in the field of Consumer Rights Protection but the litigations are found to be costly, complex and trouble-some. The procedures are complicated, cumbersome and time-consuming, and the remedies available are limited in scope due to systemic drift. That is why the impact of the benevolent consumer rights legislation enacted for protecting the consumer rights has been very minimal.

Therefore, the issues discussed above required to be taken seriously, more diligently and catiously. One of the possible suggestions to reduce the burden of Consumer Fora and for speedier justice is to refer the consumer disputes matters to Mediation Centres. In fact, the Consumer Forum can also refer the matters to Mediation Centres for peaceful settlement of disputes between the parties, as an option if the parties agreed to resolve on their own, where court feels that there is possibility of settlement of the disputes by the parties themselves.

In this the Media can play greater role in highlighting the problems of consumers and also educate the common man about the Consumer Laws, etc. The NGOs are mainly working in the areas of child rights, women rights, labour rights, etc. Only few NGOs are working seriously with dedication and commitment for Consumer Rights issues. The NGOs should actively participate in consumer affairs and in combination with media they can work hand in hand to bring consumer right revolution. I think after Green Revolution, White Revolution there is absolute need for Consumer Right Revolution in this country.

In this context, the judiciary also has a special role to play in the task of achieving the socio-economic goals enshrined in the Constitution. The Presidents/judges have to be aware of the social changes in the task of achieving socio-economic justice for the people who are running from pillar to post for just delivery of justice. I feel like highlighting four basic requirements Socrates had said long ago for a Judge to improve the process of justice delivery:

(a) to hear courteously;

(b) to answer wisely;

(c) to consider soberly; and

(d) to decide impartially.

While concluding, I would like to quote few famous lines for all the practitioners of law and stakeholders from Rabindra Nath Tagore's Gitanjali, the book that won him the First Nobel Prize in literature:

"Where the mind is without fear and the head is held high;
Where knowledge is free;
Where the world has not broken up into fragments by narrow domestic walls;
Where words come out from the depth of truth;
Where tireless striving stretches its arms towards perfection;
Where the clear stream of reason has not lost its way into the dreary desert sand of dead habit;
Where the mind is led forward by thee into ever-widening thought and action;
Into that heaven of freedom, my father, let my country awake."

Reference

1. Balakrishna Eradi: *Consumer Protection Jurisprudence,* Lexis Nexis Butterworths, 2005.

13

Consumer Protection Law in India: Some Crucial Cases on Banking—An Overview

Parmarty Venkataramana

1. The Disputes Redressal Agencies (District Forums, State Commissions and National Commission), under the Consumer Protection Act, 1986 adjudicate upon the complaints of consumers relating to defaults in products and deficiency in service. 'Service' as defined in the Act includes the provision of facilities in connection with banking.
2. The decisions of the State Commissions, the National Commission, and the Supreme Court (as the final authority), on different aspects of banking and other services offered by banks have been reported in various law journals. A short compilation of the decisions from 1995 to 2005 has been made with a view to giving a brief account of the principles laid down in these cases. Each case is given separately along with the citation for enabling access to the full text of the case, whenever necessary.
3. The principles laid down by the various decisions of the Consumer Commissions and the Supreme Court and included in the compilation can be summarised as under:

(i) Failure/Delay in Repaying Deposits: Withholding of the amount due on a fixed deposit after its maturity amounts to deficiency in service. Delayed payment of term deposits on maturity also amounts to deficiency in service. The principle applies to cases of inordinate delay in payment of proceeds of premature encashment of deposits as well.

(ii) Payment and Collection of Cheques/Drafts: Wrongful dishonour of cheques due to the negligence or mistake on the part of the bank has been held to amount deficiency in service. Dishonour of Demand Drafts due to the lapse or omission on the part of the officials of the bank like non-affixation of signatures, failure to mention code number etc. have also been held to be amounting to deficiency in service.

(iii) Loans and Advances—Refusal of Grant of Loans: Matters concerning the eligibility of parties to any credit assistance, viability of the project and continuation of the credit facilities or the operation of the account by any party, are within the discretion of the financial institution/bank depending upon various factors like financial discipline and past history of borrower and his ability to pay the loan, if such discretion is exercised bonafide. Even though the bank has the right to refuse or grant loan, causing undue delay in releasing the installments of the sanctioned loan might be held to amount to deficiency in service.

Interest: Charging interest at a rate higher than the rate stipulated in the loan agreement would also amount to deficiency in service.

Interest cannot be claimed in a consumer case under section 34 of the Code of Civil Procedure as these provisions are not applicable. However, based on the underlying principles of justice, equity and good conscience, the Forums and Commissions can grant appropriate interest in each case. Although banks cannot give interest exceeding that prescribed by the Reserve Bank, they have a duty to inform the depositor about this, the failure of which, would amount to deficiency in service.

(iv) Security for Loans

Non-return of Documents: Banks are liable for deficiency in service in cases where they fail to return the security documents even after repayment of the whole loan.

Insurance of Security: Banks are not bound to insure the security taken for a loan unless the loan agreement provides for insurance and as such, failure to insure does not amount to deficiency in service. Further, merely because the owner of a vehicle has given the cheque for insurance premium to the bank along with monthly installment of loan taken for purchase of the vehicle, liability arising out of an accident to third parties cannot be shifted to the bank.

(v) Lien: Banks have a right to exercise lien under section 171 of the Indian Contract Act against the dues from constituents/

customers. However, the banks cannot exercise lien over the personal account of a customer on the ground that money was due to the bank in another account where he acts in a different capacity, if there is no agreement to that effect.

(vi) Bank Guarantee: The failure of a bank to honour bank guarantee is a deficiency in service. However, in cases where a demand was made not in accordance with the conditions of the guarantee and therefore, the guarantee was not honoured, it would not amount to deficiency in service.

(vii) Locker: A bank is liable for loss of articles kept in the locker with the bank. The bank cannot contract out of its responsibilities in relation to a locker by describing the agreement as that between a landlord and a tenant. When locker was found emptied and contents lost, the banks have been held liable for deficiency in service. However, in some such cases, the disputes were left open to be decided by the Civil Court after taking detailed evidence.

(viii) Security in Bank's Premises: A bank is responsible for deficiency in service for lack of security in its premises and loss, caused to customers accordingly. This is on the ground that ensuring the safety of the money to be deposited and/or withdrawn inside the bank premises is implicitly a part of the service rendered by a bank to a customer.

(ix) Consumer Forum—Jurisdiction and Procedure: A consumer complaint may not be entertained by the Consumer Forums when the matter is *sub-judice* before a competent Civil Court.

A person, who acts as surety for another and does not hire/ avail service from the bank, is not a consumer of the bank and therefore, his complaint may not be entertained.

(x) Voluminous Evidence—Complicated Questions of Law and Fact: In cases involving complex questions of facts and interpretation of laws and rights and obligations of parties under various Statutes, the complainants have to seek redressal of their grievances before Civil Courts not the Consumer Forum. Similar is the case when elaborate evidence is required to be taken.

(xi) Limitation: A bank may exercise lien under section 171 of Contract Act even where the debt is barred by limitation.

A consumer can initiate proceeding against a banker for non-release of securities even after the expiry of the period of limitation. This is based on the principle that the banker holds any goods as security from a customer as trustee and the security is not intended to be transferred to him, nor can he acquire any title to it, except on the basis of legal proceedings.

(xii) Other Banking Services

Operation of Account: The stoppage of operation of account of a partnership firm on account of an arbitration award and the subsequent legal opinions obtained by the bank would not amount to deficiency in service.

Closing of Account: Closing of account without the instructions of the account holder would amount to deficiency in service.

Refusal of Cheque Book: The refusal to provide cheque book facility to a customer on the ground of not maintaining the minimum balance in his account may not amount to deficiency in service.

Service Charges: An increase in charges levied by a bank for its services does not fall within the provisions of the Consumer Protection Act. A bank may levy charges for issuance of MICR cheques, so long as it is not against the directives of the Reserve Bank. This cannot be termed 'unilateral' and taking the consent of each customer does not arise.

Rendering of Account: A demand for rendering of accounts of transactions with a bank is not within the scope of the provisions of the Consumer Protection Act.

Succession Certificate: It has been held that there is no deficiency in service on the part of a bank in insisting that the children of a deceased account holder should produce a succession certificate before releasing the amount to them in accordance with the Succession Act and the Reserve Bank guidelines.

Insistence on denomination of notes: A customer cannot as of right insist for a particular denomination of notes, as the notes provided by the bank are legal tender and therefore, no deficiency in service in failing to comply with the demand.

Forgery of Power of Attorney: Once a registered power of attorney is produced before the bank, the bank does not have to make any further verification of signature. As the bank is not expected to verify signature, it cannot be held responsible for negligence in verification of signature. The failure in respect of an act which does not form part of the service cannot be considered as a deficiency in service.

Compliance of RBI Directions: It has been held that the Consumer Forum may not direct the banks to make payment to a depositor contrary to the directions issued by RBI under section 35A of the Banking Regulation Act or allow the directions issued by RBI to be flouted.

Vicarious Liability: A bank is bound by the Act of negligence of its staff during the course of employment. Thus, where the bank cashier fails to account for the money deposited with him at the counter, the bank would be liable.

Rude Behaviour: A bank may be held liable for deficiency in service owing to rude behaviour of its officials and be ordered to pay compensation for the mental agony and discomfort caused.

Notice before Auction: A notice to pay or face auction without making any earlier demand for repayment of loan and without giving date of auction was held to constitute deficiency in service.

Non-return of Dishonoured Cheque: The failure to return a dishonoured cheque has been held to be deficiency in service where the complainant was unable to take action against the drawer without the instrument.

Strike: A bank may not be liable to pay compensation for suspension of business due to illegal strike by the employees and when no loss is caused due to the negligence of the bank. However, in a case when the strike by award staff was not such as to paralyze work and when the officers and other employees were willing to work and still the salary accounts were not credited, it was held that the bank was liable for deficiency in service.

Bank Guarantee: A complaint was filed alleging deficiency in service in not paying the amount of bank guarantee on Bank Guarantee:

A complaint was filed alleging deficiency in service in not paying the amount of bank guarantee on demand. The defense plea was that the demand was not in accordance with terms of guarantee. It was held that where bank guarantee provided conditions for its invocation then Bank would not be deficient in service in not making payment under the bank guarantee if conditions were found not fulfilled. *MP Minerals Ltd.* vs. *Bank of India and Ors* - 2003 (1) CPR 96 (NC).

The bank was alleged to have failed to issue bank guarantee despite sufficient security and the complainant suffered financial loss. It was held that the non-issuance of bank guarantee despite security deposit with the bank would amount to deficiency in service and the complainant would be entitled to interest on that security amount. *M/s. Anand Lubricating and Pneumatic Systems Ltd.* vs. *State Bank of India* - 2003 (2) CPR 53.

Banking Service: The grant of relief of rendition of accounts in relation to transactions with the Bank is not within the scope of the provisions of the Consumer Protection Act and the averments in the petition do not make out any deficiency in the service rendered by the Bank. The rendition of accounts by the Bank and the recovery of amounts that may be found due as a result of settlement of accounts are reliefs that can be obtained only by recourse to a suit in the Civil Court. *M/s. House of Dubary* vs. *New Bank of India and Others* 1991 (1) CPR 216 (NC).

The bank is liable for deficiency in service for inordinate delays in providing banking services and the customer of the bank is entitled to claim compensation for the loss and the injury suffered by him due to the inordinate delay in the payment of the amount of deposit certificate on its premature encashment. *P.N. Prasad* vs. *Union Bank of India* 1991(1) CPR 198 (SCDRC- AP, Hyderabad).

The banker is supposed to safeguard the interest of the depositors when his amount is entrusted to the custody of the Bank and the Bank is liable to return the amount with interest. In the absence of any directions from the customer, no banker can unilaterally and arbitrarily transfer the money of a depositor from his account and deposit in the account of another customer. This amounts to deficiency in service by the bank.

Dilip Madhukar Kambli vs. *Nilesh Vasant Borkar and Ors,* 1991(1) CPR 571 (SCDRC- New Bombay, Maharashtra).

The Commission ruled that adopting discriminatory practice in sanctioning loan without basis by the cooperative society or Bank amounts to deficiency in service and such practice is liable to be stopped. *Madras Prov. Consumer Association* vs. *The Registrar Cooperative Societies, Madras and Others* (Madras), 1991(2) CPR 447 (SCDRC- Madras).

They (Banks) must be ever vigilant and solicitous about the interests of their customers departure from such standard can cause inconvenience not only to stray individuals but widespread economic disaster. The Banks should, therefore, be enjoined to maintain their services efficient and above reproach. In view of the above it was held that where the bank caused unexplained delay in the mail transfer of money it amounts to deficiency in service for which bank is bound to compensate. *N. Sahadevan* vs. *Manager, Syndicate Bank* 1991(2) CPR 617 (SCDRC-Kerala).

Due to the wrongful dishonour of the demand draft the complainant was stranded at a very far off place from his home and it resulted in loss, mental agony and hardship to him. The primary duty of a Bank is to safeguard and protect the interest of their customer. It was held that if there has been a lapse or an omission committed by the officials of the Bank and if some inconvenience were caused to a customer due to the omission, negligence or default of the Bank, it amounts to a defective service according to the *Consumer Protection Act. N. Raveendran* vs. *Branch Manager, State Bank of India,* 1991(2) CPR 473 (SCDRC-Kerala).

It is a common knowledge that when an account holder draws a cheque in favour of the bank itself, it is undoubtedly for the purpose of utilising that amount by the bank for any of the specified directions of the customer and not for paying to an unknown third party, merely because the word "bearer" is not struck off in the cheque. Therefore, a cheque directing the drawer (i.e.) the bank to pay itself cannot be equated with an ordinary cheque payable to self or bearer where the bank can pay to the bearer. Hence the bank has clearly shown utter negligence in paying a huge amount of Rs. 20,000 to an unknown outsider and thus caused loss to the account holder. There is clearly lack of good faith on the part of bank. In the circumstances, the customer is entitled to the loss and costs of this complaint. *S.S. Shirwaikar, Margao* vs. *State Bank of India, Margao,* 1991(1) CPR 513 (SCRDC-Goa). It was alleged by the complainant that misappropriation by its employee from the complainant's account maintained with the bank was made possible due to the negligence and deficiency in service of the officials of the bank. It was held that the bank passbook is not a reliable piece of evidence to establish the fact of short deposit especially when it was in the custody of the employee who was convicted of forgery and fraud in the case. The short deposit has to be established on the basis of the amounts indicated in the depositor's counterfoils of the pay-in-slips. *Corporation Bank and Anr.* vs. *M/s Filmalaya Pvt. Ltd.,* -1992(1) CPR 445 (NC).

The complainant had already overdrawn the cash credit limit given by the opposite party bank and was in default in the repayment of his dues. He was also not clearing the dues which he owed to some other bank. It was held that the refusal by the opposite party bank to permit the complainant to further draw in his account was justified and there was no deficiency of service. *A.R. Narayan* vs. *State Bank of Hyderabad,* - 1992(1) CPR 534 (NC).

The complaint against the respondent bank was improper maintenance of the complainant's account and transfer of some amount from Fixed Capital Loan account to Working Capital Loan account. The statement of the bank that the transfer of the amount from one account to the other was as per the instructions of the complainant himself was accepted by the Commission. It was held that the transfer, though irregular, was to the benefit of the complainant and enabled him to reduce to an extent his exceeding the drawing power limit. The complaint was dismissed as vexatious and malicious. *M/s Classic Electronics* vs. *Punjab National Bank and Anr.,* -1992(2) CPR 128 (NC).

The complainant filed the complaint praying that the opposite party bank be directed to issue a No Dues Certificate and also claimed compensation. There was nothing on record to show that the complainant had hired the services of the opposite party for consideration for the purpose of issuing a no dues certificate. Hence, it was held that the complainant is not a consumer as defined under Section 2(1)(d) of the Act. As the Redressal Forum can grant only those reliefs enumerated under Section 14(1) of the Act, it was held that the direction which the complainant has sought against the opposite party cannot be granted to the complainant. *Pawan Kumar Birla* vs. *Branch Manager, State Bank of Bikaner and Jaipur* - 1992 (1) CPR 15 (SCRDC - Raj.).

The services of appellant, an MD Collector of the bank, were terminated and his security deposit was not refunded by the bank. It was held that since the bank had hired the services of the appellant by paying commission and not hired the services for consideration, the appellant will not be a consumer of the bank. Also, it was held that for determining the amount due to the appellant accounts will have to be taken and that can be done by a Civil Court and not by the *Consumer, Forum, Parashuram S. Veerannavar* vs.*Branch Manager, Union Bank of India* -1992, (1) CPR 329 (SCRDC - Kar).

Where the bank permitted withdrawal of a huge amount from the account of the complainant on the basis of a duplicate pass book and cheque book, it was held that complainant is a consumer and permission for withdrawal from his account by another is deficiency in service. *Premananda Nanda* vs. *State Bank of India and Anr.*- 1992(2) CPR 199 (SCRDC - Orissa).

Under the terms of loan, the borrower-hypothecator- (i.e., the complainant) is bound to insure the hypothecated assets against fire and against any other risks and endorse the policy in favour of the bank. Insuring the assets in favour of the bank is not in any way part of the service contemplated or to be rendered by the bank. Taking out an insurance policy by the bank on behalf of the complainant at his request is a gratuitous service, performed by the gratuitous Act. In the circumstances, it was held that no complaint would lie against the bank. *K.R. Krishnankutty* vs. *South Indian Bank Ltd. and two Ors.*- *K.R. Krishnankutty* vs. *South Indian Bank Ltd. and two Ors.*- SCRDC - Ker).

Where the complainant settled all his dues with the bank freely and voluntarily and sent a letter to the bank stating that "all transaction between us are fully and finally settled and there are no claims in whatsoever nature against you" it was held that the complainant's claim against the bank that certain amount has been collected in excess and hence repayable to him with interest, is an abuse of the process of *Consumer Protection Act. SMW Consumer Protection Council and Anr.* vs. *The Branch Manager, State Bank of India* -1992(2) CPR 253 (SCRDC - Mad).

The bank had given a guarantee ensuring due payment of a *Hundi/* promissory note and undertaken to indemnify the complainant in case of default by the drawer of the pro-note. It was held that the act of furnishing guarantee by banks amounts to 'service' as defined under Section 2 (1) (o) of the Act. Therefore, if a bank furnishes guarantee but fails to make the payment in accordance with the terms of the guarantee, the effected person can file a complaint against the bank under the provisions of the Act. Since the complaint has been filed on the basis of the guarantee issued by the bank in favour of the complainant, the drawer of the promissory note is not a necessary party to the complaint. *M/s Chavan Rishi International Ltd.* vs. *State Bank of Bikaner and Jaipur* - 1992(2) CPR 567 (SCRDC - Delhi).

The complainant's employer had sent some amount to him towards his traveling expenses, but the same was not received in his account with Catholic Syrian Bank, Ernakulam. The employer's banker in Middle East had sent telex payment order to the first opposite party (SBI Overseas Branch, Bombay) in favour of the complainant's aforesaid account who in turn vide telegraphic transfer remitted the funds to second opposite party (SBT, Ayiroor Branch) for credit to complainant's account. However, the said telegraphic transfer was not received by the second opposite party. It was held that not only the persons who hire any service but also the persons who are the beneficiaries of such service other than actual hirers would come within the clutches of the term 'consumer'. However, in the present case, the complainant's employer had not hired the services of the opposite parties but had hired the services of their bank in Middle East for sending the money. Therefore, it was held that the complainant was not a beneficiary of the service rendered by the opposite parties and hence not a consumer as defined under the Act. Complaint was dismissed. *P.P. Devassy* vs. *State Bank of India and two Ors.* - 1992(2) CPR 603 (SCRDC - Ker).

The opposite party bank refused to accept the deposit of motor vehicle tax by the complainant on the ground that the District Transport Authority has not opened an account with them, it was held that refusal of the bank is understandable. In any event, since the complainant did not have any account with the opposite party bank. It was held that he is not a consumer under the Act as neither any goods were purchased nor any services were hired by him for consideration from the opposite party. In the circumstances, the complaint was held not maintainable. *Nawal Kishore Sharma* vs. *The Accountant State Bank of India* - 1992(2) CPR 645 (SCRDC - Bihar).

The issue in the case was whether the Ajara Urban Co-op. Bank being a large commercial organisation and the purchase of Xerox Machine for its commercial activity as a bank could maintain a complaint under the Consumer Protection Act in respect of the Xerox Machine. The Commission held that when a Xerox Machine has been purchased by a bank for its office use and the complaint is not regarding services attached to it but rather that machine was faulty and defective then complaint does not fall within the purview of the Consumer Protection Act as machine purchased being for commercial purposes. *IDC Electronics Ltd.* vs. *Ajara Urban Co-operative Bank Ltd & Ors.* 1993(1) CPR (I) 225 (NC).

A revision petition was filed by the Bank of Maharashtra against the order of District Forum directing it to renew FDR of the respondent, to treat the amount of Rs. 20,040 withdrawn by the Respondent as having been paid under Cash Credit Facility, that Rs. 42,042 with interest due under Cash Credit Scheme be paid to the complainant and Rs. 900 be paid as expenses for hearing, Rs.1000 for mental pain and Rs. 2000 for mental torture. The bank's appeal was dismissed by the State Commission against which the revision was filed before the National Commission. The National Commission on examination of facts held that it was open to the bank not to renew the cash credit facility after one year and to adjust the amount in FDR towards amounts recoverable. It, therefore, held that the act of the bank does not amount to deficiency in service as the action is strictly in accordance with the terms of the arrangement. Branch Manager, Bank of Maharashtra Vs. Monohar Sitaram Nanadanwar (1993(2) CPR 109) (NC). The company engaged in the business of manufacturing and leasing and selling computers entered into an agreement with the Second Respondent Firm for supply of a computer system. The payment was to be made on a quarterly rental basis for a period of 60 months and the same was ensured by issuance of a bank guarantee in favour of the company.

When the complainant company invoked the bank guarantee, the Bank did not make the payment. The complainant company alleged deficiency in service on the part of the Bank. It was held that the complainant Company is a consumer as regards the Bank and the act of the Bank constituted deficiency in service. *Bank of India* vs. *HCL Ltd. and Anr.* 1993(3) CPR 31 (NC).

Bank account was opened in the name of a partnership firm with instructions to the bank that the account would be operated by two partners which would necessarily include signature of complainant. An arbitration award was passed in the meanwhile allowing remaining three partners to operate the account. The bank after obtaining legal opinion allowed the operation of the account in terms of the supplementary award. When objections were raised to the operation of account in terms of the arbitration award, the bank obtained another advice from its senior lawyer and it stopped further operation of the account. In view of the facts involved, the Commission held that it cannot be said that the Bank's action was not bonafide and the bank cannot be said to have acted negligently. *M/s. Seth Mohan Lal Hiralal* vs. *Punjab National Bank and Ors* 1993(3) CPR 209 (NC).

Where an amount of Rs. 1,85,000 lying deposited in three FDs were being claimed by the complainant in the capacity of beneficiary under registered will executed by the depositor, the bank directed the beneficiaries to establish the authenticity of will before a competent court of law and to secure a succession certificate in order to make payment. The Commission held that the bank commits no deficiency in service in asking the complainant to produce succession certificate for disbursement of amount of depositor who died leaving a will. *B.G. Krishna Iyengar* vs. *Manager, Vijaya Bank* 1994 (3) CPR 547) (SCDRC- Karnataka).

The complaint was filed for increasing in service charges levied by banks for collection of cheques, issue of demand draft, processing of loans, etc. It was held that the complaint about increase in charges levied by banks for its services doesn't fall within the provisions of Consumer Protection Act, 1986. Complaint dismissed. *Sindhi Chamber of Commerce* vs. *Reserve Bank of India and Others, CPR* (1) 756 (SCDRC - Tamil Nadu).

The complainant filed against the opposite party/ appellant under section 2(1)g, 14,19 of Consumer Protection Act for deficiency in banking service. It was held that the bank advanced loans to the complainants who are agriculturist and who wanted to install lift irrigation system.

The layout of the scheme was prepared by Mr. Autade, an Engineer (not a employee of the Bank) which was approved by the Bank. The Bank cannot be held responsible as the scheme was prepared by the *Consultant. Appeal allowed*. Maharashtra State Co-operative Agricultural and Rural Development Bank Ltd. Vs. National Forum of Consumers Education and Others, CPR 1995(3) 24 (NC).

The complainant applied for conversion of loan in Indian rupees and hedging/forward booking against exchange rate fluctuations. He filed the captioned complaint under section 2(g) and 14(l)(d) for deficiency in service for delaying two years by (RIICO) in arranging forward foreign exchange rate fluctuation. It was held that hedging was one of the devices to be adopted in the loan transaction as per the policy of the IDBI and the Central Government, and it was obligatory on the part of the opposite parties to secure hedging of the complainant's loan as early as possible. Further, it was held that RIICO is liable to compensate complainant by a sum of Rs. 50,07,609 avoidable increase in principal amount on account of depreciation of Rupee with interest at the same rate which it is charging the borrower till the date of the payment of the compensation of Rs. 50.07 lakhs. Complaint allowed. *M/s. Global Granimarmo Ltd.* vs. *Rajasthan State Industrial Development and Investment Corporation Ltd. and Another* (RIICO) CPR1995(1) 432(NC).

The complaint was filed under Section 2 and 14 of Consumer Protection Act. It was the case of the complaint/respondent that the Bank withdrew the amount in an account without instructions of the account holder and closed the account. It was held that the Bank cannot close an account and remit the amount in credit of somebody else even if, unauthorised or wrongly opened, as it is not at all function of the bank to find out as to whom the money in that account actually belongs or from which source the same is collected. Appeal filed by bank dismissed. Chief Manager, *Punjab and Sind Bank and Anr.* vs. *Punjab and Sind Staff Organisation*, CPR

(3) 1995 309 (SCDRC -Punjab). The complaint was filed under Sections 12 and 17 of Consumer Protection Act for deficiency in banking service.

The complainant Association opened an S.B. Account in opposite bank. A dispute arose regarding operation of the account and civil proceedings pending. The opposite bank had informed complainant association that they would not permit operation of account without production of specific order of the Civil Court. It was held that act of Branch Manager permitting operation of account and allowing withdrawal of Rs. 2 lakhs within 36 days is negligence and deficiency in service. Complaint allowed with cost. *Bangalore Water Supply and Sewage Board Employees' Association* vs. *The Manager, Syndicate Bank, CPR*(3) 108 (SCDRC - Karnataka).

The question whether the bank acted in contravention of the special instructions issued by the partners of a partnership firm by honouring cheques signed by one of the partners only and that too after dissolution of the firm, was answered in the negative, on the evidence produced in the case wherefrom it was found that the partnership had authorised that "partners at serial No. 1 or 3 shall operate the bank account with his signature" meaning thereby that signature of either of the said partners is sufficient and that the bank received a copy of the dissolution deed subsequent to the date up to which the account was operated. As such, it was held that there was no deficiency in service on the part of the bank. Branch Manager, *Osmanabad Dist Central Co-op Bank Ltd., and Anr.*, vs. *Ramachandra Desharath Mane and Ors.* 1996 (1) CPR 1(NC).

The Order passed by the State Commission allowing the complaint on the ground that the bank had debited the account of the complainant with interest amounts due to the bank without following the principles of natural justice, was set aside by the NC, for the reason that the guidelines governing such interest rate levy, etc., do not contemplate issuance of a Show Cause Notice to the complainant. The matter was remitted to the State Commission to pass a proper order after hearing the parties and considering all the documents produced by the parties. *Syndicate Bank & Ors.*, vs. *M/s. Bharat Appliances Corporation & Ors.* 1996 (2) CPR 212 (NC).

The question whether a beneficiary under a Bank guarantee could be termed as a consumer of the bank was answered in the affirmative and accordingly, by not making payment within one month of invocation of the bank guarantee, the bank was held liable for deficiency in service and was also directed to make good the shortfall in the amounts required to be paid under the bank guarantee. *Union Bank of India & Anr.*, vs. *M/s. Seppo Rally OY & Anr.* 1996 (2) CPR 221 (NC).

Where the salary cheques were not cleared by the Service branch of the bank due to disturbances in the Ahmedabad City (Force majeure), the same was held not amounting to deficiency of service on the part of the bank. *Madhubhai R. Patel & Ors.*, vs. *SBI & Anr.* (Pertains to November salary) 1996 (3) CPR 51 (NC).

Where the complaint sought for exemplary compensation on the ground that the complainants suffered mental agony, etc., due to issuance of fake currency by the bank, the State Commission gave a nominal compensation, the same is in order in the facts of case when *malafide* intention and deliberate act of gross negligence on the part of the bank is not established. *H.R. Davesh & Ors.*, vs. *PNB* 1996 (3) CPR 191 (NC).

Non-honouring of bank guarantee was held to be deficiency of service on the ground that honouring of the bank guarantee was a contract unqualified/independent of the underlying contract between the complainant and the contractor in whose favour the bank guarantee has been issued. The decisions of the *Supreme Court in M/s. Tarapur and Company Madras case* (AIR 1971 SC 891) and *Larsen and Toubro Ltd.*, vs. *MSEB* (AIR 1996 SC 334) were followed. The bank was directed to honour the bank guarantee issued in favour of the complainant (State), however it limited it only to the first bank guarantee which was an unconditional guarantee and the complainant was held not entitled to invoke the second bank guarantee given towards loss/damage caused or likely to be caused in the absence of the complainant invoking the same on the existence of such grounds. State of U.P. through *Executive Engineer* vs. *Corporation Bank & Anr.* 1997 (1) CPR118 (NC).

Where the bank acted contrary to the terms of agreement entered into between the bank and the complainant and released the goods in favour of a third party without realising all the amounts from that party, the bank was held liable for deficiency in service. However, the complainant was restrained from recovering the amount from the bank if the recovery is already made from that third party. *The Manager, State Bank of India* vs. *M/s. Chemist Products & Anr.* 1997 (1) CPR 156 (NC).

Where the cheque book facility was refused to the Appellant - customer (Complainant before the District Forum) on the ground that the minimum balance in his account was not maintained at Rs. 250 as required by the rules of the bank, it was held that there was no deficiency in service on the part of the bank in such refusal. *Harindra Nath Singh* vs. *Central Bank of India,* 1996 (1) CPR 384 (SCDRC-Bihar).

14

New Age Consumers in India: Challenges and Effectiveness of Redressal Mechanisms

Hari Dev Goyal

Consumer 'seeking value for money' from the traders and service providers operative in the imperfect Indian market was a desired aim of the Consumer Protection Act, 1986 that provides speedy and inexpensive three-tier redressal mechanism set up at the District, State and National levels. The Act has certain in-built weaknesses which have not only defeated the very purpose of this benevolent law but also deprived the consumer his lawful rights to be protected from market injustices. This is particularly true in the case of consumers residing in rural India who are mostly ignorant of the consumer protection law. In fact, the Right to Information Act, 2005 has set a road map for civil society activists, volunteers and Central and State Governments for educating the consumers as well at large and providing them access to redressal system. The procedural, structural and functional analyses by the subject researchers have brought out huge volume of issues and challenges. Certain strategic operations in the developed countries provide lessons and opportunities for amendments and reforms of the Act to make it consumer-friendly and all powerful.

(i) Newly Developed Free-market Scenario

Developments in international trade and commerce after the fall of Berlin Wall have also led to vast expansion of business and trade in India. As a result of which a variety of consumer goods have appeared in the market to cater to the needs of ever-growing consumers. A host of services have been made available to the consumers by different sectors like insurance, transport, electricity, housing, entertainment, finance and banking. A well-organised sector of manufacturers and traders with better knowledge of markets and psyche of Indian consumers who have tremendous tolerance of suffering having grown in a society infected by crisis of faith in the bureaucratic and judicial structure, has come into existence, thereby affecting the relationship between the traders and consumers making the principle of Consumer Sovereignty almost inapplicable. This is a growing challenge to the Indian consumers as well to government.

Advertisements of goods and services in newspapers and magazines; shopping through internet, influence the demand for the same by the consumers though there may be manufacturing defects or imperfections or shortcomings in the quality, quantity, or the purity of goods or there may be deficiency in the services rendered. Production of the same item by many firms by different brand-names has held the consumers to think about them before they can buy the best. For the welfare of the consumers at large, there is no mechanism or policy of different organised players to check the glut of adulterated and sub-standard articles in the market.

(ii) Consumer Protection Act, 1986

Various legislations enacted since 1860 to 1976 for providing protection to the consumers and stringent action against adulterated and sub-standard articles fail to provide relief to the consumers. Following United Nations' Guidelines, the Consumer Rights Protection Act, 1986 for better protection of the interests of the consumers and settlement of consumer disputes and for matters connected therewith, was enacted by the Parliament of India in December 1986. The Act seeks, *inter alia,* to promote and protect the rights of consumers such as:

(a) The right to be protected against marketing of goods which are hazardous to life and property;

(b) The right to be informed about the quality, quantity, potency, purity, standard and price of goods to protect the consumer against unfair trade practices;

(c) The right to be assured, wherever possible, access to an authority of goods at competitive prices;

(d) The right to be heard and to be assured that consumer interests will receive due consideration at appropriate forums;

(e) The right to seek redressal against unfair trade practices or unscrupulous exploitation of consumers; and

(f) The right to consumer education.

For the promotion and protection of these objects, Consumer Protection Councils have been established at the central and state levels.

(iii) Consumer Disputes Redressal System

To provide speedy and simple redressal to consumer disputes, three-tier quasi-judicial machinery has been set up at the District, State and National levels. These quasi-judicial bodies are supposed to observe the principles of natural justice and have been empowered to give relief of a specific nature and also award, wherever possible, compensation to consumers. Penalties for non-compliance of orders given by the quasi-judicial bodies have been provided in the Act.

1. District Consumer Forums have been set up at all the districts in India. Complaints involving cost of goods and services or compensation amount up to twenty lakh rupees can be made in district forum after paying the specified fee ranging from Rs. 100 to 500 depending upon the amount of compensation. There is no fee for compensation up to one lakh rupees for consumer complainants who fall under the Below Poverty Line (BPL) families holding *Antyodaya Anna Yojana* cards.

(a) Admissibility of the complaint shall ordinarily be decided within 21 days from the date on which the complaint was received.

(b) Every complaint shall be heard and decided within a period of three months from the date of receipt of notice by the opposite party and within five months, if the complaint does not require analysis or testing of commodities.

(c) Appeal against the Orders of the District Forum can be made to the State Commission within a period of 30 days. "No appeal by a person, who is required to pay any amount in terms of an order of the District Forum, shall be entertained by the State Commission unless the appellant has deposited in the prescribed manner 50 per cent of that amount or twenty-five thousand rupees, whichever is less."

2. State Consumer Disputes Redressal Commission has been set up at all State capitals in the country to adjudicate the consumer disputes and thereby protect the consumer rights.

(a) Complaints where the value of the goods and services and compensation, if any, claimed exceeds rupees twenty lakh but does not exceed rupees one crore. There are two levels of fee for the complaint amounting to rupees two thousand and rupees four lakh under the Consumer Protection Rules, 1987.

(b) Penalty under section 19 of the Act to the National Commission shall be entertained on deposit of 50 per cent of the compensation amount by the appellant or Rs. 35,000 whichever is less.

(c) Penalty of punishment from one month to three years or fine of Rs. 2,000 to 10,000 or both has been provided under Section 27 of the Act. Moreover, property attachment in case of non-compliance of orders has also been provided in the Act. But unfortunately it has never been exercised making the Act favourable to the rich, dishonest and unscrupulous manufacturers, builders and traders and non-friendly to the unorganised and poor consumers.

3. There is National Consumer Disputes Redressal Commission that functions from New Delhi.

(a) Complaints where the value of goods and services and compensation, if any, claimed, exceeds rupees one crore can be made before the National Commission.

(b) Appeal against the orders of the National Commission can be filed before the Supreme Court of India. No appeal against the National Commission shall be entertained by the Supreme Court of India unless the appellant has deposited 50 per cent of the amount of compensation awarded by the National Commission or Rs. 50,000 whichever is less.

(iv) Effectiveness of the Redressal Mechanism

The most important consideration and fundamental issue is how effective are these mechanisms set up throughout the country for better protection of the consumer rights? Their effectiveness can be analysed through a number of indicators. Important ones are: (a) functioning of the system; (b) inexpensive and speedy mechanism to deliver justice to the consumers; (c) inherent weaknesses in the system; (d) education of the non-literate, poor belonging to BPL sections of consumers, and involvement of the civil society practitioners; (e) providing easy access to different categories of consumers to the system in place like for example Right to Information applicants and (f) introducing strategic policies of level playing in Indian market.

(a) At the District and State levels, large number of posts of Presidents with legal background as well as members is lying vacant and that is hampering the functioning of the Consumer Redressal Fora resulting in huge backlog of pending cases waiting to see the light of the day. It is in this regard that immediate action is called for from the appointing authorities to make these forums fully functional and effective.

(b) Majority of urban consumers and a negligible number of rural consumers are aware of the provisions of the Consumer Protection Act, 1986. Those who approach the Fora have to wait for the results for months and years due to many reasons. It is a well known fact that the victimized consumers have to fight the rich and powerful opponents who adopt various means to deprive the consumers their lawful rights. Adjournments are one of the most common tools which these rich and unscrupulous parties use to frustrate the complainants and that delays the delivery of justice. Thereby the effectiveness of the system has been largely impacted adversely particularly its speed. Cost of adjournment when asked for by the opposite party under Section 11 of the Consumer Rights Protection Regulations, 2005 need to be enhanced to at least 10 per cent of the cost of the goods and services, and claimed amount to discourage the opposite party seeking a number of adjournments thereby delaying the finality of the case.

(c) The Consumer Rights Protection Act in the present form, as pointed out in Section-III above, has inherent weaknesses that provide ample scope to the rich and powerful persons and companies to deprive and delay the quantum of relief to the victimised consumer for months and/or years together, and thereby defeat the aim and objectives of the Consumer Rights Protection Act. Appeals shall be entertained only after the deposit of 50 per cent of the compensation award. This was an honest and well thought of provision by the authors of the Act. But the second part of the provision that "or twenty five thousand rupees against the District Forum Award, Thirty five Thousand Rupees against the State Commission Award, or Fifty Thousand Rupees against the National Commission Award whichever is less" has made the Act, a piece of amusement and joke on the consumers thereby making the system ineffective and unable to deliver the speedy justice. When the compensation award goes in lakhs and crores, builders and big manufacturers find themselves comfortable in challenging the award by paying the negligible amount and fighting and harassing the victimised consumer. This is the most urgent reform required to be introduced for amendment of the Act.

(d) Awareness of rural consumers of their rights due to low literacy level in rural India and failure of social engineering in economic development generating huge mass of poverty despite not so-bad growth of the economy is directly affecting the effectiveness of the system. Here, we need the active involvement and participation of the people for whom the development is primarily meant and provisions of the Consumers' Act. People find it more practical and close to their needs the small initiatives of civil society actors and volunteers' organisations as this is the best form of social delivery system.

(e) Civil Society Organisations (CSOs) in India have not shown sufficient interest in educating the consumers of their rights and approaching the redressal mechanism. We can learn certain things from the Right to Information Act, 2005 for increasing consumer's access to the redressal mechanism and reducing his/her suffering. The Union Ministry of Consumer Affairs unlike Ministries of Rural Development, Social Welfare or Planning Commission has lagged behind in creating infrastructure for educating the consumers.

Monthly and/or periodical advertisements like *'Jago Grahak Jago'* appearing in some media/dailies has hardly made a dent or provided consumers any effective platform to get their grievances addressed and/or redressed. The CSOs, wherever they exist, are not being involved or encouraged to participate actively in educating the consumers. Rather roadblocks are created by power centres especially in rural areas. The CSOs may be made vibrant with a policy decision so as to make them accept and perform their best in social delivery system of justice. It is certainly the need of the hour both in urban and rural areas.

(e) Location of District Forums and State Commissions are not easily accessible to the rural consumers because of geographical distances. In place of physical presence of the consumers at preliminary stages, an alternate agency like the Post Offices need to be involved for filing application for compensation as is done for applicants under Right to Information Act, 2005. Fee can be paid with the application through Indian Postal Order or Bank Draft. Post Office will assist the applicant by receiving his application and forwarding it to the District Forum or the State Commission. For the amount of prescribed fee, involvement of the civil society volunteers and members of the *Gram Panchayat* is desired. In the beginning, Post Offices may be involved on experimental basis for applications to the District Forums only.

(f) For increasing effectiveness of the system, manufacturers and traders are required to introduce 'Return Policy' and 'Price Policy' as is being adopted in many developed countries like United Kingdom and United States of America, and a number of developing countries such as Singapore, Hong Kong, Japan. No question is asked to the consumer when s/he comes for change of the goods purchased or wants refund from the trader. It is the job of the merchant trader to take up case of defective goods with the manufacturer for replacement or money back. Most of the traders assure their price as the best in the town or the city even for fifteen days or a month saying if any other trader quotes the price less than this, the consumer would be given double of the difference in price. They do really mean it and put it in practice. Many manufacturers on their own have recalled their vehicles back from the market and the consumers when they found there was some/minor technical defect in their product. India needs to learn lessons from the players in the international arena. This perfect competition market scenario may not be an immediate step/goal due to known opposition from the vested interests but should be made an important reform of economic and social development.

(v) Reforming the System

Issues and challenges before the Consumer Disputes Redressal System in India, as discussed in the foregoing paragraphs, are numerous but the opportunities for reforming the system are not limited. Of course, honesty and sincerity is the first pre-condition that is required to win over the confidence of the justice-deprived consumers of India. Most of them have almost lost faith in the overall system that has developed during the last few decades and is presently going through the crisis of faith. That is why what is urgently required is the prioritisation of reform process to make the system of consumer protection effective. The following suggestions may be considered:

First and foremost priority has to be given to making the Consumer Rights Protection Act a powerful legislative tool to infuse fear among the wrong doers. Till the inherent defects in the Consumer Rights Protection Act giving upper hand to unscrupulous traders and builders, relating to penalties are removed, money power will continue to rule and deprive the poor victimised consumers for whom the said benevolent Act was framed. The big manufacturers (domestic and multi-national) have established huge legal departments to fight any complaint against them, their products and/or services; even sometimes where compensation amount is smaller than the cost of opposing it, as they know that consumer cannot afford to go from pillar to post for a long time or in some cases even in his life-time. In a number of cases, consumers have been suffering for months and years together after the award of compensation and has to go through the same kind of grill due to uneven level playing and psyche of the rich manufacturers and builders who want to make the consumer realise that challenging them is not liked by them and will not be in the consumer's interest in the given scenario.

Second, one is making the redressal Fora at district and state level fully functional by employing the sanctioned staff and training them to understand the right spirit of the provisions of the Consumer Rights Protection Act so that they are able to deliver socially effective justice.

Last but not the least is the involvement of the Civil Society Actors in educating the illiterate and poor consumers and changing the approach to increase their access to the redressal system. Governments' R and D funds need to be earmarked for encouraging the voluntary consumer organisations to participate in this cause; seeking the help of Panchayati Raj Institutions in educating the rural consumer and the school teachers can go a long way in protecting the consumer rights. School-going students both boys and girls are the best educators of their parents and would be happy to be the ambassadors of this social cause. These suggestions may be creatively implemented to provide the consumers rightful place in the society.

15

Challenges of Consumer Fora in India: An Urgent Need for Integration of Mediation Mechanism

M.C. Paul

We all are aware that it was the horrible balance of payments crisis and the emotional effects of mortgaging of the country's gold reserves that became one of the reasons that forced the historic policy of deregulation of the economy and pursuance of the policy free-market liberalisation by the government from 1991. Since then as a result a new found consumerism culture syndrome is also set in throughout the country during this post-liberalisation and globalisation era whether we like it or not. It is a fact that millions of gullible and unsuspecting consumers are also falling prey to disgruntled free-market forces 24 × 7. The menace of wrongdoings of the market and consumer exploitation has taken different shades and types. It seems the free-market forces have got a chance to do so as the government of the day is doing precious little to evolve effective protection mechanisms in the country. I am very much sure we will not find a single person who has not been made victim by the evolving free-markets while buying goods or services. And in this process, the modern science and technologies have come to their rescue as we all know how the 24 × 7 advertisements through modern multi-media, many of which are unethical and misleading, have taken a menacing proportion, depriving people to take informed decision because most of these do not sufficiently inform the consumers.

It is a fact that the fundamental interest of modern market forces is profit by hook or by crook methods. In 1986 at the behest of UN guidelines that the Indian Government took initiative and enacted the socially benevolent Consumer Protection Act (COPRA). It came into effect in 1987 throughout the country. It was designed to protect the interests of the *aam* consumers since they suffer the menace of consumer exploitations by the disgruntled business and commerce of all hues whether these are related to goods or services. Thus, it was certainly before the new economic reform policy was adopted the COPRA was made effective. Despite COPRA, the menace of consumer exploitation has not gone down, certainly during the post-liberalisation period, but greatly-increased as a result of the new consumerism culture that is emerging with the evolution of modern markets flooding with newer consumer goods and services with several ingenious ways alluring the consumers 24 × 7. On many occasions the level playing fields are missing and/or compromised or found to be violated by the market forces that came up under the global market agenda affecting the unsuspecting consumers. The existing protection mechanisms including the Competition Commission are yet to be pro-active and consumer-friendly to effectively control or check many such violations that directly affect consumer interests. However, with increasing awareness disseminated through multi-media based technological channels, many informed-consumers are encouraged to take on the violators under the special Consumer Protection Act (COPRA), 1986.

There is no doubt that the COPRA is a unique piece of legislation through which the *aam* consumers are not only given their rights but also the redressal of the violations of the same in specially created three-tier Consumer Disputes Redressal Fora set up in different Districts of the country to protect the consumer interests. Not only that, in fact, it was due to Consumer Protection Act, 1986 that the consumer movement in our country found a new direction and took a legal shape though it is yet to develop as a force to bring justice to millions of consumers whose rights are increasingly violated in the free-market disposition.

As stated, under this Act, the Government opened three-tier Consumer Disputes Redressal Fora, popularly known as Consumer courts. We may note here that the notable role played by late H.D. Shourie and his NGO, Consumer Cause, cannot be under-estimated in this regard. These three-tier judicial fora are supposed to be quasi-judicial bodies, exclusively set up to deal with consumer disputes. The aggrieved consumers can approach these bodies when their rights are violated or challenged. Thus, they are the real victims in the hands of disgruntled marketers of goods and services. Certainly they cannot be considered as litigants like in civil courts. And as per the Act, the procedures to be followed by these quasi-judicial three-tier bodies are definitely not like the general civil courts. These bodies are headed by retired Judges and the like, as stipulated in the Act. They are designated as President of the Fora. At the lowest level, there are District Consumer Disputes Redressal Fora opened in every district. They admit and hear consumer grievance cases within the pecuniary jurisdiction of compensation values below Rs. 20 lakhs. At the middle, there is State Consumer Disputes Redressal Commission at each State and union territory which is equivalent of High Courts (in civil court format). They have pecuniary jurisdiction of hearing cases within the value of Rs. 20 lakhs to 1 crore. They are also empowered to hear appeal cases from District Fora. At the top is the National Consumer Disputes Redressal Commission. It is located in *Upobhokta Nyaya Bhavan,* 'F' Block, General Pool Office Complex, INA, New Delhi-110023. They admit and hear cases where the compensation sought is above Rs. 1 crore. Like in the State Commissions they also hear appeal cases arising from various States Commissions in the country. Thus, each tier can adjudicate matters based on the pecuniary jurisdictions fixed in the Act.

The District Forum is headed either by a retired Judge or a lawyer eligible to be a District Judge. Similarly, the State Commission is headed by a retired High Court Judge and the National Commission is headed by a retired Supreme Court Judge. As stated, all the heads of these quasi-judicial bodies are invariably designated and known as Presidents. However, each category of courts has also requisite Members drawn from the civil society, and they together conduct the summary trial or proceedings but except the Presidents, the members are not empowered to deliver final verdict. These three-tier bodies should redress consumer disputes/grievances within 90–150 days as stipulated in Consumer Protection Act. In principle and spirit, these quasi-judicial bodies are not supposed to follow civil court procedures while adjudicating the consumer complaints like in civil courts. Thus, it should not be operated to prove legal matters by involving the lawyers but as a rule they should follow simple procedure based on the summary trial and proceedings. So, resorting to technical and procedural complexities of civil courts including the witnesses and other legalihs are not to be the rule.

These Fora should believe in dealing cases without involvement of lawyers and by the complainants themselves. Thus, the adjudication format of these quasi-judicial bodies has to be simple, inexpensive and pro-consumer in orientation unlike the civil courts so as to deliver speedy justice to the aggrieved consumers who have been victimised by the disgruntled market forces. In other words, these quasi-judicial bodies must not practice cumbersome legal paper works, complex formalities and procedural technicalities as in civil courts. Thus, the intention of the Consumer Protection Act is crystal clear: save aggrieved consumers from cumbersome procedures, on the one hand, and affording them simple, cheaper and speedy justice delivery system, on the other, because they were aware that involvement of lawyers in ordinary circumstances would make them resort to cycle of adjournments as a matter of course and thereby delay the simple summary trial/ proceedings.

The Consumer Protection Act, 1986 brought under its ambit a vast variety of subjects that affect *aam* consumers in day to day market whether it is related to purchase of goods or hiring of services. In other words, the subjects fall under the purview of this Act are numerous. Thus, the benevolent Consumer Protection Act was passed with high hopes that a consumer will get quick, inexpensive and simple justice based on summary proceedings but today it seems to be a far cry as the objectives and purpose of the Act are found to be gradually defeated in many ways. Many times, it is pretended that all is well and that adds to the woes of the aggrieved consumer victims. It is only the aggrieved consumers who only know where his/her shoes are pinching. Majority aggrieved consumers find their complaints put in cycles of dates and grilling processes till the verdict is seen the light of the day. They invariably suffer not only the delay but also the complicated procedures in the process of justice delivery like in civil courts. The adjournments and delays are the order of the day though it is reasoned that numerous factors are responsible for it which are beyond the capacity of the forums. But in the process it is the aggrieved consumers who invariably suffer from double-victimisation syndrome as rather than heaving a sigh of relief they feel frustrated since as quick, inexpensive and simple summary justice is an illusion and only found in the Act.

This extra-ordinary delay in delivering justice by the Consumer Forums to the aggrieved consumers within the stipulated time-frame is generating undesirable 'double-victim syndrome' among the consumers who dare to take the violators to the court for redressal of their grievances. When the gullible and unsuspecting consumers, whose rights are violated by the unfair dealings of the markets, go to the Court for redressal of their grievances, they suffer again in the hands of the justice delivery system as it fails to deliver justice within the stipulated time-period of 90 to 150 days as mentioned in the Consumer Protection Act. Several studies and experiences by the various consumer organisations, including individual consumers, do show that frustrations of the aggrieved consumers at the hands of Consumer Forums are real and it is necessarily a cause of concern that needs urgent attention and strategies to strengthen the justice delivery as enshrined in the said Act. One of the reasons for delay in the delivery system may be due to the fact that the Forums are over-burdened with the rising number of cases against the growing disgruntled marketers of goods and services whose only interest is to make 'profit' at the cost of consumers who are the very purpose of their 'business'.

With the generation of awareness among the consumers by the media and/or otherwise, we need to find, if not an exact alternative, but then an appropriate additional arm to the existing Consumer Fora so that the delay in delivering the much-desired consumer justice, within the time-frame, against the violators of the Consumer Protection Act could be made more a reality than a dream-proposition. In fact, the writer himself has got the first-hand bitter experience of this 'double-victim syndrome'. If not the same, many must also be feeling the pinch somewhere in the process of getting justice delivered as it was thought off in the beginning of the legal process. It is really frustrating and disheartening that the righteous consumers, who would like to genuinely see that justice is delivered as per the benevolent Consumer Protection Act, find that it is unthinkable, if not impossible under the present juncture. Many times, a feeling does come in the mind of the consumer-victims that it is a cursing destiny that must have brought them to the door of justice delivery for redressal of grievances against the consumer rights violators. In fact, a year-long study sponsored by the Ministry of Consumer Affairs conducted by the author adequately shows that many of the aggrieved-consumers suffer agonies and frustrations more from the courts compared to the violations of their rights from the wrongdoings and unfair deals of marketers of goods and services. What results ultimately in the consumer-victims compromise with the reality and/or eventually forgetting about taking the powerful violators headlong even if they wish it. Many of those who have not undergone the agony of the legal process may not know how the hope of the complainants is belied due to several in-built systemic ills, limitations and overall constraints. There is another serious issue that obviously gets lost in the process and that is the untrained manpower who have been entrusted to adjudicate justice as per Consumer laws. Then it becomes herculean task for them to do justice with the consumer courts as they are well-versed more with the Civil Procedure Code (CPC) laws, but on their retirement after their selection as Judges of the Consumer Courts and without adequate knowledge of the spirit of the Act and the consumer jurisprudence, they sometimes feel more as a 'fish-out-of-water' than probably in the civil court environment where they spent better part of their careers. Thus, their being inadequately trained manpower in the consumer jurisprudence creates a 'vicious circle' in which the consumer-victims of the market become the 'first-victim' of the consumer court where rule of the law is specifically supposed to be simple, speedy and more 'pro-consumer' in approach, unlike the CPC where legality and not the 'summary proceeding' that matters most. Keeping the growing anathema among the informed-consumers in mind, it would be a good remedy if the Government of the day innovatively thinks of some pragmatic approach like, for example, the much-desired training in consumer jurisprudence for the people who desire to serve and/or believe in participating in the consumer court affairs/services may be selected through the autonomous selection body like Union Public Service Commission (UPSC). Moreover, the various Law colleges and universities must be roped in at the earliest to generate pro-consumer legal manpower who would be well-versed in consumer jurisprudence to tackle the mighty free-market economic forces who are smarter and provocative in action-orientation to believers and/or upholders of the consumer rights.

We all know that the menace of rising consumer rights violations of all shades and types as well as the propensity of consumers' approaching the quasi-judicial bodies in accordance with rising consumer rights awareness are not proportionate yet in any way. In other words, rising of consumer cases through increasing in the Consumer fora is disproportionate to the rising menace of wrongdoings of dubious marketers who sell all types of goods and services under the global free-market agenda as there are no effective checks or enforcement by the regulatory bodies of the government. The palpable governance-deficit and corruption is a well-known facts of life. Under this circumstance, unlike in the past, many the free-marketers are seen using several ingenious methods and tactics to fleece the unsuspecting *aam* consumers through 24×7 multi-media-based advertisements including misleading and unethical misleading ones. In fact, it is an integral part of free-market strategies to allure the unsuspecting consumers and has taken menacing proportion. Due to the misleading advertisements the *aam aadmi* cannot help making informed-choice or decision to buy goods and services in this technological era. They often fail to get value-for-money while buying goods and services. Thus, the vulnerability of millions of consumers is certainly a major challenge unless proper protection mechanism is evolved to protect consumer interests. Moreover, millions of consumers find such unethical and misleading advertisements are bombarded through multi-media channels are yet to be effectively prohibited as these are yet to be legislated to check the rising menace of consumer exploitation. However, under the non-regulatory free-market syndrome and culture when all types of consumer rights violations are seen and experienced by *aam* consumers in the market one gets the impression that the consumer rights given under the Act are really under siege in the market.

Challenges of Fora: However, in this emerging scenario, the challenges of quasi-judicial consumer disputes redressal bodies have also been multiplied with increasing number of grievances/complaints are filed unlike in the nineties. Despite the best intention of the legislatures, the three-tier quasi-judicial bodies have failed to come up to peoples' expectations. We may highlight what A.P. Shah, former Judge of Madras High Court has said while delivering in a Refresher workshop for core consumer courts functionaries in Chennai: "unfortunately, consumer forums have adopted the same work culture and ethos that prevail in other law courts in the country.... That's why consumer forums are not getting accolades from the consumers."

Thus, it is ironical to see that the consumer courts conceived 25 years ago in 1986 as a dedicated body to easily afford aggrieved consumers simple, cheaper and speedier alternative became another extension of civil court system with heart-breaking civil court procedures and in its ambience, orientation, ethos and attitudes. For example, the presence of more lawyers than the aggrieved consumers is seen every day in any court in the country. That means the quasi-bodies are gradually becoming lawyer's paradise and these are not exceptions. It defeats the high expectations of the law-makers who thought that keeping them out-of-bounds would facilitate the *aam admi* to avoid the ills the civil courts pose. But it is unfortunate that it has crept into the quasi-judicial consumer bodies too. In other words, the reliance on lawyers is not rare and the presence of lawyers certainly complicates the scenario as they generally try to complicate the matter to win against the opponents resorting to cumbersome technical or legalistic procedures. And invariably it is the powerful marketers of goods and services who usually hire the best legal eagle or senior corporate lawyers to fight their cases against the poor aggrieved consumers. The former possibly cannot see them losing cases filed by *aam* consumers who dare to file complaints and challenge them in the court of law. As a matter of course their lawyers routinely seek adjournments, often on flimsy grounds since they ordinarily have vested interests to serve. This undoubtedly not only complicates the process but prolongs the matter in the courts depriving the consumer-victims from getting speedy, simple and inexpensive justice in terms of time, energy and money. This is a very disheartening situation for the *aam* consumer-victims who dare to file dispute cases for adjudication but the delays they are forced to undergo through cycle of dates and adjournments most cannot afford unlike their opponents. This is due to this fact that the 90 to 150 days time schedule as stipulated in Consumer Protection Act, 1986 could not be materialised. For example, Section 19(1) of Consumer Protection Regulations, 2005 says, "A Consumer Forum is expected to dispose of at least 75 to 100 matters per month" is not followed by these bodies. It has become a myth costing the aggrieved consumer-victims dearly. Thousands of consumer-victims have heart-rending stories to tell who are losing confidence in these quasi-judicial bodies all over the country. What we need is serious introspection as to where are the flaws that must be failing them to perform their best. These need to be rectified and if necessary the Act must be amended based on the changing scenario.

It is true that the consumer courts do suffer from many inbuilt challenges while playing their roles. It is also true that these quasi-judicial bodies are headed by the retired Judges who are trained in complicated civil/criminal court procedures. They are certainly in law profession for a long time both as lawyers as well as Judges in different courts, it is but natural that they are used to civil court ethos and work culture. This possibly makes them habitually fall back on the civil technical formats while dealing with consumer cases as well. This fact may be denied openly by many but in confidence many confided that there is some truth in it. Because it is difficult for many retired Judges on getting selected and appointed as Presidents in the quasi-judicial bodies to de-learn many civil court culture and ethos at this ripe or retired age. We all know Consumer Protection Act is not very complicated unless it is interpreted in right spirit developing consumer jurisprudence to serve the consumer interest. Many Judges may not be well-versed with consumer laws and its jurisprudence to pragmatically deal with consumer cases where consumer factor is prominent. For many it may be difficult to come to terms with simple non-technical formats and nuances of Consumer Protection Act, 1986 and that too when the lawyers persist or insist on technicalities to win cases against the opponents. It is, but, natural for many to de-learn the culture, attitudes, ethos and mindset acquired over the years which usually die hard. It is said that for many these quasi-judicial bodies are the parking place for retired judges who usually do not show much seriousness and responsibility to the post. Many are reluctant to de-learn and re-learn the critical consumer jurisprudence necessary to understand state of mind of consumer-victims and their interests. That's why probably it makes many Presidents of these quasi-judicial bodies to put consumer complaints through several procedures and stages like in civil courts where each stage consumes enormous precious time of consumer-victims and exceptions are rare.

Thus, the concept of summary trials and/or proceedings is defeated or become a misnomer since the whole process becomes more complicated and legalistic; though sometimes it is argued that since each case is unique it cannot be adjudicated uniformly without applying legal civil court format. But this argument should not come in their way to deliver pro-consumer justice with adequate compensation taking into consideration the tremendous mental agony and harassment as a result of enormous time consumed in justice delivery by these quasi-judicial bodies as per consumer law. It should be remembered that consumer fora is not bound to follow principles of natural justice. They are supposed to dispose cases through summary proceedings only without too much technicalities. But it rarely happens this way. Every complaint must be filed in affidavit form including the reply of the opposite party to save time. There should not be any filing of rejoinders, etc. by the parties. But it does not happen this way.

It is high time that the concerned Ministry and/or Department must consider the challenges of these bodies seriously so that the benevolent Act is not allowed to be defeated so as to fulfill consumer expectations as prescribed in consumer law. If necessary, as stated, the consumer law may be amended. Certainly there are needs to ponder over the fact whether the appointment of retired Judges is the best to run these quasi-judicial consumer fora? Whether time has come we may think of appointing qualified senior lawyers and/or non-retired Judges who are well-versed with consumer jurisprudence and adequate knowledge of consumer laws. They may be selected by the Union Public Service Commission (UPSC), or other appropriate body through open competition and fair selection. There is a high requirement of effective trainings and rigorous orientation to the staff of these bodies and they should be appropriately provided the salary at par with other courts with service regulations. A judicial accountability system needs to be introduced and practiced in true sense. In other words, a proper accountability is to be necessarily fixed and discipline has to be underlined for those who man these bodies. As it is the case these bodies are kept under the Food and Civil Supply Department/Ministry who guide and not the Presidents who are at the mercy of the whims and fancies of government officials who in turn are controlled by their political masters of the day. This creates the tug-of-war situation between the two power centres of different bodies. The vacancies are not filled-in time and posts lie vacant causing tremendous disaffection among the stakeholders. In some courts it is found that files go misplaced, missing or are clumsily kept to harass the complainants. These incidences though rare need to be taken seriously. A proper system of maintenance of file with accountability has to be evolved. It will only then make it possible by these quasi-judicial bodies to properly extend simple, inexpensive and speedy pro-consumer justice under the consumer protection law much to the relief of the aggrieved consumers who approach these bodies with high hopes. It must be remembered that we all are consumers since we have opted free-market society and in this regard we all have a stake in these bodies so the quasi-judicial bodies cannot but play pro-actively pro-consumer roles to the satisfaction of aggrieved consumers without resorting to more technicalities but on merit. The Presidents have to develop a mindset to protect the consumer interest as they have been made victims by the marketers of goods and services. The intention to find adequate relief to consumer disputes must be central in the process of justice delivery.

As stated, these quasi-judicial courts suffer from inadequate infrastructure facilities, their salaries are meager and devoid of other benefits etc. which the general courts command. These quasi-judicial bodies also should be necessarily refurbished with adequate facilities and adequate staffs like in other courts. Certainly these quasi-judicial bodies are not inferior to other courts. They are certainly pro-consumer in spirit and bias as intended in the Consumer Protection Act, 1986. Under no circumstances, we may allow the pro-consumer prescription of Consumer Protection Act defeated. As stated earlier, the Presidents of these quasi-courts must appreciate that those who come to them are not the litigant *per se* in strict sense of the term but are victims of the disgruntled marketers of goods or providers of services whose rights are violated or seized. It is keeping in view the above scenarios we strongly feel that all the functionaries of these bodies urgently require massive doses of innovative and effective refreshers' training/orientation courses to pragmatically man these pro-consumer courts. What they need is to practice the pro-consumer nuances in true spirit as enunciated in the benevolent Act while dealing with consumer complaints otherwise notion of simple, inexpensive and speedy justice delivery will be only on paper and cannot be materialised to reduce the sufferings, pain and agony of ever-rising aggrieved consumers in this global era of free-market economic disposition which in turn may encourage the consumer exploitations in the market.

Moreover, as per rule the final verdict can only be passed by the President. This clause puts a break to early justice delivery when the Presidents go on leave and new extensions of dates become a routine affair in this circumstance costing the aggrieved consumers dearly. On condition of anonymity many core functionaries opined that adjudication and declaration of verdict within 90–150 days is not possible as it is absolutely unrealistic to expect it in view of the rising number of cases filed in these courts in our country as a result of rising consumer awareness. They feel it normally needs at least two-to-three years if not more to pass the final verdict. Thus, many of these courts have to cope with not only the piled-up cases but also the newly filed cases but there is no provision for more benches to take care the rising number of cases. What is required are more benches in District redressal fora based on number of cases filed. Furthermore, as stated, the non-filling of vacant positions in time certainly adds to more problems. Moreover, the backlog including the rising number of new cases over-burdens the existing structure with inadequate manpower. In fact, many quasi-bodies look so shabby like any other district government offices in some remote village and it does not inspire confidence to complainants. As stated, the record keeping in most courts is poor and are not at all standardised and/or kept up-to-date. Usually this is done by people who are periodically transferred from one department to another based on the whims and fancies of the bureaucrats empowered to do so with exceptions.

The scenario of harrowing experience of aggrieved consumers can be easily seen in the corridors of quasi-consumer redressal forums/courts in the country. Thus, thousands of aggrieved consumers are badly trapped in the cycle of long dates and hearings and other complicated technical procedures and legalities. By and large, the aggrieved consumer-victims feel tired of waiting for the final verdict against the wrongdoers of market. In other words, most of them are also forced to go through bumpy roads to get proper justice. If it happens in their favour they feel their dream ultimately could come true. These experiences definitely do not augur well as it does not give rise to much confidence among the *aam* consumers who approach these bodies with tremendous hope raised by multi-media based *'Jago Grahak Jago'* sloganeering by the Government of India. However, the statistical data rolled out by the ministry and the concerned departments do show that the success rates/records of these quasi-judicial bodies in different parts of the country are good but what these statistics hide is that they don't mention the actual time taken to settle the matter from the date the cases are filed. It is here that the fault lines or decay of consumer courts lie as they have been mandated that all cases be settled within 90–150 days.

It is also a known fact that the Act was passed 25 years back with good intent and it was also amended last in 2002 but it seminally failed to check the menace of consumer rights violations in the market due to several inherent factors as highlighted above. The reality checks by discerned people only show how the developing scenario is pathetically against the needy aggrieved consumers who file grievances with tremendous hope for proper justice. It is not to tarnish anybody's image but to highlight a fact that the novel quasi-judicial redressal system set up under the Act is gradually brought to this condition by the lack of political will and bureaucratic apathy and complexities in checking the downslide over the years. This is despite legislature's best intention to protect the interest of consumers from wrongdoers in the market. It seems the quasi-judicial bodies are yet to find a Godfather to come to their rescue. The regular blame game between the States and the Centre including the governance deficit has now become chronic. For instance, the States argue that the Centre does not give them enough funds to properly run these quasi-consumcr courts. The Centre counters that they can't dictate terms because the consumer affairs are a state subject. Moreover, when Centre gives them financial grants, the states neither use them well nor do they supplement them with their own support.

Thus, in the midst of the Centre and the states orchestration of charges and counter-charges to each other the real victims of the market, i.e., the *aam* consumers who suffer perennially from the denial of the simple, cheaper and speedy justice that have been costing them very dearly.

Even Justice A.P. Shah opined that in many states the sanctioned funds are not utilised. The question that arises is that why the bureaucracy and/or its political masters don't take prompt actions to strengthen the pro-consumer forums in the states even though it is a known fact that the menace of consumer exploitation is on the rise is unfathomable. It seems it has something more to it than what meets the eye. Therefore, unless the political leadership rise up to the occasion and the bureaucracy is made to act pro-actively to deal with the situation, we hardly can do anything to strengthen the quasi-judicial forums, protect consumers as well as to forward the consumer movements in this country. Thus, tackling of rising menace of consumer exploitation in the global free-market era through half-hearted approach only encourage the market wrongdoers and exploiters. Thus, despite various positive steps and legislative and administrative measures the consumer protection remains a dream to be true for millions.

Keeping in view the above scenarios we can safely infer that in most cases the problems derive from lack of Ministerial will and administrative apathy including chronic governance-deficit. Moreover, it seems the consumer protection is not a priority area for many states otherwise why consumer rights protection issues are not yet made central by many Ministries both in the Central and the States even though most Ministries and Departments do produce goods and provide services to the consumers. Why this consumer protection is still languishing within the Ministry or Department of Food and Supplies in many states including the Central without full-fledged Ministers to look into the consumer rights protection issue even though billions of our consumers fall victims to wrongdoers in the market. It is also said that most of the staff runing the quasi-judicial consumer Fora are transferable from other government departments and they are often transferred whimsically by the Department of Food and Supply. It is also said that sometimes this staff is transferred by the relevant Department without the knowledge of the Presidents of consumer forums.

We find several examples in the National Capital Territory of Delhi. Such. This only shows that the proper appointments to these bodies are of low priority for many states. They fail to appoint Presidents and/or Members in time even though requests for filling the vacant posts are made known to the relevant departments and state governments in time. Moreover, it is said that appointment of members and retired Judges are mostly the political appointees and the like. Many members are poorly paid despite suitable recommendations by the P.D. Shenoy Committee in 2008. For example, in Delhi Fora a member is paid Rs. 9000 per month, in Maharashtra it is Rs. 8000, in Odisha it is Rs. 6500, in Uttarakhand Rs. 4000, in Gujarat and Sikkim it is Rs.3000 p.m., in Manipur Rs. 2500 p.m., in Nagaland Rs. 2000, etc. All these sad narratives do not augur well for the health of the quasi-judicial bodies that are entrusted with a serious business of consumer rights protection. However, with exception, this scenario often fails to generate enough enthusiasm to many Fora members who want to play pro-active roles in justice delivery but fail to do so. It is said that sometimes this pittance ultimately help breeds corruption and/or they may fall into the trap of powerful companies who often act desperately to win them to win cases against the complainants. However, most retired judges are well paid as they receive their last salary drawn minus pension and/or get fixed honorarium. It is also found that many times consumer courts are forced to meet their running expenses on their own. Sometimes the complainants are also asked to deliver the notice in *dasti* (by hand) or pay for it to send their notice.

Being a bone of contention between the States and the Centre, there is clear-cut decision on the share of contribution and/or the disbursal of funds and in its absence the problem aggravates. The State's contribution essentially determines the funding levels which are invariably low and/or inadequate. Shortage of staff or timely filling up of vacancies often leads to piling up of cases and since, as said, for many states consumer affairs is not a priority area; it is mostly handled by small department of consumer affairs under the Ministry of Food and Civil Supply. The latter seems to be of high value affairs and lucrative for many Ministers and officials. Thus, unless many of the chronic teething problems are urgently rectified the challenges highlighted in above paragraphs cannot be solved and ultimately become a death-knell to many quasi-judicial bodies in States. The indications of these are already seen how aggrieved consumers are hankering for cheaper, simple and speedy justice against the wrongdoers of the market as enunciated in the benevolent Consumer Protection Act, 1986. Thus, the states as well as the Centre conflict cannot be allowed to be an enduring phenomenon and both cannot possibly shirk the responsibility to deal with the challenges as noted above since these are affecting the interests of *aam* consumers under the law. The one-upmanship only weakens the consumer courts and consumer movements in the country. Just by celebrating March 15, as annual ritual and multi-media publicity slogan *'Jago Grahak Jago'* at a huge cost to exchequer will not be meaningful and fruitful to serve consumer interests whose rights are under siege in this global era by the dubious market forces. This cannot but create a mismatch between the Act and the reality.

It is true that some of the informed consumers only go to consumer courts when they felt cheated or their rights are violated by the sellers of goods and/or providers of services and, as said, they approach court as victims only and not otherwise. Without genuine cause consumers may not dare to approach quasi-judicial bodies by spending time, money and energy. They possibly don't go to court for fun and that the consumer courts should operate and on this premise only that the Consumer Protection Act has prescribed the pro-consumer approach to deal with cases. Moreover, the Consumer courts have the same power as in civil courts. Thus, if a dispute goes to consumer courts, s/he should be presumed to be right unless it is proved otherwise so it is very much like 'unless prove guilty a person cannot be convicted'. It is seen that seldom do companies pay heed to consumer courts. For example, the consumer court verdicts, orders, summons and reports are routinely ignored on one pretext or the other. This is also proving to be a menace. The popular opinion is that as in family courts, in consumer courts too advocates should be discouraged from entering consumer courts as it is they who vitiate the matter by bringing legal technicalities as a part of strategy to prolong the matter through various tactics like adjournments, etc., to serve their interests as well as their rich clients in the name of equal justice to harass the complainants. Various pro-active actions and initiatives for consumer protection is the need of the hour. All these initiatives can possibly work better if enough teeth with statutory powers to deal with consumer cases are given.

There must be compulsory comprehensive complaints redressal policy as a part of corporate social responsibility agenda. The industry and commerce associations should have some kind of ombudsman. But these initiatives must have legal powers otherwise it is a futile exercise having limited utility. Their decisions should be taken on-record by the consumer courts. For the consumer courts remain the only option but they seem to be not in a position to deliver justice as highlighted above. Many times, the big companies who fight cases with their corporate legal eagles don't fear consumer courts and their verdicts and go for appeal adding to further costs and agony to weak consumer-victims. This has been underlined in several studies and reports. The World Wide Web is full of heart-breaking stories on this count given the sorry state of consumer cases. Social media, worldwide web sites as well as the voluntary consumer bodies need to be more pro-active to voice the consumer issues like in the western developed countries. One heartening fact is that there is a growing awareness about the consumer rights in our country but awareness alone is not panacea under the prevailing circumstances. What is required is to give more statutory powers to consumer courts as they are the last hope for the aggrieved consumers to deal with consumer matters and disputes.

Under the prevailing situations when the consumer courts are facing many heats due to several weaknesses identified above that we may think of pragmatic system in terms of strengthening Mediation system unlike many stray initiatives here and there both by the government and/or autonomous bodies. These Mediation bodies we are proposing here are qualitatively different and act as complementary and supplementary wings of the existing quasi-judicial bodies since they are to be placed directly under the court's jurisdiction. All the consumer complaints are to be necessarily filed with all the relevant documents in affidavit forms to the Mediatory Cell for mutual settlement with the help of professionally qualified mediator within a month's time without lawyers as a rule. This Mediatory Cell will operate under the jurisdiction of the court. They will certainly not be technical but go by the complaints. Many vexed legal issues that usually crop up during hearing by the consumer courts can be brought to its limit as well as to help deliver speedy justice to the needy. This Mediation system, as said, must not allow lawyers as in the case of family courts. Both the parties would mutually try to solve the disputes within a month's time and failing which it automatically moves to next stage, i.e., quasi-judicial consumer courts for adjudication. This would unburden the quasi-judicial bodies as it will act a filter/screening process. Since it works under the direct court jurisdiction it will not have separate power structure. The Mediatory Cell will accrue power to pass rulings that will bind both the parties to comply. This filter process will abolish the cycle of dates and hearings.

It may not be out of place to mention here that there is a high need to develop separate consumer jurisprudence which is different from existing civil jurisprudence as it is still in its nascent stage. It is possible only when the quasi-judicial consumer courts adopt fresh and unconventional approach while interpreting the provisions of law providing consumer justice. Justice M.B. Shah, Former President of NCDRC has rightly said that the 'proceedings in a Consumer Fora cannot be adversarial in nature. Thus, for any breach of obligations, there has to be consumer factor or consumer surplus as one may call it to which consumer is certainly entitled'. This may arise from matters dealing with goods and services. For example, deficiency of services in banking services, airlines services, carriers and courier services, educational services, electricity and financial services, franchisee, housing, delay in delivery, failure to provide amenities, postal and telegraph services, health and insurance services, legal services, medical negligence, railways, transport services, etc., are consumer matters. Thus, the. arena of consumer court is very vast. Thus, given the challenges in this era of consumerism, all efforts must be made to strengthen the consumer protection in the light of rising complaints against the sellers of goods and providers of services and role of consumer forums is tremendous. It is in the light of above harsh realities that we need to think and explore complementary and supplementary justice delivery system because one system alone will not suffice to tackle the menace of wrongdoings in the market. It is here that the mediatory system as a possible pragmatic complementary.tool can come to our rescue to save the aggrieved consumers from heart-breaking situation in consumer courts.

Increasingly the unsuspecting consumers are feeling the heat in the hands of disgruntled free-market forces and many are recognising the fact that the free-market forces are not acting as pure manna from heaven but a fiendish attempt to exploit the unsuspecting consumers because their primary objective is profit-making. In other words, the *aam* consumers are increasingly becoming the object of exploitation and as Justice Bhan said, today getting justice in this country is a very expensive affair. Moreover, the consumer courts are also not in a position to dispose complaints in time. Under this circumstance, it is essential that we promote internal complaint redressal mechanism under the court's jurisdiction through the proposed Mediatory system to assist and solve the grievances of aggrieved poor consumers. It may be highlighted that under Section 89 the Code of Civil Procedure (CPC) lays down the mandate for all disputes of civil nature to be settled through the provision of arbitration, conciliation, Lok Adalats or Mediation. Therefore, since Section 3 of the Consumer Protection Law lays the rule that Consumer Protection Act is not in derogation of any other law for the time being in force it may be difficult to follow Section 89 of CPC while opting for mediatory system as a viable complementary mechanism even though Consumer Protection Act, 1986 is silent and/or not explicit on this issue. It may be necessary to amend the Consumer Protection Act, 1986 to incorporate Mediation mechanism as an integral part of the quasi-judicial consumer forums. In other words, the mediatory mechanism must be placed under the overall jurisdiction of the President of consumer courts to have its legal sanctity and strengths. It must be autonomous but under the control of the courts to appropriately resolve/ redress grievances *of aam* consumers mutually with the help of professionally trained Mediator to arrive at a win-win situation satisfying both the parties in disputes. As said, lawyers must be debarred from appearing in the mediation cell except the parties in disputes.

We may also opt for Mobile Mediators to expeditiously solve *aam* consumer's grievances having the power since they work under the command and jurisdiction of quasi-judicial consumer courts. These Mobile units will have web-based complaints registration, report generation system and common knowledge-data base networking system. We may also rope in public-spirited bodies and/or genuine voluntary consumer organisations to get involved in this mediation advocacy process if necessary since it is work of public welfare. We may evolve comprehensive suitable guidelines for their pragmatic and innovative involvement.

The additional networking in terms of roping the committed pro-active NGOs should be encouraged to facilitate consumers through the multi-tasking activity-oriented programmes like helping the consumer-victims through the awareness generation among them and, with the help of volunteer-lawyers, helping the Court-annexed mediation to sort out grievances of the consumers. Thus, proper incorporation of Alternative Dispute Resolution (ADR) system in right spirit can to a large extent, reduce the burden of burgeoning cases in consumer courts all over the country. This will certainly make the aggrieved consumers breathe a sigh of relief.

It is a sort of mediation tool to be adopted to unburden the Forums from piling up of cases of the aggrieved consumers as well as to give an option to parties to sort their grievances in front of the Court-annexed and/or monitored mediators within a time-frame of a month or so. It is in this context that an out-of-box thinking and innovative measure can make it possible to sort out the growing grievances of aggrieved consumer-victims and/or get the much-desired justice at a faster pace. So, a more professional approach and strategy would only bear fruits against the mighty marketers who care less in regard to consumer right protection affairs. Therefore, the role of volunteers and NGOs cannot be under-estimated provided they are legally empowered to do the 'special job' under special situation of global economy. There are many committed NGOs who may be interested to help, from their own premises in mediation and expedite the justice delivery, at the doorsteps of the consumers, as most of them may be conveniently located in the residential/nearby market areas. In these consumer welfare matters, the dedicated Residents Welfare Associations (RWAs) may feel happy to join by providing their community facilities/space if they can find that their services are desired on private-public partnership basis. In fact, they will also ultimately gain in this joint welfare venture as one of the beneficiaries. Thus, the court-annexed and monitored ADR mediation may act as a catalyst in bringing much change in the market run by disgruntled elements who are taking the burgeoning consumers for a ride, rather than an exception, in their run for profit at the cost of consumers, society and environment.

However, on failing to solve the court-annexed and monitored grievances by the parties themselves, keeping in view the mediator's commentaries/remarks, etc., the aggrieved consumers would be entitled to automatically transfer their complaints to the regular Consumer Forums for adjudication of the same. It is said that after the judgement delivery, it is a real problem to get the final outcome (meaning the compensation, etc., awarded by the court). This situation adds to another third dimension to victim syndrome. So, a stringent legal framework has to be placed for the benefit of immediately getting the 'award' implemented. Only then the things will be expected to be improved, otherwise the whole purpose of consumer laws will be defeated, or at best be read like a novel.

The above welfare-oriented proposition may act as a filtration system to the existing 'burden-ridden' courts. Most of the petty low compensatory cases can be solved remarkably within a little time. It will have 'broom effect' in terms of sweeping/cleaning/weeding out the disgruntled/dubious business people who hardly respect laws, and/or help modify their *modus operandi* of business dealings for fear of being hooked and punished. Henceforth, they will certainly become more cautious about not repeating the same wrongdoings leading to consumers' rights violation. Moreover, their names, addresses, etc. must be telecast and/or put on the websites for everyone to know. They may be forced to modify/change their way leaving the ingrained tradition of consumer rights violations as a birth right, while doing their business and flourishing at the cost of 'poor' consumers. Only then, the consumer welfare can easily find a new meaning and centrality to the dubious business class.

Thus, it is in this context that we see the centrality to consider 'Mediation' as a possible viable tool for achieving justice for the consumer-victims. As stated, since there are ever-rising consumer grievances resulted from the operation of many dubious market forces which are desperate to make profit by hook or crook, their violating consumer rights in various ways and means, needs to be checked. Otherwise, the menace of consumer rights violation in the market arenas will grow with the help of modern science and technological tools. We need to strategise through checks and balances as already the syndromes of wrongdoings in the markets are not a rare phenomenon. Globalisation has, no doubt given us, by and large, certain benefits of getting quality consumer products and services which we were unknown to before, and/ or we could ever imagine of even a decade before. But along with availability of quality of goods and services in the market all over the country, there are also a huge amount of goods and services of doubtful qualities that are made available with several inbuilt unfair trade practices and with the help of unethical/ misleading advertisements alluring the unsuspecting consumers to fall into their trap. The exploitation of consumers in the market places, particularly by the dubious marketeers, is seen to be believed in the nascent globalised Indian free-market scenario. It is ironic that despite India being an emerging economic power with phenomenal growth of profit-making industry, trade and commerce in the midst of palpable 'governance-deficit and corruption syndrome' it is yet to wholeheartedly check the menace of consumer rights violations. Everywhere the unsuspecting *aam* citizen-consumers are facing the consumer rights violations in the markets.

I am sure we will not find a single soul who can vouch that s/ he has not been exploited by any dealer in her/his life time and thereby their rights were not violated. It is also true that many upright consumers, whose rights and dignity as 'consumers' have been violated often do not feel to get their grievances redressed. Glaringly, they are cheated and their value of money is not appropriately compensated and they fear to tread the path of Consumer courts to fall into another trap of unending dates and hearings as well as due to other limitations or reasons. In fact, millions may not be aware that there exists a three-tier Consumer Dispute Redressal Fora exclusively set up by the Government, under the aegis of Consumer Protection Act, 1986, in different districts of the country to redress the consumer rights violations. Under this Act each complaint must be redressed and/or justice delivered within a stipulated period of 90-150 days from the date of filing the complaint. Unfortunately, it is usually not the case due to several known and unknown reasons and circumstances. For many aggrieved consumers, even if the cases are filed under the CP Act, it becomes a mirage to get their complaints redressed within the stipulated period. Thus, the unlimited delay in adjudicating the cases under the CP Act for one reason or the other is noted in many studies. Among many other reasons, it is also seen how the aggrieved consumers fall victims to the whims of the Judges who are not in a position to see the merits of cases. This may be due to their inadequate knowledge and understanding of the spirit of benevolent CP Act or lack sufficient sensitivities or they habitually fall back upon the civil technicalities and ethos to delay adjudication of consumer complaints. Thus, under this circumstance, the victim-complainants suffer from double-victimisation syndrome: once in the hands of dubious marketers when her/his rights are given scanty respect and secondly, the delay in deliverance of justice by the Consumer Fora. This becomes heartbreaking for the consumer-victims who lose confidence on the quasi-judicial bodies while seeking justice endlessly like in civil courts. Such scenario is seen everywhere in the country and our Government seems to be not unaware of it. Thus, ostrich-like decisions and policy strategies leaving the *aam* consumers to defend themselves in the free-market scenario as well as to the quasi-judicial bodies without effective monitoring can only sustain and allow heartbreaking vicious circle of injustice to flourish. How to solve this vicious circle of injustice and/or double victimisation syndrome of the aggrieved consumers? What can be the best possible alternative or complementary solution to give relief to the consumer-victims? Can we think of other pragmatic ways to protect the consumer rights in the right earnest as well as to strengthen them? As stated earlier, the Consumer courts are overburdened with cases is a fact since they too suffer from many challenges like lack of better/proper infrastructural facilities to perform their duties, vacant posts not filled-up in time by the government, inadequate understanding of the benevolent CP Act among the majority functionaries of these quasi-judicial bodies, running quasi-bodies whimsically transfering staff from government departments including from hospital/mortuary staff who have no understanding and sensitivities to guide aggrieved consumer-victims or about consumer law, inadequate salaries, non-release of funds, and many other challenges and bottlenecks that often cause piling up of cases in different consumer courts in the country. Under this scenario no amount of *Jago Grahak Jago* slogan through the multi-media can bring confidence to consumers to seek justice at the right earnest in the event of wrongdoings done by the marketeers of goods and services. Instances of not getting fast justice despite the stipulation in the Act delude the consumer-victims the most and this scenario certainly dissuades the informed-consumers from approaching the Consumer Fora for justice. Thus, when their hopes belied and they suffer from disillusionment. It is in this context it may be necessary or desirable to look into the strategies the developed countries have opted to face the rising challenges of consumer rights violations in the free-market economies. Can we pragmatically incorporate some of their good practices to relieve our aggrieved consumer-victims whose rights have been challenged by the market? However, it is a fact that the developed countries do encourage the mediation as a viable tool to ensure faster delivery of justice.

The mediation mechanism that helps resolve the grievances/ matters in an out-of-court process is termed as Alternative Dispute Redressal (ADR), as stated earlier. Thus, the recognition, acceptance and strengthening of ADR system can possibly be the viable alternative where the parties are encouraged to resolve their own grievances without approaching the quasi-judicial Consumer courts at the first instance. This method or technique seems to be convenient also for our multi-ethnic, multi-cultural and multi-lingual country like ours. We must think seriously about the possible integration of this process to resolve rising consumer complaints in our country. It is certainly necessary when the globalisation of free market which is in its nascent stage or it is creeping into our life so fast that the dubious marketeers are having a field day to exploit the unsuspecting consumers day in and day out. Therefore, Court-annexed amicable settlement mechanism and logically integrating it under the jurisdiction of

Consumer courts can be a big relief to *aam* consumer-victims. It must be tried as a pre-trial stage mechanism allowing the aggrieved parties to mutually settle the disputes failing which they will automatically move up to the second stage, that is, for adjudication by the quasi-judicial Consumer Fora. Thus, Court-annexed ADR system or method or technique may give some hope to the aggrieved consumers to redress their complaints with the help of professional Mediators. In this process both the parties are offered opportunities to work out amicable solutions at the first instance without the involvement of lawyers. The latter must be barred in this process as it hampers the solution as the lawyers usually have vested interests to serve at the cost of consumers.

Many studies all over the world also show how by using ADR-methods the consumer grievances can be settled more economically and efficiently by investing time, energy and money in the precinct of the courts by bringing the parties face-to-face to find win-win situation mutually with the help of trained Mediators. In fact the ADR methods were introduced in 1980s all over the developed world for the resolution of commercial disputes and the advantages of ADR techniques were quickly recognised. It was also found to be drawing widespread attention and interest. Mediation is the most common form of ADR system. It offers the opportunity for a fresh approach to negotiations as well as to reduce the cost of conflict in time, energy and money of the aggrieved consumers and thereby helps them getting their grievances redressed/resolved.

It may he noted that in the ADR, the flexibility and confidentiality are important features. The mediators have to take a neutral role here but will, without expressing any opinion, often persuade the parties to re-evaluate their own positions by asking challenging questions to the parties. In conventional sense, it is named as 'reality testing'. For example, questions usually asked are: Have you considered the options'? What if single option does not work ? What do you think about other option? What other options do you think might be available to you? and so on. Thus, the mediator allows the parties to search together and find a best possible solution to come to a settlement and/or resolve their disputes on their own terms. In fact, the role of a mediator is to assist the parties exploring suitable options by measuring the strengths and weaknesses of their respective cases. In this mediation system, the parties can certainly save time, energy and money, and thereby minimise both in financial and emotional cost of resolving a dispute. It also helps assist the parties to re-establish trust and gain respect, and thereby develop or prevent damage to the ongoing relationships between them. It is desirable to strengthen the consumer-seller symbiotic relationships and it must be protected because ultimately both the marketers and consumers get benefited in the long run. But in reality, it helps more to the marketers by reposing the consumers' trust and loyalty for the goods and services the company markets.

Usually, conflict occurs when people disagree or get cheated, shattering their expectations. It occurs as a natural part of life and business, particularly in cases where business ethics are either not strong or given a go-bye or are violated, or if the business falters to respect consumer's rights who is interested to get the value of his/her money, while buying goods and services in the market. In common parlance, conflict is understood as a negative occurrence and it is often accepted or seen as a negative or destructive force. But it may not be necessarily so. Otherwise also, conflict has a negative effect when people disagree, knowing fully well the possible causes or they don't want to redress or resolve it. It is only then, it hurts feelings and thereby fractures the symbiotic consumer-business relationships. Knowing the causes is not always impossible and to deal with consumer-business conflict in a positive way, if both the parties approach the problem to come to win-win situation without ill feelings. This, in turn, creates considerable 'goodwill' for both and helps the business to grow and to consumers satisfy their needs and purposes.

Thus, mediation may necessarily be accepted as an option for finding a positive way to deal with any conflict; and it may be incorporated in the CP Act of 1986, if required by amending the same. It not only offers the possibility to improve communication between business and customer, but also helps build trust between the parties to solve the dispute amicably in an efficient, sensible and cost-effective way, unlike in the present dispensation through consumer courts where the delays in adjudication of disputes are anybody's guess. It is already causing enough discouragement and frustration among the rising number of consumer-victims in our fast pace of life in the society. Moreover, the fact is the conflict resolution only through legal approach usually follows a win-loss model of conflict resolution. But in mediation mechanism, every conflict has both a winner and a loser side simultaneously with wide options without tremendous feeling of win or loss syndrome. However, in real life a 'winner' in court may not always be truly a winner. The following story may highlight what it can ultimately lead to at the end?

"Two brothers were trying to share an orange, failing they both started fighting over it. They thought of taking the case to court where the judge simply imposes on them the decision of cutting it into half, giving each one his share. It looks to be a fair enough decision, but it leaves one with a feeling each one of them took something away from the other. Thus, they leave the conrt with hurt feelings towards the other. It is definitely a win/loss situation. Back home, one brother takes half of the whole orange, squeezes out the juice and throws away the rind to the waste basket. The other brother grates the rind from his half share and throws away the rest as he does not want it". Thus, we can easily understand the morale of the episode between the brothers-in-quarrel ?

Thus, what we see above, the judgement is an adversarial court procedure. The only measure for decision was the obvious position taken by each one, 'I want the orange.' In a mediating process, both of them would have been asked for the reason they wanted the orange, and very quickly the simple solution would have been obvious to both of them as one brother was thirsty and wanted to drink orange juice, whereas the other one wanted to bake cake and hence wanted the orange with rind. Both could have had 100 per cent of what they wished for, and it would have left with a win/win situation for both through mediatory process. Moreover, there would not have had any hurt feeling between both the brothers. Thus, the precondition of any mediation is to be a fair, impartial or neutral process without taking sides. It must believe and practice principles of objectivity and thereby develop a sense of natural justice with giving proper attention to the rights and obligations of the parties in dispute. There is no scope of moral judgement, favouratism, bias or prejudices but only conducted with respect and deference in a neutral fashion while treading the path to arrive at a solution in a participative manner. However, in this process the parties may not be discouraged to show anger or hurt feelings, but they have to make sure that no one crosses the proverbial *Laxman Rekha*, that is, not to cross a line using abusive languages because the whole purpose cannot be allowed to be defeated by any party in the "process of mediation. Thus, proper decorum has to be strictly followed without allowing it to de-rail the process to attain the ultimate objective of finding a solution amicably and honestly otherwise blame-game may polarise the parties against each other. Thus, what is highly essential in this venture is to look at the matter from parties' viewpoints and/or allowing oneself being in the shoe of the other. It is only then a solution can be found. These are the basic rules for mediation which must be appropriately and necessarily adopted and/or followed to come to any amicable settlement of the grievances of the parties for which they are found to be agitated. Usually, one of the fundamental reasons for any conflict is the breakdown and/or lack of communication. In fact, mediation can be a suitable process to open communication which may not always be possible in courts as they stand opposite to each other with a strand of winning over the opponent by hook or by crook methods. The consequences of this are not rare to see for the discernable eyes. It is here the role and duty of mediator is significant to facilitate communication between the parties to amicably find satisfactory/win-win solution to their problems on their own terms.

We all know that a process of new consumer market syndrome has set in the country in wooing the *aam* consumers 24 × 7 offering them newer products and services whether we like it or not. In the process, millions of gullible and unsuspecting consumers do regularly also fall victims to disgruntled market forces as 'profit' is their prime consideration even if the consumer rights are violated. We all know the evolving free-market syndrome is increasingly turning from 'sellers' to a 'buyer's market' but the menace of consumer rights violations in the market is a rising phenomenon taking different shades and types.

References

1. Bhanu Pandey: "Are consumer courts really serving the consumers ? in *The Economic Times,* 12th April, 2011.
2. M.C. Paul: "Role of Consumer Disputes Redressal System in India: Issues, Challenges and Opportunities" in *Consumers Power,* Inaugural Issue, May 2010.
3. "Protect consumer movement from evils of court culture", in *The Hindu,* October 31, 1999.
4. P. Venkatesan : "Strengthening the Consumer Movement" in *The Hindu,* 31 October 1999.
5. "Ban the appearance of lawyers in consumer courts', in *The Financial Express,* March 24, 2002.

16

Challenges and Prospects of Consumer Rights with Special Reference to Rural India

Vinod Kumar

India is a country with diverse tastes and attitudes which are reflected in the socio-economic and cultural scenario of India. The best prospects of consumers' rights can be understood when one explores the huge gaps prevalent in India in terms of urban consumers and rural consumers. Out of more than 70 per cent of population of India who live in rural areas, a majority of the consumers come from the rural areas. And most of the time, disparities in terms of social, political, economic and physical inaccessibility result into a greater vulnerability for millions of these population as market often behaves cruel as an institution. If left unregulated and unchecked market can follow their own ways to violate their rights; so it becomes much more important in Indian context that at least consumers should be made aware of their rights and responsibilities as various types and serious kinds of frauds and unethical practices are prevalent in this competitive age of market and the lack of awareness and information can play havoc for the rural innocent masses.

The strength of a consumer is echoed in Mahatma Gandhiji's voice *"A customer is the most important visitor on our premises. He is not dependent on us. We are dependent on him. He is not an interruption in our work he is the purpose of it. We are not doing him a favour by serving him. He is doing us a favour by giving us an opportunity to serve him."* By keeping the above commitment of our beloved national leader who considers the consumer as *Daridra Narayana,* the first Act of consumer rights protection of 1986 came into force to ensure protection of consumers from unscrupulous sellers, traders and the service providers who cheat vulnerable sections of consumers through various unfair trade practices and means in service delivery. Government of India has constituted a separate Ministry, known as Ministry of Consumer Affairs. The government has also established consumer courts at national, state, district level. But due to many factors like dilly-dallying, weak infrastructure and inadequate manpower a large number of cases are pending in the courts. So, it is pertinent keeping in view the above scenario to create consumer awareness in the country. In this present study. the author has tried to examine the guidelines provided by the United Nations and how these guidelines correspond to Consumer Protection Act, 1986 of India. Author has also brought out rights and responsibilities of consumers, regional pattern of consumer courts, and spatio-temporal analysis of budgeted amount released for the welfare of consumers including the prevalent loopholes in implementation of consumer rights and the policy implications.

Who is a Consumer?

As defined in the Consumer Protection Act, a consumer is a person who purchases goods and services for consumption by himself/herself or by someone else from the market or set of institutionalised sellers. Goods may include both consumable goods like wheat, flour, salt, sugar, fruits, food, grams or other consumer durable goods like television, refrigerator, toaster, mixer, bicycle, etc. from a shop or other outlet or sources. While services include electric power, telephone, transport services, theatre services, beautician, hairdresser, mechanic, electrician, etc. A 'consumer' may also be defined as "anybody who chooses goods and services, spends money to obtain them and uses them to satisfy his or her own needs".

What are the Rights of Consumers?

Serious kinds of frauds and unethical Practices are prevalent in this competitive age of market and the lack of awareness and information can invoke havoc for the consumers. So, it becomes indispensable for a consumer to know one's rights while making purchases of goods and services and protect oneself from losing one's precious wealth.

Let us now discuss the various rights of consumers that are recognised by Government of India under the said Act.

- ***Right to consumer education:*** Every consumer has a right to know the rules and regulation regarding the purchase of goods and services, quality standards, efficiency and reliability, compensation in case of inferior quality of goods and services and damage cost by them.

- ***Right to safety:*** Consumers have a right to be protected against marketing of goods which are injurious to health and life. Every manufacturer must guarantee the safety measures laid down by the concerned authority.
- ***Right to be informed:*** Consumers have right to know the ingredients, components and parts of the goods and services, they are going to buy. Information regarding ingredients and components must be properly labeled on the cover of the goods.
- ***Right to choose:*** Consumer has the right to choose from the large number of goods as he /she wants according to price, quality.
- ***Right to be heard:*** Consumers have a right to consult with Government and non-government bodies regarding rules and regulation laid down in the consumer protection act and if they are satisfied with the decision, they can appeal to the higher level of consumer courts.
- ***Right to seek redress:*** Consumer can redress the complaint through the telephone or in writing for being cheated, charged higher prices, irregularity in services, and inferior quality of products.

United Nations Guidelines for Consumer Protection

United Nations has initiated some guidelines for the protection of consumer rights in terms of social, economic, cultural, and environmental and the demographic aspects across the globe.

- ***Physical safety:*** This is the responsibility of nation to encourage the adoption of certain issues, including legal systems, safety regulations, domestic/international standards, voluntary standard of production, etc., to ensure the physical safety of goods, services and consumers.
- ***Promotion and protection of consumers' economic interests:*** Adequate distribution system and satisfactory production, fair trade/business, performance of standard and the information of the market affects the consumer. So the promotion and the protection of consumer rights is necessary.

- ***Standards for the safety and quality of consumer goods and services:*** Formulation and the implementation of rules and regulations regarding the standard of goods and services to the safety and quality is the responsibility of Governments to save the consumers from market frauds.
- ***Distribution facilities for essential consumer goods and services:*** In developing countries proper distribution system must be ensured as they lack in proper infrastructure, e.g., road connectivity.
- ***Measures enabling consumers to obtain redress:*** Establishment of legal/administrative measures to enable consumers to protect their rights and to fix the responsibilities their upon, through formal or informal procedures which are expeditious, fair, inexpensive and accessible especially to the low income group of consumers.

Fig. 16.1: According to UN Guideline for Protection of Consumers

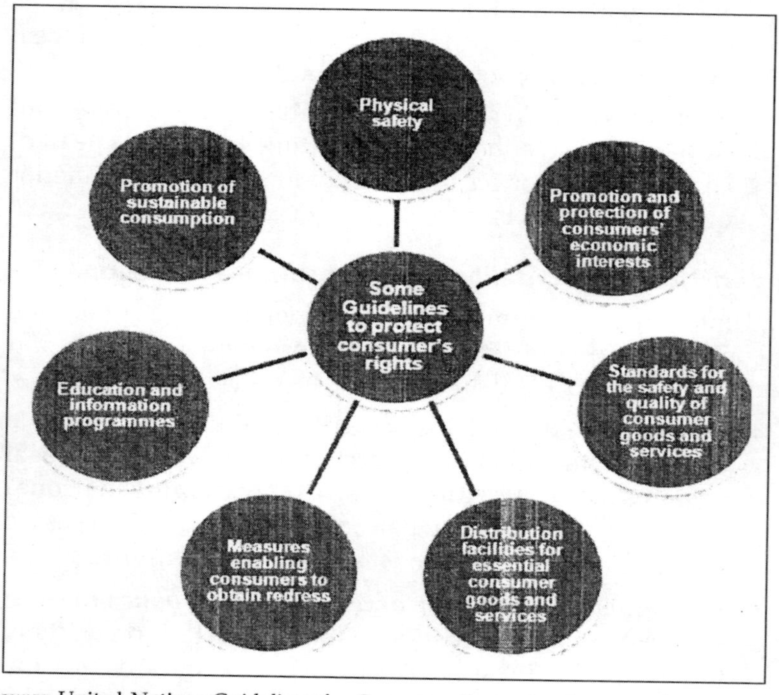

Source: United Nations Guidelines for Consumer Protection (as expanded in 1999), Department of Economic and Social Affairs.

- ***Promotion of sustainable consumption:*** Sustainable consumption and promotion is very important to keep the balance between the population and the resources. If it is imbalanced, it will create some problems in future. So it is important to keep in mind that goods and services for the economically, socially and environmentally backward sections in society should be available sustainably.

National Consumer Policy 1986 in India

This policy for the consumer protection was introduced for the empowerment of consumers through education and awareness, enforcement framework for legislation providing rights to consumers and mechanism for resolution of disputes. Some principles to ensure security of consumers are:

- *Empowering Consumers:* Through the proper knowledge of rules and regulations and awareness of the consumers by the government as well as the non Government organisation, especially taking into consideration the most vulnerable consumers, i.e., rural masses.
- *Competition:* The purpose of the maximum retailing of the product with the other retailer in the market. So that consumers have larger options with standard quality for goods and services.
- *Government as a Service Provider:* Government must provide the goods and services at reasonable rates so that the consumers coming from the weaker sections also enjoy quality products.
- *Partnership with Voluntary Organisations:* To enhance the accessibility in terms of distribution, accountability, government must go hand in hand with voluntary organisations.

Implementation Strategies: Government has formulated some policies and programmes to implement the Act of 1986 regarding consumer protection rights through the ministry, non-governmental organisations, and volunteer organizations and through freelance individuals, after consultations with eminent scholars and policy makers. These strategies would have the following components (*Source:* Draft - 6th November, 2009, National Consumer Policy):

3 Internal dispute resolution mechanism for all manufacturers/service providers;

3 Use legislation for enforcement of the rights of consumers;

3 Use of EC Act for non-market interventions;

3 Ensure better harmonisation of standards, national and international, to promote better choices.

The following Tables 16.1 and 16.2 show the Budget Estimates and Amount Released for Consumer Welfare Fund in India and Number of Cases Filed/Disposed of/Pending in National/State Commission and District Fora under Consumer Protection Act, 1986 in India.

Table 16.1: Budget Estimates and Amount Released for Consumer Welfare Fund in India

(2005-2006 to 2007-2008)

Year	*Budget Estimate (Rs. in crore)*	*Amount Released (in Rs. in crore)*
2005–06	31.5	8.5
2006–07	17.35	6.7
2007–08	20.6	8.7

Table 16.2: Number of Cases Filed/Disposed of/Pending in National/ State Commission and District Fora under Consumer Protection Act, 1986 in India

Agency Filed	*Cases Since Inception*	*Cases Deposed of since Inception*	*Cases Pending*	*Percentage of Total Disposal*
National Commission	53310	43488	9822	81.58
State Commission	440102	328911	111191	74.74
District Fora	2519282	2286543	232739	90.76
Total	**3012694**	**2658942**	**353752**	**88.26**

Source: Lok Sabha Un-starred Question No. 4926, dated 28.04.2008. and Department of Consumer Affairs, Government of India.

The following Figure 16.2 and 16.3 show Budget estimates and released for consumer welfare fund and Number of cases filed/disposed in National/State Commission and district fora in India.

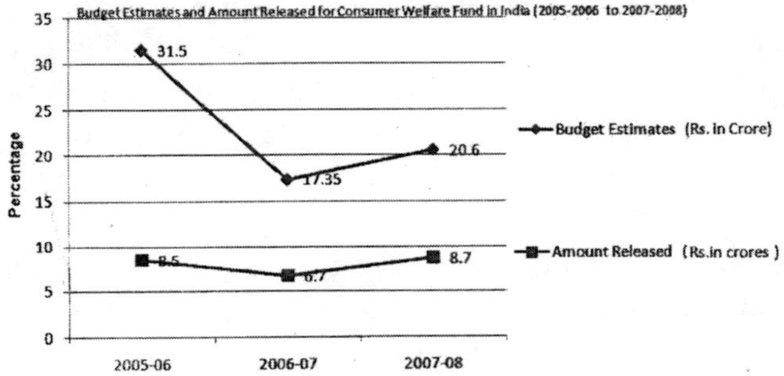

Fig. 16.2: Budget Estimates and Released for Consumer Welfare Fund (2005 - 2006 to 2007 - 2008)

With the increasing demand and supply, government of India has set up Ministry of Consumer Affairs to look into the welfare of consumers. It is clear from the above graph that the amount of money released for welfare of consumers has been fluctuating over a period of time. Government is not releasing adequate funds for the welfare of consumers. In 2005–2006, the amount of funds required was 31.5 crores. but only 8.5 crores had been released. Same situation was witnessed in 2007–2008, we can't imagine the welfare of consumers without the adequate fund and infrastructure. Thus, it is important in the light of the above mismatch between demand and supply of funds related to consumer rights protection issues to strike a balance between the same.

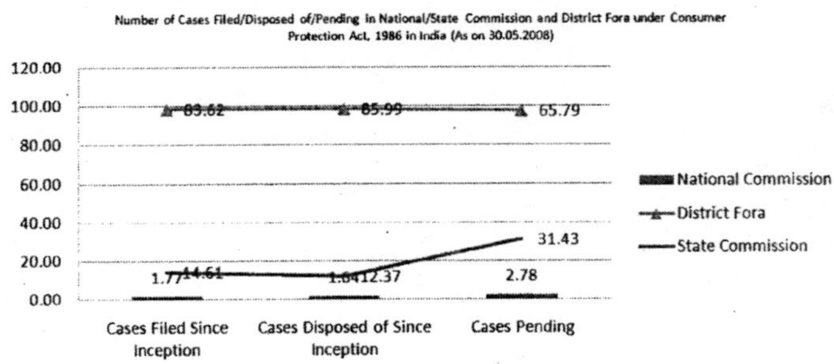

Fig. 16.3: Number of Cases Filed/Disposed/Pending in National/State Commission and District Fora on 30.05.2008

Under the 1986 Consumer Protection Act to resolve the cases at national, state, and district level forums have been set up which are not functioning properly to serve the population because of the shortage of manpower, infrastructure and adequate funds which is reflected through the data as on 30-05-2008 (see in Tables 16.1 and 16.2 and Figure 16.2 and Fig. 16.3) which show that a total of 3012694 cases were filed by aggrieved consumers at different consumer courts in India only 2658942 of these cases were disposed of and 353752 cases were pending for proper adjudication. If the pace of pending cases remains unsolved, the prospects of protection of consumer rights would be shattered and end up in a deplorable future.

Table 16.3: State-wise Number of Functional/Non-Functional Forums in India

(*As on 31.03.2008*)

States/UTs	*No. of District Fora*	*Functional*	*Non-Functional*
Andhra Pradesh	29	29	0
Andaman and Nicober Islands	1	1	0
Arunachal Pradesh	16	15	1
Assam	23	23	0
Bihar	38	17	21
Chandigarh	2	2	0
Chhattisgarh	16	16	0
Daman & Diu	2	2	0
Dadra & Nagar Haveli	1	1	0
Delhi	10	10	0
Goa	2	2	0
Gujarat	26	26	0
Haryana	19	14	5
Himachal Pradesh	12	12	0
Jammu & Kashmir	2	2	0
Jharkhand	22	22	0
Karnataka	30	30	0
Kerala	14	13	1

Lakshadweep	1	1	0
Madhya Pradesh	48	47	1
Maharashtra	39	39	0
Manipur	9	9	0
Meghalya	7	7	0
Mizoram	8	8	0
Nagaland	11	8	3
Odisha	31	31	0
Pondicherry	1	1	0
Punjab	17	11	6
Rajasthan	33	27	6
Sikkim	4	4	0
Tamil Nadu	30	24	6
Tripura	4	4	0
Uttar Pradesh	74	65	9
Uttarakhand	13	8	5
West Bengal	21	21	0
India	**616**	**552**	**64**

When we examine the regional situation of consumer rights protection in India, out of the 616 districts only in 552 forums are functioning across the country. Many of the States have higher number of non-functioning forums. So we have tried to analyse state-wise prospects of the consumer forums in terms of the number of functioning and non-functioning forums and the inadequate budget they are getting for the welfare of consumers at grass root level. India has a unique diversity in terms of environmental, social, cultural, and in economic aspects. Rural and urban areas are characterised by a huge gap in terms of literacy, health, and other factors which help to empower and aware the consumers in India. In the Northern, Southern, North-Eastern, Western part of the country some states have more functioning forums while some states such as Bihar, U.P., Rajasthan , Uttarakhand, Nagaland and Haryana have more number of non-functioning forums, e.g., in Bihar out of 38 district only 17 forums are functioning hence 21 forums are not functioning. Vide Table 16.3.

Table 16.4: State-wise Amount Released for Awareness of Consumer Rights

State wise Scenario of Amount Released	*Released Amount for Awareness of Grass-root Consumer Protection in India*
Andhra Pradesh	28.75
Andaman & Nicober Islands	3.75
Arunachal Pradesh	18.75
Assam	28.75
Bihar	46.25
Chandigarh	6.25
Chhattisgarh	20
Daman & Diu	2.5
Dadra & Nagar Haveli	1.25
Delhi	11.25
Goa	2.5
Gujarat	170.5
Haryana	23.75
Himachal Pradesh	15
Jammu & Kashmir	17.5
Jharkhand	27.5
Karnataka	33.75
Kerala	17.5
Lakshadweep	1.25
Madhya Pradesh	60
Maharashtra	41.25
Manipur	11.25
Meghalaya	8.75
Mizoram	10
Nagaland	10
Odisha	37.5
Pondicherry	5
Punjab	21.25
Rajasthan	40
Sikkim	7.5
Tamil Nadu	36.25

Tripura	5
Uttar Pradesh	87.5
Uttarakhand	16.25
West Bengal	125.75
India	**1000**

Source: Department of Consumer Affairs, Government of India. and also Lok Sabha Unstarred Question No. 5240, dated 14.05.2007.

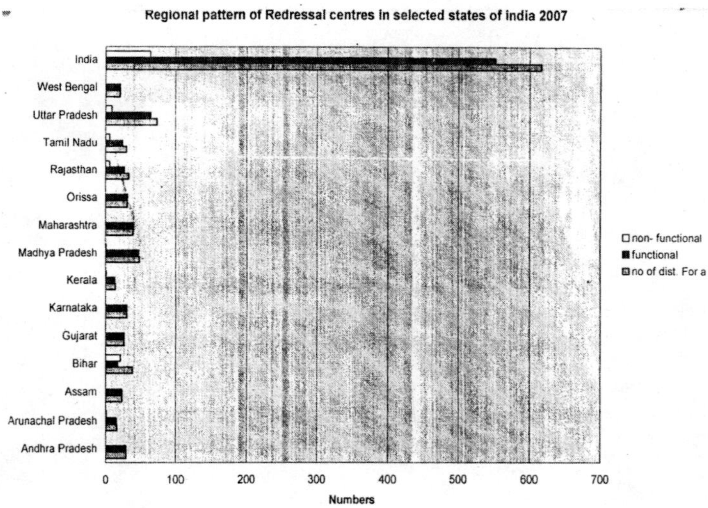

Fig. 16.4: Regional Pattern of Redressal Forum in Selected States of India 2007

In terms of 46.25 lakh budget released to spread awareness at the grass root level to empower the consumers, Bihar was not up to the mark. Many of the states wherein all the district forums are functioning, e.g., in Tamil Nadu only 36.25 lakh rupees budget was released to maintain this functioning properly. In almost all the North-Eastern states of India each district has a consumer forum which is functioning properly but the budget varies drastically from state to state owing to the demographic, socio-economic, and developmental level of the state. In the light of the above discussion in terms of consumer protection forums there is a greater need of solid preparation at the grass-root as well as at the regional and national level. There is an urgent need to create awareness about their consumer rights not only in the citizens but also at the supply side, i.e., at the government level which is responsible to implement the rules and regulations and for adequate fund release.

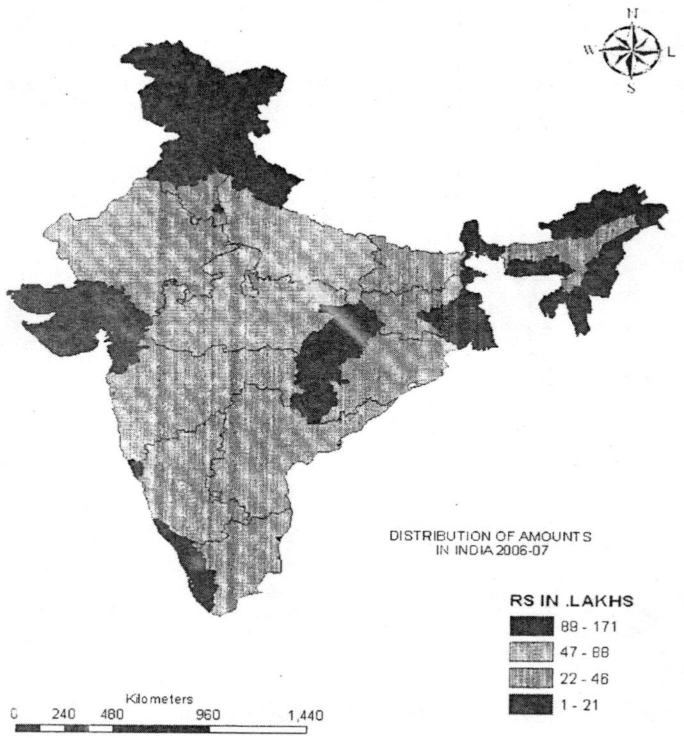

Fig. 16.5: State-wise Amout Released for Creating Consumer Awareness at Grass-root Level for Consumer Protection and Welfare in India 2006-2007

Responsibilities of Consumers: There is a well known proverb that "there cannot be rights without responsibilities by themselves". So for the proper solution of the problems consumer have some responsibilities on their part to exercise his/her rights. Consumers must try to obtain maximum information concerning the goods and services he/she is using and he/she must be very careful about the procedure to be followed in case of any damage or fraud.

Responsibility of self-help groups: It is always desirable that a consumer should not depend on the seller for information and choice. As far as possible, a consumer must also consult fellow consumer as one's life is not enough to get all the experiences so one must learn from other's experiences.

Proof of Transactions: The second responsibility of every consumer is that the proof of purchase and documents relating to purchase of durable goods should be invariably obtained and preserved. When consumer holds the proper documents the procedure of getting justice becomes easy and speedy or fast.

Proper Claim: Another responsibility that consumers are expected to bear in mind is that while making complaints and claiming compensation for loss or injury, they should not make unreasonably large claims. They must refer to previous cases if they can or they should consult the proper authorities and channels regarding the claim.

Proper Use of Product/Services: Some consumers, especially during the guarantee period, make rough use of the product, thinking that it will be replaced during the guarantee period. So guarantee period must not be taken for granted. Consumer's rights are not there to create unnecessary hurdles to the manufacturers or shopkeepers. They are there to assist the consumers to get the quality services from manufacturers and shopkeepers.

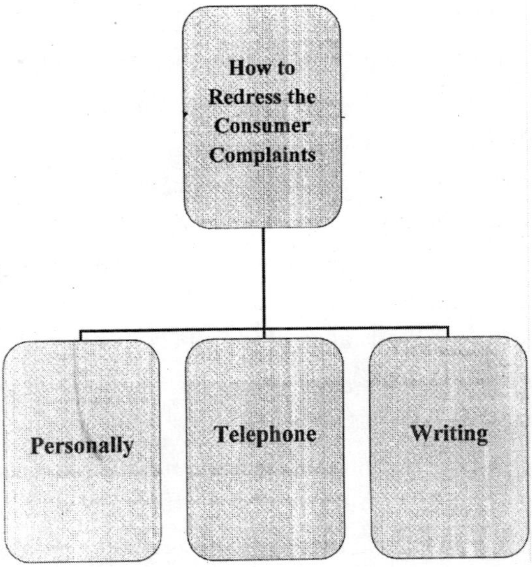

Fig. 16.6: How to Redress Grievances

• **Personally:** Approach the person from who provided you goods & services. And make witness to manage proper documents against the services provider when consumer visits personally shopkeeper or manufacturer gets no chance to make excuses and the things become much clear as they can be discussed openly.

• **Telephone:** Firstly, consumer can talk through phone that he has purchased the goods and services and note down all the discussion. This method works when consumer buys any goods or services from far off places and cannot visit the place again and again or he/she is a professional highly busy in his/her work.

• **In Writing:** This is the effective way to solve the problem because through the proper document and following the proper legal and institutional means a consumer problem can be solved. Manufacturers and shopkeepers cannot manipulate the things very easily when consumer deals everything in writing it becomes a very effective proof and consumer can get justice within no time.

Why there is lack of efficiency in the functioning of consumer courts in India

- Insufficient availability of fund in the government budget.
- Shortage of manpower/staffs in courts at every level.
- Inefficient functioning due to malpractices of corruption, complacency, etc.
- Courts are not friendly for rural masses in terms of time, lawyer, money, etc.
- Courts are established at District/state headquarters while 70 per cent of the population lives in rural areas as well in slums. For them accessibility becomes a big question.
- Lack of proper awareness in consumers regarding the redressal process.
- Judges are engaged simultaneously in two or three courts in a week which reduces the efficiency of decisions.
- Lack of infrastructure as well as over political intervention posses hurdles in smooth functioning of courts.

How consumer courts/consumers can be more efficient in India

- Map and Identify the area where the consumers are acute sufferers.
- Create/Decentralise awareness through electronic media and print media, e.g., Radio, Television, newspaper, Mobiles, disseminate functioning and consumer awareness through Self-Help Group, Anganwadi, School, Health like Population Policy function.
- Make consumers aware through M.C.D., Nagar Palika, and Panchayat as well as through NGO's.
- Facilitate legal rules and regulations which may prove to be consumer friendly and equips them with rights to fight the Rich, Traders, Sellers, Manufacturers.
- To define the timeframe to resolve cases as fast as possible so that it may be helpful to change consumers' behaviour in terms of delaying cases.
- Establish the consumers courts in remote areas at Panchayat level and nearby to the slums to facilitate the access of consumers coming from the weaker sections of the society.
- Promote RTI Act 2005 to bring much more transparency, accountability, and authenticity regarding consumer cases.
- Promote Mobile courts for the speedy functioning of redressal process.

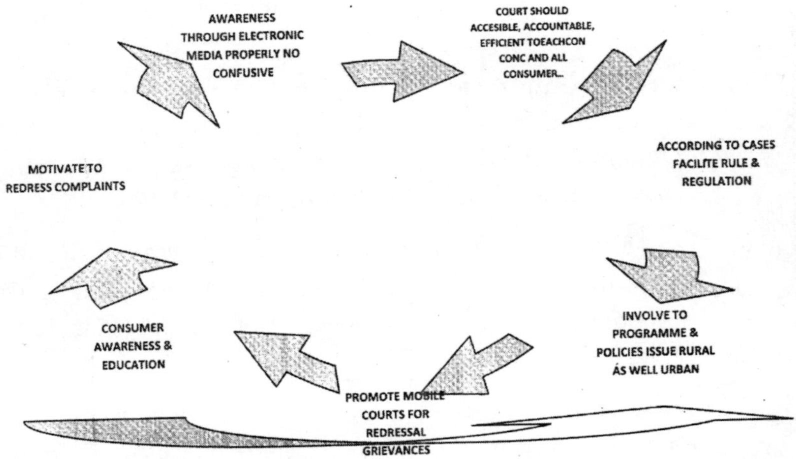

Fig. 16.7: Consumer Courts how can be More Efficient in India

Conclusion

It can be concluded that there are many loopholes in the protection of consumers right one of them is inadequate dissemination of consumer's rights awareness among the rural consumers. When problem begins at the very initial level, a chain of problems is witnessed. Government authorities as well as inactive consumers are responsible for inadequate functioning of consumer courts. The above points highlighted bring out the reality in rural India and its policy implications in regards to consumer right protection in India.

References

1. *The Consumer Protection Act, 1986* (68 of 1986), 24th December, 1986.
2. *Annual report of 2008-09,* Ministry of Consumer Affairs, Food and Public Distribution, Department of Consumer Affairs, Krishi Bhawan New Delhi-110001.
3. *United Nations Guidelines for Consumer Protection* (as expanded in 1999), Department of Economic and Social Affairs, UN.
4. Draft-6th November, 2009, *National Consumer Policy.*
5. Lesson 25, - Rights and Responsibilities of Consumers Business Study.
6. Hauser, John R. and Kenneth J. Wisniewski, (1982) "Application, Predictive Test, and Strategy Implications for a Dynamic Model of Consumer Response" in *Marketing Science,* Vol. 1, No. 2 (Spring, 1982), pp. 143-179.
7. Kerssens, Jan J. and Peter P. Groenewegen, (2005) "Consumer Preferences in Social Health Insurance", *The European Journal of Health Economics,* Vol. 6, No. 1 (Mar. 2005), pp. 8-15.
8. Brinkmann, Johannes, (2004) "Looking at Consumer Behavior in a Moral Perspective", *Journal of Business Ethics,* Vol. 51, No. 2, Promoting Business Ethics (May, 2004), pp. 129-141.

9. Majumdar, Amita, (1986) "Consumer Expenditure Pattern in India: A Comparison of the Almost Ideal Demand System and the Linear Expenditure System", *Sankhyā: The Indian Journal of Statistics,* Series B, Vol. 48, No. 1 (April, 1986), pp. 115 -143.
10. National Consumer Helpline Number: 1800-11-4000.
11. Websites: *www.fcamin.nic.in, www.core.nic.in.*

17

Collective and Individual Consumer Redressal in Germany: How Effective Role is Played by NGOs

Gerd Billen

The Federation of German Consumer Organisations (VZBV) is situated in Berlin. It is a non-governmental organisation acting as an umbrella for 42 German consumer associations including 16 consumer centres of the German Federal States, the "Verbraucherzentralen". It represents the interests of consumers in public and vis-a-vis legislators, the private sector and civil society. Its goal is to protect and empower the consumer. It is done by lobbying and campaigning at national and European levels, by taking collective legal action on behalf of consumers and by ensuring that its message receives broad media coverage. Though VZBV is prominently a non-profit organisation but it is financed by the German Government, precisely by the Ministry for Consumer Protection. In 2009, the institutional aid amounted to more than nine million Euros. Beside the institutional aid that it receives annual project funds usually are also in a similar amount.

Let us know deeply the legal enforcement system in Germany. German consumer protection laws are primarily anchored in civil law. This has consequences. Government authorities such as in France or Great Britain, which control and implement consumer rights, are not provided with civil law. In Germany, individual rights are to be disputed in court on a case by case basis, particularly collective legal enforcement is basically delegated to qualified entities. VZBV and the consumer centres play a key role in this field. With the right to sue as an association, VZBV acts a "lawyer for consumers" trying to contribute to legal security and refinement of the law. The advantage is, as a private organisation we can react immediately avoiding red tape.

Individual Redress

The 16 consumer centres, promoted by public funds, are allowed to give legal individual advice to consumers out of court corresponding to their duties and responsibilities and ensure high quality advice in more than 190 consumer advice centres by providing training and establishing uniform advice throughout the country. They claim for individual consumer rights and defence also claims from the company's side. In the past we could help many consumers by out of court correspondences with the companies. To guarantee this high quality advisory service we have special networking groups preparing different topics and providing all consumer centres with the same high standard information. VZBV itself does not give individual advice to consumers but we provide professional training for the staff of consumer organisations.

Collective Redress: regarding collective redress VZBV has different options to enforce consumer rights.

Collective Actions for Injunctive Relief

The private enforcement system in Germany has a long and proven tradition. Already in 1965 the *Law of Unfair Competition* established the right for consumer associations to initiate collective litigation against misleading and dishonest advertising. Since 1977, consumer organisations are entitled to file actions for injunction due to unfair contract terms and conditions and since 2000 they may claim for injunction in cases of consumer laws as for instance the right to withdraw in distance selling contracts or when missing information in online offers have been violated. The consumer organisations which are qualified entities in the sense of the EU-Directive on injunctions used these legal instruments during the last decades steadily and intensively and they still do so. In 2009, VZBV along with the consumer centres initiated more than 2000 written warnings and achieved about 1400 cease and desist declarations. Normally about 75 per cent of our written warnings concern the infringement of competition law, about 25 per cent of them concern unfair terms and conditions and about five per cent of the litigations concern cross-border cases.

Airline Proceedings

During the last years we have focused on misleading advertising of airline companies. We criticised for example that additional charges were hidden or the companies did not indicate the final price at the beginning of the online booking process. After November 2008 the EU-Regulation on Common Rules for the Operation of the Air Services in the Community (EC No 1008/ 2008) came into force we have initiated even more proceedings concerning the pricing frauds on the basis of this Regulation as they have been using default boxes for insurances or costs for payment by credit cards which are given only at the end of the booking process.

Cost Traps on the Internet

Another field we have been working on affects price transparency of online services. Since 2006, many consumer companies have reached VZBV concerning deficient price transparency on internet pages which we call "cost-traps". Companies offer different services such as intelligence tests, calculation of life expectancy, a route planner or a computer software. The costs concerning the contract are hidden in the contract conditions or written so small that consumers would overlook them. As a consequence the consumers who are used to receiving services like these free of charge press the button to accept the conditions without being aware of the price. A couple of days later they receive invoices for a two-year subscription. Later on some companies threaten the consumers to pay otherwise they would employ a lawyer to encash the money. Even if there is no legal right to demand the payment some consumers pay the bill as they have the impression that they better pay. We got a number of cease and desist declarations and won many lawsuits against these companies. Unfortunately, the companies often build up new websites under new names after they have lost the lawsuits or they upgrade and change their internet page in a way it is on the borderline of legality but still betraying the consumers.

As Germany and also the European Commission noticed the problem it is now intended to implement new legal regulations in Germany. In the future consumers are supposed to be bound by the contract only if they give explicit confirmation concerning the price of the service in certain manner on the webpage. VZBV who has been pleading for a legal ruling for a couple of years now naturally appreciates this initiative of the German Government.

Food

We have made the experience that the food packaging is often confusing for consumers. So we initiated several proceedings as there is a product called "Wasabi peas". In reality there was no Wasabi in the product. The seller was sentenced not to offer such product anymore and the producer has changed the package in the meantime. Another example is tea which was called "strawberry-blackberry tea". In fact, the tea contained hibiscus, shell of rose hips and only natural flavour of strawberry and blackberry. Now the company wants to change the ingredients and put real strawberry and blackberry into the tea. We are going to intensify our activities in this area within a special internet project which is supported by the Federal Ministry for Consumer Protection and is going to start soon.

Cold Calls

"The home is inviolable". That is what the German Constitution states. The Federal High Court (Bundesgerichtshof) also read it that way. Telephone advertising is a particularly serious breach of constitutionally protected privacy. Unfortunately, the advertising industry has not always conformed to this legal verdict. For millions of consumers "Cold Calling"—or unsolicited advertising calls on private phones—is a frequent annoyance. With the law change in 2004, VZBV succeeded in ensuring that the protection of privacy explicitly applies to advertising too. Since then, unwanted advertising calls have been legally prohibited. As the unsolicited phone calls went on stronger legal measures came into force in August 2009. Now consumers have explicitly to agree to the call beforehand. Companies can be punished by a fine up to 50,000 Euros if they do not stick to this. Moreover, companies who call people are not allowed to blank their phone number. This can also lead to a monetary fine up to 10,000 Euros. Between March and June this year the consumer centres asked about 40,000 consumers and found out that just one per cent of them agreed to the call. Many of them were bothered by lottery and prize advertising. In order to cut the economic incentive for such unsolicited marketing VZBV has argued for a confirmation of the contract in text form measuring that consumers have to confirm the agreement made on the phone, by letter or at least by e-mail and we are optimistic to get another legal improvement shortly. Summing up we can tell actions for injunction are an essential part of a competition controlling system in order to guarantee legal consumer protection on an enduring high level.

Recovery of Ill-gotten Gains—Profit Skimming

However, we recognise that the benefit from a collective action system mainly based on injunctions is limited. We still have to face that companies being sentenced to change their misleading or unfair advertising are not forced to compensate any individual damage of consumers caused by the infringement. In this context, we have to take into account that unfair practice infringements usually lead to small losses for a large number of consumers. So even if they had the right to claim for damages many consumers supposedly would refrain from going to court because the litigation costs would exceed the damages by far. The German legislator has recognised this problem and adopted a legal instrument for skimming in July 2004. According to that rule, consumer organisations as well as organisations representing the interests of competitors have the possibility to skim the profits of companies gained by unfair competition methods. The idea is that a competitor who does not behave according to the law must not benefit from this behaviour.

However, the efficiency of this instrument has still to be proved. VZBV has initiated 19 court cases for profit skimming by now but could skim money just in two cases. The reason is that the legal requests for the plaintiffs are high, they have to prove that the defendant company has violated the law deliberately and furthermore that the increase in sales has been caused by the infringement. Both acting deliberately and causality between the development of the turnover and the legal infringement are hardly to prove. Intention has been affirmed for example in litigation against a big discounter which had promoted matresses with an outdated test result. This litigation ended in a court settlement;

the company had to pay 25,000 Euro. Because of the further court risks including the high litigation costs VZBV accepted money on the basis of unfair competition practices. VZBV has calculated a gain of more than 4,00,000 Euro.

The profit skimming model has been criticised as there might be no incentive for organisations to sue knowing that the full amount to realise by the action belongs to the government. However, if the consumer organisation loses the case it will have to cover all expenses by itself. As such legal proceedings as the above described can carry with them the risk of an enormous financial loss we are allowed by the governmental authority which is *Bundesamt fur Justiz* to find an agreement with an insurance company in that way that they will cover the financial risk in case VZBV loses the litigation. On the other hand, VZBV would have to pay a certain percentage to the insurance company if the defendant is sentenced to pay. So far VZBV has not worked together with an insurance company. So, we can say that we do appreciate the system of profit skimming but we would prefer a facilitation of bringing forward as we think it is difficult to prove that the companies acted deliberately.

Sammel or Musterklage—Claims by Assigned Rights

Since 2002, Consumer organisations are entitled to file monetary claims in a law suit on behalf of the consumers. Precondition is that a collective consumer interest is affected. To use this legal instrument for a larger group of people poses an enormous administrative burden so the consumer organisations have used this instrument mainly for test cases for a manageable number of consumers in order to clarify fundamental questions.

Example 1: Scope of Guarantees

After the Directive on Sale of Consumer Goods and Guarantees 1999/44 EC had been implemented in German law in January 2002 we have received a consumer complaint concerning a well-known German catalogue company. The consumer had bought a new stove which became defective after one and a half years. The company replaced the stove by a new one and asked the consumer to pay 120 Euro as a compensation for using the stove during the time before it was exchanged. We were of the opinion that this claim would not be justified because it is stipulated in the directive that repair and replacement are free of charge for the consumer during guarantee period of at least two years.

Aften the consumer who had paid the amount has assigned her reclaim to VZBV we filed an action for payment. In August 2008 we won this case and the Federal Court of Justice, decided that the exchange of a defective product must be done free of costs. As a result the German law had to be amended to be in line with the EU Directive.

Example 2: Airline Section

In March 2005, a group of thirteen persons had booked a flight from Oslo to Munich with Lufthansa. The flight was scheduled to start at 2 pm and arrive in Munich at 4.30 pm. The flight was cancelled which was announced to the travellers by a notice at the departure gate. Contrary to the EU-Regulation the passengers did not receive any assistance. With support of other attendants at the airport they managed to change their reservation for a flight with Scandinavian Airlines. This flight started between three and four pm and arrived in Munich at 10 pm which is five and a half hour later than intended.

Due to later complaints vis-a-vis Lufthansa and the National Enforcement Body Luftfahrtbundesamt costs for refreshment and meals were reimbursed. However, their claim for a compensation of 400 Euro each (the route longer than 1500 km) was rejected. The airline argued that the flight had to be cancelled due to "unforeseen technical problems". In 2007, VZBV sued the company for payment. After this, the airline changed its opinion and paid the amount requested to stop the legal proceeding. These examples may show that claims by assigned rights can definitely be used for the benefit of a large number of consumers even if the consumer organisation was assigned by only one or a small group of consumers. But by all means we need a claim for payment. That means that we can only sue if we can reclaim money for consumers with the consequence that we have to prove not only the ground of each claim but also the total figure of the amount. That means that we have to collect all receipts by the consumers. The amount of the individual claims, however, mostly differs and is not of public interest.

Result: The litigation by assigned rights could be disbursed from individual amounts of damages. What we need is an action for a declaratory judgement.

Capital Markets Model Case Act (KapMuG)

Last but not least I would like to mention the latest legal instrument for collective redress: In 2005, the German legislator introduced and passed a bill relating to claims for damages as a result of wrong or misleading capital information by the company, for instance damages due to wrong or omitted ad-hoc-disclosure. With the Capital Markets Model Case Act, the German law provides a way to handle capital market mass proceedings. The Act has introduced a model case procedure into German Law - not a class action.

The most famous case concerns 15,000 investors claiming for rescission of their contracts with *Deutsche Telekom* due to wrong information about the value of the property they had invested in. The Higher Regional Court (Appellate Court) in Frankfurt was called by the regional court to decide the question for one representative plaintiff: whether or not the information was true. After the decision of the appellate court the regional court will decide the outstanding questions for all plaintiffs.

The German government extended the monitoring until the end of October 2012 to see how useful this instrument proves in the future. If positive, it will investigate how to use it for other domains as well.

As a result we can say the Capital Markets Model Case still has to stand the test of time. The idea is worth if it could be considered as a role model for group actions in general.

Our Comprehensive Survey

Result 1: Actions for injunction are an indispensable part of a competition controlling system in order to guarantee legal consumer protection on an enduring high level.

Result 2: Facilitation for the entitled organisations of bringing forward proofs as well as gross negligence instead of intent would help to enforce profit skimming proceedings.

Result 3: The litigation by assigned rights could be disburdened from individual amounts of damages. What we need is an action for a declaratory judgement.

Result 4: The Capital Markets Model Case still has to stand the test of time. The idea is worth considering as a role model for group actions in general.

Future prospects: Which are the next political steps in Germany and in the European Union?

The German Ministry for Consumer Protection is currently running an evaluation of the existing collective action system in Germany. In Europe the discussion about collective redress mechanisms has just been revitalised: As there is still no coherent system for collective redress existing in Europe, the EU Commissioners for Justice, Competition and Consumer Policy have now announced to launch a new public consultation on a European approach. Goal is to identify which forms of collective redress could fit into the EU legal system and into the legal orders of the 27 EU Member States. It was intended to start the consultation in November 2010 and run them until the end of February 2011.

18

Relevance of Alternative Dispute Resolution (ADR) and Consumer Disputes Redressal in India

Shiv Kumar

The Consumer Protection Act (CPA) when introduced was considered an innovation in the field of consumer rights. It was intended to provide for an expeditious disposal of disputes of consumers on the one side and manufacturers of goods and service producers on the other. Having recognised that the Act had severe shortcomings, amendments were introduced in the hope that consumers' grievances would be redressed more effectively than before. Whether or not this object has been achieved is debatable. The dispute redressal mechanism provided under the Consumer Protection Act leaves much to be desired. Lack of adequate powers of enforcement of orders to ensure that consumers actually realise the fruits of an order passed by the Consumer Court has resulted in negating the positive provisions of the Act.

In the context of present-day free-market economy the average consumer is becoming more aware and belligerent to protect his rights provided under the said Law. It is accompanied by a willingness to fight for such rights. The consumer can no longer be taken for granted or persuaded into believing that he has no enforceable legal rights. Consumer education and awareness have witnessed phenomenal growth and have led to a qualitative change in the profile of the consumer.

The focus of the Indian Consumer, as in any legal system, is today on Rights. Decades of suppression and unethical business/trading practices, have converted the average Indian consumer into being indignant and militant. The spending power of average consumers has seen an exponential growth leading to an equally increased demand for better quality goods and services. Wealth creation is no longer considered either unethical or undesirable. On the contrary, it has assumed the status of a legitimate economic activity. Cumulatively, therefore, the Indian Consumer has become empowered, and is willing to confront the service providers and suppliers. The Indian consumer is willing and happy to carry the battle forward.

In this perspective, the questions that arise are:

(a) Has the Law recognised the new profile of the consumer or his needs, aspirations and the need to be vindicated?

(b) If so, has the Law/Statute, particularly the redressal mechanism, been suitably amended to reflect the present needs?

(c) Does the consumer receive quick, efficient and satisfactory redressal of his grievances?

(d) If not what is the alternative remedy for the consumer?

It is obvious that the Law has failed to understand or recognise the needs of the "new profile" consumer. For example, the Law has failed intentionally or otherwise, to understand that to-days consumer demands greater focus on "service" than on goods *per se*. It fails to take cognisance of the critical need to satisfy the consumers need for assured quality and quality control mechanisms. It fails to recognise and protect the average consumer against exploitation by not being empowered to prohibit manufacture and sale of defective goods or dangerous goods. It has not recognised cross-border commercial transactions. Not having understood or gauged the needs of the modern consumer; the Law has done even less in enhancing the redressal mechanism. Consumer Courts have not been vested with adequate power to render them effective. Cumbersome procedures and technicalities haunt these Courts thereby diluting the efficacy of the redressal system. Adequately qualified persons are not appointed to man the Courts and the procedures have become conducive to delays. Consumer Courts claim helplessness in executing their own orders and most often the complaint is that of a consumer holding a "paper decree or order". The power to order arrest of a defaulter is now to be exercised through a Criminal Court. Complicated and disputed questions of fact are decided in a perfunctory manner due to lack of specialised knowledge and/or relevant skills. As a result, the consumer rarely gets what it richly deserves viz., an effective and meaningful redressal of grievances.

The right to quick, efficient, speedy and qualitative justice is a fundamental right granted to every citizen under the Constitution of India. The present justice delivery system has failed to achieve that objective. Courts all over the country are overburdened and the long wait for justice is quite often frustrating. The reasons for such stupendous arrears are varied, but reaffirm that the delays in disposal of cases in the mainstream of justice delivery is far from satisfactory. The present judicial system, including the Consumer Court System, offers little or no hope to the litigant/consumers.

The existing system of justice delivery is adjudicatory and adversarial in nature. It focuses primarily on "right" and "wrong". It tends to enquire into the violation of a right by one and seeks to compensate the violation. It precipitates conflict between two or more litigants for example, between—a consumer and supplier. It is founded on conflict and is eminently suited to assert a "right" of one over the other. It ensures a legal victory for one while leaving the other either unhappy or dissatisfied. It facilities concepts of vengeance of one against the other and does not make any distinction between "law" and "justice". It is based on the letter of the Law and not on the "spirit" of the Law or on larger concepts of justice. It fails to realistically deal with or recognise the measures and importance of human relationships and adopts a "legalistic" approach to resolution of disputes. It is circumscribed by technicalities and cumbersome procedures which, by their inherent nature, promote delays.

Cumulatively, the result is inordinate delay in disposal of cases and judgements/decisions of questionable quality and faulty reasoning. The end-user, namely, the consumer is, therefore, the last priority in this scheme leaving him completely frustrated, angry, disappointed and indignant. It has eroded his confidence in the justice delivery system.

Need for Alternate Disputes Resolution

In this dismal scene, the advent of the Alternate Dispute Resolution (ADR) mechanism is more than welcome. ADR comprises Arbitration, Conciliation and Mediation. Fundamentally ADR emphasises quality resolution of disputes, at minimal cost and time and provides an alternate platform. A facet of ADR is known to be Pre-litigation mediation. This presentation will focus briefly on Mediation and Pre-litigation Mediation.

Mediation: Mediation is an interventional process where a third neutral party facilities resolution of a conflict/dispute. In the USA about 93 per cent of cases are resolved by mediation. A Mediator, who is appointed by consent of all parties to a dispute, is a neutral person who does not adjudicate on the dispute. He acts purely as a facilitator, promoting a settlement through a process of collaborative negotiation. He is trained in communication and negotiating skills and identifies the real and true interests of the disputants. The Mediator endeavours through a structured but informal process to identify a solution which is acceptable to all the disputants. The process eliminates a judicial determination of "right" and "wrong" but concentrates on identifying the interests of each disputant. It addresses the basic conflict rather than the apparent disputes.

Mediation Process: The Mediation process accords prime importance to the disputants and it ensures that they are the essential and critical participants in the resolution process. Mediation is a voluntary process and is based on the consent of parties to participate thereby allowing them the freedom to withdraw from mediation at any time without assigning any reasons. The decision to settle a dispute as also its terms is, therefore, entirely within the discretion of the disputants. The process promises confidentiality, inter se the disputants and hence encourages them to identify their real interests which need to be resolved. It allows to the disputants unrestricted freedom to evolve a variety of solutions without being constrained by technicalities of law. The Mediation shifts focus from "people" to "issues" or "problems" and with no emphasis on negative emotions, solutions become substantially easier. The Mediation, therefore, offers a comprehensive solution to conflicts and disputes with the added advantage that once settled in mediation viz., through the consensual process, no further appeals are possible. The Mediation, therefore, recognises a fundamental principle of dispute resolution, viz., that a consensual process is always the most desirable.

The cases before Consumer Courts are usually adjudicated substantially in accordance with procedures applicable to civil cases. The approach is adjudicatory in nature, that is, an investigation into the 'right' and 'wrong' of a given situation. The focus continues to be on determining the "right" of a complainant. Applying the mediation process to pending consumer cases could, therefore, be the answer to the present problem of delayed justice in Consumer Courts. This would be defined as Court-annexed Mediation. The process of introducing the Mediation process would mean identifying a panel of trained Mediators. The Hon'ble Supreme Court, as a part of its nationwide project of training Advocates as Mediators, has already trained a large number of Mediators across the country. Empanelling them would be the first step. Their services could be utilised to mediate in all cases pending before the Consumer Courts, with a specified time (usually 60 days) for resolution. The Consumer Courts would need to refer pending cases to a Mediator.

The Mediator could be located either at separate room within the Court Complex or at an outside location. Both parties before the Court would be instructed to appear before the nominated Mediator on a specified date to participate in the mediation process. To ensure transparency in the selection of a Mediator, the parties could be offered the right to select a Mediator of their choice, as all Mediators, as a rule, are trained to be neutral and impartial. A trained Mediator would apply the skills of mediation and attempt to resolve the dispute within 60 days. If settled, the terms could be reduced to writing and retransmitted to the Court, which would then pass a decree/order in terms thereof. If a settlement is not resolved, the case would continue before the Court. Considering the success of mediation in most States where Court annexed mediation has been introduced, (which is around 67 per cent) there is every reason to believe that mediation will succeed in Consumer Courts.

A distinct advantage in applying Mediation proceedings to cases in Consumer Courts is that the consumer is afforded an opportunity to come face to face with the opponent/supplier/service provider for the first time. The consumer is able to "identify" the supplier and interact with him on a "one to one" basis before the Mediator. Additionally, it provides an opportunity for the consumer to understand (and perhaps appreciate) the view point of the supplier, thereby substantially increasing the possibilities of a negotiated settlement. Mediation creates a platform for both the consumer and supplier to meet on equal terms and arrive at a negotiated settlement after having understood each other's point of view. The consumer feels empowered by the process and, therefore, feels secure that he/she has been able to successfully negotiate and receive what he/she perceives as his/her needs or wants. The Mediator who acts as a facilitator is also enjoined to ensure that the parties are not under any misconceptions of applicable law or facts or that they have no misinformation or beliefs about the reliefs that they could actually obtain from the Court. The Mediator would, whenever necessary, use the Reality testing process to remove any unrealistic expectations of justice from the Courts. The process, therefore, promotes a fair settlement, more so, as the consumer is given the freedom to determine the relief he/she would be happy with. Without complicated procedures the applications, affidavits, evidence, cross-examination etc., settlements would be achieved efficiently and in double quick time.

The Law today has also provided for pre-litigation intervention and settlements. It is eminently possible to introduce the process of mediation even before the litigation process is set in motion by a consumer. Trained Mediators could be appointed, and attached to Consumer Courts. Availability of such a process viz., of Mediation before the legal process is activated and could be advertised. Consumers with complaints could approach the accredited/appointed Mediators who would initiate a dialogue with the service provider and commence and complete the mediation process. It is believed (realistically) that a large number of complaints could be resolved by this process, as it would consume minimal time, effort and resources and would dispense with procedures and technicalities.

As both, Mediation and Pre-litigation Mediation are party-centric processes; there is adequate incentive for disputants to actively participate in the process without incurring substantial legal costs and undergoing the inconvenience of the adjudicatory process. The primary incentive to resolve disputes through

Mediation would, therefore, be the efficacy and expeditious disposal of disputes. The realisation that a third unknown person would not decide on the terms of resolution of a dispute but instead that it vests entirely in the hands of the disputants would create an environment of trust, faith and confidence.

NGO-sector and Consumer Rights Protection

In the NGO-sector the growth of consumer service organisations and associations has been substantial. There are innumerable specialised consumer service groups that are not only empowering consumers in their fight for justice but are also keen to participate in the process of alternative dispute redressal. Most of these associations deal with common consumer related issues and, therefore, possess substantial expertise, knowledge and skill in dealing with consumers and their rights. The present Act does not provide for an effective utilisation of such skills from the NGO Sector. It would be worthwhile to examine whether selected representatives of such NGOs could be trained in the skills of mediation thereby creating a body of effective Mediators to assist Consumer Courts in disposal of pending cases.

It would become necessary to empower selected NGOs to officially enter upon the Mediation process by appropriate amendments to the Consumer Protection Act. If this were to be done NGOs would become the intervening organisation and would implement the process of pre-litigation Mediation. Such NGOs could be empanelled and statutorily recognised as Mediation Centres where a consumer would be able to lodge a complaint for initiating mediation process or pre-litigation mediation process. The existing Law would need to be amended to ensure that such NGOs are vested with power to compel appearance of service providers/opponents so that the mediation process could be implemented. It is possible to argue that if such NGOs are vested with powers of compelling appearance of parties there could be large-scale misuse and the voluntary nature of the process would be compromised. Consequently, two precautions would necessarily have to be put in place:

(a) a fool-proof comprehensive selection procedure under which NGOs are selected for their credibility and impartiality;

(b) A process of monitoring by either the State Commission or a statutory entity created for this purpose.

As an alternative what could be examined is the possibility of such NGOs approaching the Consumer Courts, for issuance, of summons or notice to the opponent parties so that the power to compel appearance is retained by Consumer Courts. The process of registration of such NGOs could be prescribed so that only credible organisations are recognised as Mediation Centres for assisting the Consumer Courts in resolution of disputes.

It is, therefore, recommended that, as Mediation has been recognised as an effective dispute resolution process by an appropriate amendment to Section 89 of the Civil Procedure Code, the process be incorporated into the Consumer Protection Act, so that dispute resolution through Mediation becomes the vehicle for expeditious delivery of justice to consumers.

19

Consumer Rights Protection and Consumer Redressal Fora in India: Why an Alternative Dispute Resolution in India is Necessary?

Apurva Dave

Introduction

There has been all round realisation that the court litigation is very expensive, very time consuming and to some extent uncertain. These factors of delay, uncertainty and cost deter the parties from approaching the court and they seek alternative methods for resolving their disputes. The well organised system of negotiations, conciliation, mediations is found to be more satisfactory, expeditious and inexpensive. As we all know that there have been revolutionary changes in business environment: instantaneous communications, transportation, multi-modal transportation of goods and such other economic activities, but civil courts procedures have hardly changed. They still act in accordance with old rules, procedures and customs. The Court reform is a distant dream in India.

In USA, The American Arbitration Association (AAA) was founded 75 years ago in the year 1926, rendering services to resolve wide range of dispute through mediations, arbitrations, election and other out-of-court settlement procedures. AAA is an established autonomous, non-profit making and self governing body. An American author observes that they had inherited English common law system that was already obsolete, and ill-suited to accommodate the new and emerging mercantile concepts. This evolution had brought the concept of alternative methods of dispute resolution.

In the last five years, there has been steady growth of inclusion of ADR provision in business contract and it is very important to establish such kind of model in the consumer fora also. The need of satisfactory dispute resolution in any society cannot be denied or underestimated. It can significantly contribute to the development of harmonious international economic relations, and it is essential in the changing circumstances.

In a judgement of the Supreme Court of India, Mr. Justice D. A. Desai had observed about the Arbitration Act:

The need for simplifying and making more effective laws of United Nation's commission on International Trade Law the new arbitration and conciliation Act; 1996 has been enacted. It is certainly a positive legislative step in furtherance of ADR. The other legislation is Legal Service Authority Act, 1987. Corresponding to the American Arbitration Association, there is an International Centre for ADR in India. The patron is the Chief Justice of India, and the chairman and members are the eminent lawyers and business men in India. This act was a result of resolution adopted by the Chief Justice and the Chief Ministers of the States in the joint conference held in New Delhi in December 1983. The resolution stated that courts were not in a position to bear the entire burden of justice system and that a number of disputes lent themselves to resolution by alternative modes such as arbitration, mediation and negotiation. The area in which the ADR could work cover disputes involving joint venture construction projects, intellectual property rights, personal injury, product liability, professional liability, real estate, securities, contract interpretation and performance, and insurance coverage.

Why Fast-track ADR?

It is common belief that justice delayed is justice denied. Arbitration is generally intended to provide speedy, economic and fair results. But international arbitration has now become too time-consuming. It is generally said that the ICC arbitration may take two to three years to be completed. Many a time, it is felt that the arbitral process has been judicialised and it is as slow as courts. Like arbitration is governed by rules and practices which are becoming more and more sophisticated and complex. The detailed rules and prescribed procedures may be fairer and more just but these do not serve the purpose of commercial arbitration because of delay in the resolution of disputes. As observed by the Supreme Court of India in M/s. Guru Nanak Foundation Vs. M/s. Rattan Singh & Sons:

'Interminable, time-consuming, complex and expensive court procedures impelled jurists to search for an alternative forum that is less formal, more effective and speedy resolution of disputes avoiding procedural claptrap and this led them to Arbitration Act, 1940 'Act' for short). However, the way in which the proceedings under the Act are conducted, and without an exception challenged in Courts, has made lawyers laugh and legal philosophers weep. Experience shows and law reports bear ample testimony that the proceedings under the Act have become highly technical accompanied by unending prolixity, at every stage providing a legal trap to the unwary. Informal forum chosen by the parties for Expeditious disposal of their disputes has by the decisions of the courts been clothed with 'legalities' of unforeseeable complexity'.

Necessity to provide for speedy decisions in commercial matters caused development of special type of arbitration—Fast-track ADR which is becoming popular day-by-day. Traditional arbitration is an improvement over traditional litigation in the courts and Fast-track ADR is an improvement over traditional arbitration. The outcome of a case does not change much if the case is completed in six months instead of 24 months but it can cause substantial time and cost saving for the parties. Establishment of hard, fast and speedy case management deadlines has a tremendous impact on the management of resolution of disputes by arbitration.

The ADR techniques such as conciliation, mediation, negotiation and mini-trials have the benefit of less time and less cost but there is no assurance that it will result in a legally binding settlement of disputes. These techniques bring the parties together but the settlement is not compulsory. Any party may walk out of such proceedings at any time or may not agree even to a very fair settlement. It happens many times that for the respondent it is a case of either total liability or no liability, and to avoid liability he may refuse the settlement. But fast-track ADR is an effective technique which ensures speed, economy and binding settlement of disputes. The award given in fast-track ADR is equally binding as an award given in traditional arbitration.

Main Features of ADR

(a) Faster. It ensures resolution of disputes within an agreed period. The time management technique prevents continuation of proceedings for years and ensures completion of the same within the prescribed period. The causes of excessive delay in arbitration are well known. The Fast-track ADR gives parties a chance to secure a settlement of disputes in a given time frame by eliminating abuses and delays of traditional arbitration. It causes meaningful reduction in length of proceedings. The parties need not waste time on unimportant matters and they can focus their attention on key issues in the dispute.

(b) Economical: The costs of ADR are comparatively low due to reduction in the length of arbitration, elimination of abuses and delays of arbitration and general avoidance of oral hearings. The cost management techniques prevent multiplication of actual costs to the parties.

(c) Final and binding settlement: Fast-track ADR agreement is binding on parties and it can be enforced as any other arbitration agreement between parties. Similar, arbitral award is final and binding on parties.

Procedure Needs to be Changed for Consumer Fora

The Arbitration moves faster not because of skipping of any vital step in the process of arbitration but mainly because of the cutting of delays and long procedures. Arbitral tribunal is constituted as per provisions of agreement between parties; claimant submits statement of facts and claims, and respondent submits his defence and counter claim. Both parties file documentary evidence with the pleadings and also accordingly submit written submission/argument/summary. The arbitral tribunal applies its mind and may ask for further documentation, submission or information, if any required by it and, thereafter, makes an award. Similarly, in Consumer Fora, also there is a requirement of fast proceedings. The only difference is the period of time for particular steps to be taken in the course of the proceedings and enforced. The oral hearings are generally avoided.

Application Method for Consumer Fora

As we all know, the Fast-track arbitration is best suitable in majority of cases which can be decided on the basis of documents, and in which the oral hearings and witness are not very necessary. The oral hearing can be held in Fast-track arbitrations, if necessary, for exceptional cases. ;

The Fast-track arbitration is not suitable in cases involving large scale discovery of documents, very lengthy presentations, numerous submissions, numerous witnesses, or expert analysis. The success of Fast-track arbitration depends on the law applicable to arbitration and its tolerance of the freedom of parties to contract. The Arbitral Model Law on Internal Commercial Arbitration (Model Law) provides for faster arbitration and it has in-built provisions for accelerated arbitration. Model Law and Fast-track arbitration are compatible.

Article 11(2) of Model Law provides that parties are free to agree on a procedure for appointing the arbitrator. Hence, there is complete freedom to the parties to agree to any faster procedure to appoint an arbitrator. Article 13(1) gives freedom to parties to agree on a faster procedure for challenging an arbitrator. Article 13(4) provides that, if a challenge is not successful, the arbitral tribunal shall continue the proceedings and make an arbitral award. Article 23(1) gives freedom to the parties to agree on time-limits for filing of claims, replies and counter-claims; and hence fast-track rules can operate without risk of infringement of any provision of Model Law due to short periods allowed to the parties to submit claims, replies and counter-claims under fast-track arbitration rule. Article 24(1) gives freedom to parties to agree that no oral hearing shall be held. Article 25 allows arbitral tribunal to continue proceedings in case of default by a party. Article 29 provides that questions of procedure may be decided by the presiding arbitrator. These provisions of the Model Law are very useful in accelerating arbitration and permit parties to agree on fast-track rules. The Fast-track arbitration rules can operate safely within the limits laid down by Model Law. The Arbitration and Conciliation Act, 1996 is largely based on Model Law; and hence the fast-track rules are also compatible with the Act. Similarly, the Consumer Fora may also help develop the Model Law to facilitate the time-bound result.

Segmentation of Disputes

Segmentation of issues for settlement by Fast-track ADR and the general ADR is also possible to meet the special requirements in big contacts, such as Unfair Trade Practices in which certain urgent disputes can be settled immediately by Fast-track ADR. It is required that the Forum works on segmentation of disputes.

Study the Model of Institutional Arbitration

The Institutional arbitration is usually fast-track arbitration. The institutions help in enabling faster communications among the parties, appointment of the arbitrators, handling the administration of the cases and in cost-effective manner. The institutions exercise a supervisory and supportive role over the arbitration conducted in accordance with rules and thereby effectively deal with delays and defaults of any party; and ensure speed in settlement of disputes.

Conclusion

The Fast-track arbitration provides final and binding settlement of those disputes which are required to be resolved urgently. It is the need of the hour when a large number of cases are pending in the consumer fora. It can be applied in most of the cases without risking the fairness to finally arrive to any settlement between parties in disputes.

Appendix–I

Recommendations to Strengthen Consumer Redressal Forums by the Participants of Two-day National Seminar on "Role of Consumer Disputes Redressal System in India Issues, Challenges and Opportunities"

M.C. Paul

A two day national seminar was organised by Jawaharlal Nehru University, New Delhi on "Role of Consumer Disputes Redressal System in India Issues, Challenges and Opportunities" on 12-13th March 2010. The Coordinator of the seminar was Professor M.C. Paul, School of Social Sciences of JNU in co-operation with Professor Bupinder Zutshi, CSRD. We are happy to note here that the Hon'ble Minister, Prof. K.V. Thomas, MOS, Consumer Affairs, wished to come to inaugurate the National seminar on the topic which has been close to his heart. As he said, "nevertheless, in view of some unavoidable, unforeseen, urgent and important Parliamentary commitment" he was unable to avail the opportunity. We were very thankful to the Hon'ble Minister for his "best wishes and compliments for the successful conduct of the seminar". Professor B.B. Bhattacharya, Vice-Chancellor, Jawaharlal Nehru University, has chaired the Inaugural Session.

The seminar participants have discussed and debated host of issues related to consumer rights protection in India and the role of consumer forums in protecting the aggrieved consumers whose rights are increasingly snatched away by the powerful marketers. About 93 participants attended the National seminar for two days from all over the country belonging to faculty and students from IIPA, universities like Pondicherry, Delhi University, JNU, Government of India, Judiciary, Senior Advocates, NGOs/VCOs, Mass Media. They are Justice J.D. Kapoor, former President of Delhi State Consumer Commission, Hon'ble Justice R.K. Batta, Member NCDRC, Shri Anupam Dasgupta, Hon'ble Member, NCDRC, Mrs. Rajyalaxmi Rao, former Member of NCDRC,

Dr PK Agrawal, former Principal Secretary, Department Consumer Affairs, Government of West Bengal, Sri Debasis Bagchi, former Inspector General of Police, Dr. Prem Lata, Member West District Fora, P.A. Krishnamoorthy (GTZ), Patrick Von Braunmuehl, GTZ (Germany), Prof. Pranab Banerjee, Prof. Sheetal Kapoor, Prof. P. Moorthy, Prof. Meenu Agrawal, Advocate Rajeev Saxena, Advocate Apurva A. Dave, P.A. Krishnamoorthy (GTZ), Prof. Savita Hanspal, Brig. Manaktala, Capt. Dasgupta, Col. Angad Singh, Col. Dua, Pankaj Singh, Advocate Biraja Mahapatra, Advocate Atulesh Kumar, Prof. Hari Dev Goyal, Dr Ajay Kumar, Prof. M.C. Paul, Hitoshi (Japan) *et al* including many students and faculty members and concerned *Aam* Consumers.

The House discussed several issues, challenges and opportunities of the Consumer Fora, rightly set up by the Government, so as to revamp and strengthen the same since the consumers feel that due to several inbuilt limitations, and weaknesses that must have crept in later on, have made the world's best Consumer Disputes Redressal system gradually become ineffective/dysfunctional; and thereby losing *aam* consumers' confidence. Many aggrieved consumers find it hard and sometimes scared to enter the portal of justice as 'consumer of justice'. It is in this context, the participants feel it crucial to unanimously recommend the following to august body like NCDRC, Central and State governments and other government authorities, for fruitful amendment of the unique Consumer Protection Act, 1986, if required, to attain its very object keeping its spirit intact.

The Recommendations are:

1. That the format for filling of Petition under the Consumer Protection Act needs to be further simplified (like in the case of RTI) and the supporting documents in self-certified format be accepted for all practical and judicial purposes before Fora petition On-line may be allowed and accepted.
2. That the Complainant should send a copy of the Complaint to the Opposite Party at the address that has been incorporated in the Complaint and a proof of dispatch of Complaint by way of Registered/Speed Post/courier E-mail with Acknowledgement due be filed along with the Complaint at the time of initial filing of the Complaint itself.

3. The Complaint filed before 11 AM on a working day before the District Forum may be listed for hearing before the Forum by 1 AM on the same day and if admitted the official Notice to the other party be directed to be issued forthwith by issuing a copy of the Summons for Appearance/Notice to the party by *Dasti* process.
4. The Complainant shall upon receiving the *Dasti* Summons ensure the dispatch of the same along with Copy of the Complaint and annexure thereto within three working days of the issue of the *Dasti* notice for service upon the opposite party and the Complainant shall file an affidavit of Compliance of the process on the next date of hearing fixed before the Forum. This will considerably simplify the whole process.
5. A copy of the Summons/Notice must also be sent by the Forum within three working days of the date of admission of the complaint.
6. The opposite party shall, within 10 days of the receipt of the Summons/Notice file its appearance before the Forum with an advance intimation to the Complainant; and shall within a period of 30 days of the receipt of the summons of appearance/Notice of the Complaint by any process, file its Counter/Reply to the Complaint with an advance copy of the same to the Complainant, before the Forum within the said period of thirty days, along with the proof of dispatch of the advance copy to the Complainant.
7. The Complainant shall within 30 days from the date of receipt of the Counter/Reply from the opposite party file his/her rejoinder by way of affidavit with an advance copy of the same to the Complainant, before the Forum within the said period of thirty days, along with the proof of dispatch of the advance copy to the Complainant.
8. In the eventuality of the opposite party failing to put an appearance within 10 days of the date of service of the Notice, the matter shall be proceeded further on the date of hearing fixed before the forum *ex-parte* without fail, unless good reason for non-compliance of the process to the satisfaction of the forum is shown, the matter shall be decided as summary trial as prescribed in the CP Act.

9. Since Cyber-shopping or e-made or online/e-purchase of goods and services are becoming the order of the day and where the location of the company or dealer offices are at for off places it is difficult for the consumers to file any complaints against them. For example, a villages from Assam buying goods or services through e-commerce from a company office located in Mumbai can't be asked to file complaint in Mumbai Consumer Fora since the company office is located in Mumbai. Thus, under the changing times, we need to amend the CPA, 1986 to enable the rising aggrieved consumers who buy goods through e-commrce.

That the definition of the "Consumer" as envisaged under Section 2 of the Act" be expanded to include.

1. A person availing the benefits of medical or any other service free of any consideration including amongst other a treatment in Government/Semi-government Hospital, dispensary, medical centers, etc. including in a Private Hospital, Nursing Home, Medical Centre. Clinic or Camps organised by Social, Government/Semi-Government/Non-Government organisations, institutions etc., which have availed of the support, subsidies, grants, grants-in-aid, and/or have been allotted land, building structure etc., on subsidised rate or special rates from the state or under any scheme of the State or some other Government/Non-Govt. organisation, institute, foreign grants, foreign indirect or direct investment or service arrangements.
2. The Complainants pending before the Forum/State Commission/National Commission be disposed off within the prescribed time frame. The Presiding officer should record reasons for delay in disposal of each complaint specifically.
3. There should be an effective mechanism for the orders of National and State Commissions to be communicated to the concerned District Fora. It is observed that the communication from district level to State commission takes longer time for the case-file to move when appeal is initiated to higher commissions. So under this circumstance, copy of the orders must be provided to the Appellant/Revisionist/Complainant under the signatures of the Court Master on the day of passing of an interim order. IT software is to be used and responsibility be fixed for its under-use and/or non-use.

4. The President of the/District Forum/State Commission/ National Commissions should take up cases *suo moto* in matters affecting the *enmasse* consumer on account of an apparent failure of the Manufacturer, Producer, Service Provider and/or any such person whose action, conduct or dealing has caused or has been instrumental to cause or adversely affect a sizeable number of population and/ or may manifest symptoms of disease later in his/her life causing him/her to suffer in any manner. It will definitely check the further misdemeanour.
5. The District Forum may be assigned the task to attend the hearing of the matters in *Gram Panchayats* at least once in a week-basis or within such a time-frame as would ensure the availability of the benefits of CP Act to the underprivileged and/or distantly placed sections of consumers as well because complaints of rural consumers are on the rise. It is in this regard that the *Panchayat* system needs to be roped-in through concrete networking process like by opening Consumer Advice Centres in various districts/Panchayats next to the fora with Helplines and/ or any other ways suitable to pragmatically help the needy consumers.
6. The Complaint from the rural areas may be directed to be accepted by Post/Courier mail, etc. Wherever the Office of the BDO/*Gram Panchayats*/Post Office, etc., are equipped with On-line facilities the Complaints must be sent to the concerned District Forums forthwith and the dates for hearing the cases of the particular Village/*Panchayats*/Post Office/*Taluka* should be fixed so as to avoid repeated service of Summons/Notices of the Hearings time and again and thereby reducing the avoidable delay.
7. Consumer Fora/Commission should be provided proper accommodation at easily accessible and visible venues with all suitable infrastructural facilities. One Member of the Forum/Commission be vested with the duties of the Custodian for the said facilities as would ensure proper upkeep and maintenance, and availability of the said facilities at the venue.
8. The staff of the Forum should be appointed through a Judicial Service Commission so as to ensure availability of

a motivated personnel trained/skilled in CP Act and, all the facilities like Promotion, Increments, Regular Performance Related Assessment and Appreciation Schemes be mooted so as to keep the staff motivated, on the one hand, and cautious, on the other.

9. The system of deploying only retired Judicial Officers as President of the Forums should be reviewed forthwith. People from all walks of life be encouraged and considered for placement at the level of the President and the disparity of the remuneration amongst the Members of the Forums and the Presiding Officers must be removed forthwith and, all the Members be placed and considered for promotions strictly on the basis of their performance during their tenure of initial placements at the Fora.
10. All members of consumer fora/commission should be appointed after they go through a properly structured training module/programme. Periodical skill upgradation has to be an on-going programme. All efforts shall be made to ensure that the Judicial Officers, if appointed to the Fora, must shed their civil court personality and demeanor, and act as the pro-active guardians of the consumers and understand, observe and implement the consumer law in its true letter and spirits rather than following the legal and/or technical intricacies rather than the substance.
11. Selection of the Members for the District Forums/State and National Commission should be made through a transparent process and each of the members selected for such a placement be given similar training to create cohesive and balanced relationships for the interest of justice because every complainant is also a consumer of justice.
12. Provision should made in the Act for Senior Member of the Forum/Commission to Preside in the absence of the President and to conduct all the proceedings, except passing of the final orders dismissing the Complaints in the absence of the President. Sense of procrastination has to be eradicated.
13. Not more than one adjournment, that too for a short period of time, should be granted to either of the parties, unless

it be for reasons shown to the satisfaction of the Forum which should record the same in writing during the complete trial of the matter especially for the purpose of completion of pleadings, affidavits in evidence, etc., and adjournments otherwise should only be granted against imposition of heavy costs as per Rules and Regulations.

14. An independent autonomous National Consumer Protection Authority be constituted and all the matters related to Consumer Protection be dealt with by the said authority, except disposal of consumer complaints under the CP Act.

15. All appointments to the Forums should be made by the three member committee consisting of President State Commission, Law Secretary and Secretary in Charge Consumer Affairs Department of the State Government through a transparent system of placement without any interference.

16. Continuing Legal Education, Training should form as a crucial part of the Service and no officer be allowed to skip or avoid such education, orientation and training, etc. Weightage may be given for the Members undergoing such educational training especially for consideration of continuation or promotion.

17. The reputed and dedicated NGOs connected with the Consumer Protection and Movement must also be made part of the structured audit for assessment of their performance and efficiency in promoting of the Consumer Protection Movement, and shall further be required to submit annual reports to the State Commissions for its appraisal and/or by independent agencies like universities and civil society groups involving selected retired activist judges *et al.*

    NGO/VCOs should be encouraged to pro-actively involve in consumer awareness and movement activities; help consumers in filing complaints for any market violations of consumer rights in a cost-effective way.

19. The recommendation of the Shenoy Committee set up by the NCDRC should be accepted by the State Governments and suitable funds be made available.

20. Adequate provisions be made to ensure the availability of free legal aid to the Consumers in association with the Local Bar Associations or otherwise with the help and assistance of the District Level Legal Aid Service Authorities or by appointing lawyers from Consumer Welfare Fund by the Commission or Fora in appropriate cases specially for the poor.
21. Court-annexed pre-litigation mediation process as envisaged u/s 89 of CPC may be introduced and qualified/ skilled mediators after thorough training/orientation be appointed so that it unburden the forums to a large extent as well as to expedite the redressal. It must be appropriately placed under the judicial body and/or under the constitutional body like National Consumer Protection Authority which should be created by the Parliament amending the Consumer Protection Act, 1986. The Consumer Affairs Department of the States may also open Mediation Cell with qualified mediators at various levels to help in pre-litigation stage. In several countries consumer complaints are handled through NGOs at pre-litigation levels and the results are quite impressive. The successful experiment of West Bengal government carried out by Principal Secretary Dr P.K. Agrawal successfully in regards to mediation may be replicated in other parts of the country. So allowing the Alternative Disputes Resolution (ADR) system in India thorough amendment of CPA would definitely bring boon to the aggrieved consumers and it will go a long way in protecting the consumer rights in India. Law colleges/universities may be entrusted also if necessary as a part of 'Extension education' programmes to the community. At JNU level, we will be interested to do this on a trial basis.
22. In fact, the participants sincerely felt that one of the ways to reduce the pressure on consumer fora could be the adoption of a suitable Alternative Disputes Redressal Mechanism/system (ADR), like mediation and conciliation to resolve the dispute between parties before they go before the consumer fora. It should be a mechanism to settle a matter of dispute at the pre-litigation phase with the help of trained/professional mediators. If it is

introduced and effected, even with the help of business associations of any hue, will not only reduce the burden of Fora but also definitely usher in a new era of consumer protection in India. However, ADR techniques can only be used only when both the parties are eager/willing to take a pro-active part in the process otherwise its very purpose will be defeated. It may be noted that ADR techniques may not be appropriate to resolve all kinds of disputes.

23. Academic institutions, Law Colleges/universities like Jawaharlal Nehru University may be involved to conduct Evaluation studies/research in different areas so as to identify the effectiveness of the system, status and prospects of consumer redressal system at national, state and district level. National Chair and scholarships/ Fellowships, etc., may be provided to the MPhil/PhD research scholars of different universities to do focused research/study in this emerging area. They may be entrusted with funds to organise consumer awareness education programmes in and around their campuses in various ways, providing training programmes to mediators, prepare training modules, involve NGOs, etc. A pilot project may be designed to begin with.

24. The State Governments must be directed to create Consumer Affairs Department separately and not as part of the Social Welfare or Public/Civil Supplies/Food and Supplies allocations.

25. Adequate facilities for putting up National Level Product Quality Testing Facilities/Medical Boards, etc., must be placed suitably and ensured at all State Levels functioning directly under the aegis of the State Commission.

26. Expeditious, efficient and corruption-free mechanism for execution of the orders of the Fora be ensured by incorporating adequate provisions under the C. P. Act with the assistance of Local police and/or SDMs or the District Collectorate or any other empowered authority in a time bound manner and the concerned offices be made accountable/answerable for any inaction.

27. Strict actions and/or penalty be contemplated for perjuries committed by either of the party during the proceedings before any Fora or Commission under the CP Act so as to keep the spirit of the most progressive and benevolent Act of 1986, the Indian Parliament could ever enact, intact. We all have responsibility to do our mite since we have equal stake in it.

28. The slogan *"Jago Grahak Jago"* alone will not cut ice with the business class. We need to have a new slogan like *"Jago Vyaparis Jago grahak adhikar ko samman karo"* which must be adopted and forced upon the traders through business organisations and associations like FICCI, CII and/or remind them Gandhi's saying that: "A customer is most important visitor on our premises. He is not dependent on us. We are dependent on him. He is not an outsider on our business. He is part of it. We are not doing him a favour by serving him. He is doing us a favour by giving us an opportunity to do so". It needs to be accepted as part of a good business ethics.

Note: **Report prepared by:** A team of academics, lawyers and students under the Coordination of Prof. MC Paul, Jawaharlal Nehru University, New Delhi-110067.

Bibliography

1. Abe, Yoshiya: *Globalization and Indigenous Culture,* Institute of Japanese Culture & Classics, Tokuo, 1997
2. Advani, Rani: Patients Know Your Rights, CERC, Ahmedabad, 1992
3. Agrawal, Meenu: *Consumer Behavior and Consumer Protection in India,* New Century Publications, New Delhi, 2005.
4. Agarwal, V.K.: *Consumer Protection in India,* Deep & Deep Publications, New Delhi, 1989
5. Ahmad, Farooq: *Consumer Rights in India,* APH Publishing Corporation, 1999.
6. Andrews, Sonia and Sailesh Mohan: "User Charges in Health Care: Some Issues", *Economic and Political Weekly,* September 14, 2002, pp. 3793-95
7. Applbaum, Kalman: "The Sweetness of Salvation: Consumer Marketign and the Liberal-Bourgeois Theory of Needs", *Current Anthropology,* vol. 39, no. 3, June 1998, pp. 323349
8. Arora, Renu, *Consumer Grievance Redressal under the Consumer Protection Act,* Manak Publishers, Delhi.
9. Asch, Peter: *Consumer Safety Regulation: Putting a Price on Life and Limb,* Oxford University Press, NY, 1988.
10. Azmi, S.S.H.: *Sale of Goods and Consumer Protection in India,* Deep & Deep Publications, Delhi, 1992
11. Bakshi, P.M.: *Consumer Protection Law,* Ashoka Law House, Delhi.
12. Bal, Arun: "Consumer Protection Act and Medical Profession", *Economic and Political Weekly,* March 13, 1993, Vol. 28, No.l 1, PP.432-435.
13. Balakrishna Eradi, V: *Consumer Protection Jurisprudence,* Lexis Nexis Butterworths, 2005

14. Balchandran. S.: *Customer Driven Services Management*, Response Books, New Delhi.

15. Bana, Ravinder, *Housing & Consumer*, Indian Institute of Public Administration, Delhi.

16. Banerji, Pranab: *Environment & Consumer*, Indian Institute of Public Administration, Delhi.

17. Barksdale, C. Hiram and William R. Darden: "Consumer Attitudes toward Marketing and Consumerism", *The Journal of Marketing*, Vol. 36, No. 4, October, 1972, pp. 28-35.

18. Barowalia, J. N.: *Commentary on The Consumer Protection Act*, Universal Law Publishing Co. Pvt. Ltd., Delhi, 2008

19. Basara, L.R.: "Direct-to-Consumer Advertising: Today's Issues and Tomorrow's Outlook", *Journal of Drug hsues.* Vol. 22(2), 1992, pp. 317-30.

20. Bateman, C. R.: 'Framing Effects within the Ethical Decision Making Process of Consumers', in *Journal of'Business Ethics*, Vol. 36, 2002, pp.119.

21. Bazerman, H. Max. "Consumer Research for Consumers" in *The Journal of Consumer Research*, Vol. 27, No. 4 (Mar., 2001), pp. 499-504.

22. Beales, Howard, Richard Craswell, Steven C. Salop: "The Efficient Regulation of Consumer Information", *Journal of Law and Economics*, Vol. 24, No. 3, Consumer Protection Regulation: A Conference Sponsored by the Center for the Study of the Economy and the State (Dec.. 198S), pp. 491-539.

23. Berg, Maxine and Helen Cliford (Eds.): *Consumers and Luxury: Consumer Culture in Europe: 1650-J850*, Manchester, 1999

24. Bhattacharya, N. and B. Mahalnobis: "Regional Disparities in Household Consumption in India", *Journal of American Statistical Association*, Vol. 62, 1967, pp. 143-161

25. Bhattacharjee, S. R.: *Law of Standards of Weights and Measures*, Law House, Delhi.

26. Bhaumik, T.K.: *WTO- A Discordant Orchestra*, Sage, New Delhi.

27. Bloom, P.N. and R. Belk Smith: *The Disadvanlaged Consumer*, Free Press, New York, 1975

28. Bloom, Paul N. and R. Belk Smith (Ed.): *The Future of Consumerism*, Lexington Books, Lexington, MA, 1986

29. Borrie, Gordon and Aubrey L. Diamond: *The Consumer, Society and The Law*, 1964

30. Brakel, Samuel J.: "Free Legal Services for the Poor-staffed Office versus Judicare: The Client's Evaluation" in *Wisconsin Law Review*, 532, 1973.

31. Brewer, John and Roy Porter (Eds.): *Consumption and World of Goods*, London, 1994

32. Brinkmann , Johannes: "Looking at Consumer Behaviour in a Moral Perspective", *Journal of Business Ethics*, Vol. 51, No.2, Promoting Business Ethics, May, 2004, pp.129-141.

33. Bugge, Lawrence J.: "Is Consumer Protection Becoming Legal Pollution?'" in 49 *Wisconsin Bar Bulletin*, 15 June, 1976.

34. Buhler, George: *Manu-The Laws of Mann* (Trans.), 1990

35. Burroughs E. James and David Glen Mick: "Exploring Antecedents and Consequences of Consumer Creativity in a Problem-Solving Context", *The Journal of Consumer Research*, Vol.31, No.2, Sep., 2004, pp. 402-411.

36. Burton, Elaine: *The Battle of the Consumer*, London, 1954

37. Caplovitz, David: *The Poor Pay More: Consumer Practices of Low Income Families*, The Free Press, New York, 1963.

38. Chahar, S. S. : *Consumer Protection Movement: Problems and Prospects*,

39. Chaudhary, R.N.P.: *Consumer Protection Law*, Deep & Deep ublications, Delhi, 2006

40. Chitkara, M.G.: *Consumerism: Crime and Corruption*, A.P.M. Publishing Company, New Delhi.

41. Chowdhary, T.H.: "Telecom Regulation and consumer Welfare" in *Economic and Political Weekly*, October 26, 2002, pp. 4354-4356

42. Church, Virginia Anne: Innovations in Legal Counseling", *Florida Bar Journal*, January 10, 1975

43. Cohen, Dorothy: "Remedies for Consumer Protection: Prevention, Restitution or Punishment", *Journal of Marketing,* 24 October, 1975

44. Corrigan, Peter: *The Sociology of Consumption: An Introduction,* London, 1997

45. Danzig, Richard and Michael J. Lowy: "Everyday Disputes and Mediation in United States" in 9 *Law and Society Review,* 675

46. Das, P.K.: *Handbook on the Food Safety and Standards Act, 2006,* Universal Law Publishing Co. Pvt. Ltd., Delhi, 2006

47. Day, R.L.: 'Relationship between life satisfaction and consumer satisfaction[1], in A.C. Samli (ed.), *Marketing and Quality-of-Life Interface* (Greenwood Press, Westport), 1987, pp. 289-311.

48. Deaton, A. and Muellbeaur, J.: *Economics and Consumer Behaviour,* Cambridge University Press London, 1980.

49. Desroches Brigitte and Marc-Andre Gosselin: "Evaluating Threshold Effect in Consumer Sentiment", *Southern Economic Journal,* Vol.70, No. 4, April, 2004, pp. 942-952.

50. Diener, Betty J. and Stephen A. Greyser: "Consumer Views of Redress Needs" in 42 *Journal of Marketing,* 21 October, 1978

51. Divita, Sal, and Frank McLaughlin: *Consumer Complaints: Public Policy Alternatives.* Washington, D.C., 1974.

52. Dutta, N.: *Origin and Development of Criminal Justice in India,* 1990

53. Ettenson, R.: "Brand Name and Country of Origin Effects in the Emerging Market Economies of Russia, Poland and Hungary', *International Marketing Review,* 59, 1993, pp. 14-36

54. Farooq, Ahmad: *Consumer Protection in India,* APH Publishing Corporation, New Delhi.

55. Featherstone, Mike: *Consumer Culture and Post-Modernism,* London, 1991

56. Fiadjoe, Albert: *Alternative Dispute Resolutions; A Developing World Perspective,* Routledge-Cavendish Publishing Ltd., NY, 2006.

57. Fitzgeral, Naill: "Harnessing the Potential of Globalization for the Consumer and Citizen", *International Affairs* (Royal Institute of International Affairs 1944-), Vol. 73, No. 4, Oct., 1997, pp. 739-746.

58. Ford, Gary: "State Characteristics Affecting the Passage of Consumer Legislation" in *Journal of Consumer Affairs,* Vol.11 (Summer 1977, pp. 177-82.

59. Fox, Richard W. and T.J. Lears (Eds.): *The Culture of Consumption,* Pantheon, New York, 1983

60. Foxall, G.R.: "Sociology and the Study of Consumer Behavior", *American Journal of Economics and Sociology,* Vol.33, No.2, Apr. 1974, pp. 127-135.

61. Friedman, Jonathan: *Consumption and identity,* Chur: Harwood, 1994

62. Galanter, Marc: *Law and Society in Modern India,* 1997

63. Galbraith, J. K.: *American Capitalism: The Concept of Countervailing Power,* (Revised Edition), Hamish Hamilton, London, 1957

64. Galbraith, J. K.: *The New Industrial State,* Penguin Books, Harmondsworth. England, 1967

65. Galbraith, J. K.: *The Affluent Society,* Harmonds worth, 1998

66. Gambhir, Cheena: *Consumer Protection Administration: Organization and Working*

67. Giri, H.N.: *Consumer's Crimes and The Law,* Ashish Publications House, Delhi, 1987.

68. Girimaji, Pushpa: *Consumer Rights for Everyone,* Penguin, New Delhi, 2003.

69. Girimaji, Pushpa: "Misleading Advertisement & Consumer" *Indian Institute of Public Administration,* New Delhi.

70. Glickman B. Lawrence: "The Consumer and the Citizen in Personal Influence", *Annals of the American Academy of Political and Social Science,* Vol. 608, (Nov.2006), Politics, Social Networks, and the History of Mass Communications Research: Rereading Personal Influence, pp. 205-212.

71. Goldberg, Stephen B., Frank E.A. sander, Nancy H. Rogers and Sarah R. Cole (Eds.): Dispute Resolution: *Negotiation, Mediation and Other Processes,* Aspen Publishers Inc., NY, 2007

72. Goode M.R.: "The Consumer Credit Act 1974", *The Cambridge Law Journal*, Vol.34.No.l, Apr. 1975, pp. 79-130.
73. Goodhart, Philip et al: *Choice: A Report on Consumer Protection*, London, 1961
74. Goodhart, Philip: *A Nation of Consumers*, London, 1965
75. Gordon, Borrie and Aubrey L. Diamond: *The Consumer, Society and The Law*, 1964
76. Gordon, Borrie: *The Development of Consumer Law and Policy: Bold Spirits and Timorous Souls*, 1984
77. Goyal, K.N.: *Consumer Protection Act, 1986*, Eastern Books Co., 2008
78. Grainer, M. A., K. A. McEvoy and D. N. King: "Consumer Problems and Complaints: A National View", *Advances in Consumer Research*, 6, Association for Consumer Research, (1979), pp. 494-500.
79. Gulliver, P.H.: "On Mediators" in lan Hamlett (ed), *Social Anthropology and the Law*, Academic Press, New York, 1977
80. Gupta Anil: *Consumer Behavior in India: A Study of All- India Consumption*, Anmol Publications, New Delhi, 1986.
81. Gupta, M.C.: *Health and Law*, Kanishka Books, New Delhi.
82. Gupta, M.C.: *Treatise on standards of Weights & Measures*, Commercial Law Publishers.
83. Gupta, R. and Singh, V.: "'Case Laws on Medical Negligence", *Indian Institute of Public Administration*, New Delhi.
84. Gupta, S.N.: *Banks and Consumer Protection Low*, Universal Law Publishing Co. Pvt. Ltd., Delhi, 2007.
85. Haefner, James and John Leckenby: "Consumers' Use and Awareness of Consumer Protection agencies", *Journal of Consumer Affairs*, 9, 205,1975
86. Hai, Maulana Hakim Syed Abdul: *India During Mughal Rule* (Mohiuddm Ahmad trans.); 1977
87. Halve, Anand Bhaskar: *Planning for Power Advertising*, Sage.
88. Haque Ohidul Mohammed: "Estimating Increase in Consumer Demand from Household Expenditure Survey Data", *Sankhya: The Indian Journal of Statistics*, Series B, Vol.53,No.l, Apr., 1991, pp. 134-149.

89. Harap, Henry: "Why Consumer Education?", *Journal of Educational Sociology*, Vol. 11, No. 7, Education for Wise Consumption (March 1983), pp. 387-397.

90. Harrison, Rob and others, *Ethical Consumer*, Sage Publications.

91. Hauser, John R.: "A Normative Methodology for Modeling Consumer Response to Innovation", *Operations Research*, Vol. 25, No. 4 (Jul. - Aug., 1977), pp. 579-619.

92. Hazard, Geofrey C. Jr.: *Ethics in Practice of Law*, Yale University Press, New Haven, 1978

93. Hildebrand, H. George: "Consumer Sovereignty in Modern Times", *The American Economic Review*, Vol. 41, No. 2, Papers and Proceedings of the Sixty-third Annual Meeting of the American Economic Association (May, 1951), pp. 19-33.

94. Himachalam. D.: *Consumer Protection and Law*, AHP Publishing Corporation, New Delhi, 1998.

95. Himachalam, D.: *Consumer Protection in India*, Associated Publishers Co., 2009.

96. Horowitz, Daniel: *The Anxieties of Affluence: Critiques of American Consumer Culture: 1939-1979*,, Amherst: University of Massachusetts Press, 2004.

97. Howes, David: *Cross-Cultural Consumption*, Routledge, London, 1996

98. IOCU: *Consumer Solidarity: For A Better World* (Proceedings of XIIth World Congress), London, 1987

99. Islam, Nurul: "Studies in Consumer Demand", Vol. I, *Bureau of Economics Research*, Dacca University and Oxford University Press, Dacca, 1965.

100. Iyer, S.: "Consumer Awareness at School Level" in *The Hindu*, April 16, 2002.

101. Jaiswal, J.V.N.: *Postal and Courier Services and the Consumer*, Eastern Book Company, Lucknow.

102. Jasper, Margaret C.: *Consumer Rights Law*, Oxford University Press, NY, 2008

103. Jaffrelot, Christopher & Peter van der Veer: *Patterns of Middle Class Consumption in India and China*, Sage, NY, 2008

104. Jeferies, James: "Protection for Consumers against Unfair and Deceptive Business", *Marquette Law Review*, 57, 559, 1974

105. Jena, Susant Kumar: "Globalization and Popular Culture: Reading Advertisement Sociologically" (Unpublished paper), 2004

106. Joshi, Navin Chandra: "Consumers' Apathetic Attitude and Ignorance" in *Central Chronicle*, 11.9.2002.

107. Joshi, Navin Chandra: "Need for Spreading Consumer Movement" in *Central Chronicle*, 22.12.1999.

108. Joshi, Navin Chandra: "Consumers Apathetic Attitude and Ignorance" in *Central Chronic*, 11.9.2002.

109. Kabir: *RTIAct and the Rules* (CD 1 & 2), Kabir, E-169, Shanti Marg, Delhi.

110. Kamath, K.P.S.: *Servants, Not Masters: A Guide for Consumers Activists in India*, Consumers' Forum, 1987

111. Kangle, R. P.: *TheKautilyaArthashastra*, Part-Mil (2nd Edition), 1972

112. Kapoor, G.K.: "Defective Goods & Deficiency of Service vis-a-vis Consumer", *Indian Institute of Public Administration*, Delhi.

113. Kapoor, J.D. Justice: *Commentary* on "Arbitration & Conciliation Act", Universal Law Publishing Co. Pvt. Ltd. CFF-IA- Dilkush Industrial Estate, G.T. Karnal Road, Delhi-110033, Year 2009. pp. 1-1466

114. Kapoor, Sheetal: "Consumer and the Market", *Indian Institute of Public Administration*, Delhi, 2005.

115. Kapoor, Sheetal: *Understanding Buying Behaviour of Indian Families*, New Century Publication, Delhi.

116. Kataria, R.P.: *Law of Consumer Protection in India*, Orient Publishing Co., 2002.

117. Kaushal, Anoop K.: *Medical Negligence and Legal Remedies*, Universal Law Publishing Co. Pvt. Ltd., Delhi, 2009.

118. Kaushal, Anoop K.: *Practical Guide to Consumer Protection Law*, Universal Law Publishing Co. Pvt. Ltd., Delhi, 2010.

119. Kaynak, Erdener and Ali Kara: "Consumer Ethnocentrism and Lifestyle Orientations in an Emerging Market Economy", *Management International Review*, Vol. 38,Special Issue, 1998/1, pp. 53-72

120. Khandela, Man Chand: *Consumer Protection in India,*

121. Kumar, Neeraj: *Consumer Protection Act,* Himalaya Publishing House, New Delhi, 1999.

122. Labarbera A. Priscilla and Edward L. Melnick: "Consumer Protection Laws: Violator Detection and Enforcement Strategy", *Management Science,* Vol. 33, No. 10, October 1987, pp. 1348-1356.

123. Lewis Sclipper: *Consumer Discretionary Behaviour,* North-Holland Publishing Company, Amsterdam.

124. Liefeld, John P., Fred H. C.: Edgecombe and Linda Wolfe: "Demographic Characteristics of Canadian Consumer *Comp\a\ners", Journal of Consumer,* 1975.

125. Linda Wolfe (n.d.): *How Complaints Are Handled by Canadian Business,* Department of Consumer Studies, University of Guelph.

126. Lingat, Robert: *The Classical Law of India,* 1998

127. Lury, Ceila, *Consumer Culture,* Oxford, 1996

128. Macaulay, Steward: "Lawyers and Consumer Protection Laws", *Law & Society Review,* Vol. 14, No. I (Autumn, 1979), pp. 115-171.

129. Mackay, Hugh (Ed.): *Consumption and Everyday Life,* London, 1997

130. Mahajan, B.M.: *Consumer Behaviour in India,* Concept Publishing Company, New Delhi.

131. Maira, Arun: *Remarking India- One Country, One Destiny,* Sage Publications, Delhi.

132. Majumdar, Amita: "Institute Consumer Expenditure Pattern in India: A Comparison of the Almost Ideal Demand Systmand the Linear Expenditure System", *Sankhya: The Indian Journal of Statistics, Series B,* Vol.48, No.l, April 1986, pp. 115-143.

133. Malik, P.L.: *Law Relating to Weights and Measures,* . Eastern Law Book Company, Lucknow.

134. Malik, Surendra: *Supplement to Supreme Court on Arbitration*, Eastern Law Book Company, Lucknow.

135. Malik, Surendra: *Supreme Courts on Educational Institutional Cases*, Eastern Law Book Company, Lucknow

136. Malik, Vijay: *Drugs and Cosmetics Act, 1940*, Eastern Law Book Company, Lucknow.

137. Marsh, Gene A.: *Consumer Protection Law In a Nutshell*, West Group, MN, 2003

138. Matadin: "Insurance and Consumer," *Indian Institute of Public Administration*, Delhi.

139. McGiliis, Daniel and Joan Mullen: *Neighbourhood Justice Centres: An Analysis of Potential Models*, Government Printing Office, Washington, DC, 1977

140. McKendrick, Neil, John Brewer and J.H. Plumb: *The Birth of a Consumer Society: The Commercialization of Eighteenth-Century England*, London, 1982.

141. McMeel, Gerard: *Modern Law of Unjust Enrichment and Restitution*, Eastern Law Book Company, Lucknow

142. McNeil, Kenneth and Richard E. Miller: "Th£ Profitability of Consumer Protection: Warranty Policy in the Auto Industry" in *Administrative Science Quarterly*, Vol. 25, No. 3 (Sep., 1980), pp. 407-427.

143. Mehta, Subhash C.: *Indian Consumers- Studies and Cases for Marketing Decisions*, Tata McGraw Hill Publishing Co. Ltd., New Delhi, 1974.

144. Mehta, Vinod: "Consumer Becoming King in India", *Assam Tribune*^ 10.7.99.

145. Meier, Kenneth: "The Political Economy of Consumer Protection: An Examination of State Legislation", *Western Political Quarterly*, Vol.30 (June 1987), pp. 343-59.

146. Mendenhall, E. James and C. Maurice Wieting: "Consumer Education Through the Curriculum", *Journal of Educational Sociology*, Vol. 11, No. 7, Education for Wise Consumption (March 1938), pp. 398-404.

147. Menkel-Meadow, Carrie J. et al (Eds.): *Dispute Resolution: Beyond Adversarial Model*, Aspen Publishers Inc., NY, 2005

148. Millar, Robert: *The Affluent Sheep: A Profile of British Consumer*, London, 1963

149. Miller, C. J.: *Consumers and Trading: Law Text, Cases and Materials*, Oxford University Press, Oxford, 1998

150. Miller, Daniel: *Material Culture and Mass Consumption*, Basil Blackweil, Oxford, 1987

151. Mitchell, Jeremy (Ed.), *Marketing and the Consumer Movement*, 1978

152. Moffit, Michael L. & Robert C. Bordone: *The Handbook of Dispute Resolution*, Jassey-Bass, 2005.

153. Moffit, Michael L. & Andrea K. Schneider: *Dispute Resolution: Examples and Explorations*, Aspen Publishers Inc., 2008.

154. Moore L. Roy and Lowndes F. Stephens: "Some Communication and Demographic Determinants of Adolescent Consumer Learning", The *Journal of Consumer Research*, Vol. 2, No. 2 (September 1975), pp. 80-92.

155. Mooiji, Maridke de: *Consumer Behaviour and Culture*, Sage publications, New Delhi.

156. Mookerji, Radha Kumud: *Chandra Gupta Mauriya and His Time*, 4th Edition, 1966

157. Moore, Christopher W.: *The Mediation Process: Practical Strategies for Resolving Conflict*, Jossey-Bass, 2003

158. Mowen, John C.: *Consumer Behaviour*, Macmillan Publishing Co., New York, 1990.

159. Moyer S. Mel: "Characteristics of consumer Complainants: Implications for Marketing and Public Policy" in *Journal of Public Policy and Marketing*, Vol.3, 1984, pp. 67-84.

160. Mueller, E.: "Effects of consumer attitudes on purchases", *American Economic Review*, 1957, pp. 946-65.

161. Muncy, J. A. and S.J. Vite: "Consumer Ethics: An Investigation of the Ethical Beliefs of the Final Consumer". *Journal of Business Research*, Vol. 24, 1992, pp. 297-311.

162. Myers, Norman & Jennifer Kent: *The New Consumers: The Influence of Affluence on the Environment*, Island Press, Washington DC, 2004

163. Nader, L.: *Law in Culture andSociety*, Chicago, 1969.

164. Nair, Suja R.: *Consumer Behavior in Indian Perspectives*, Himalaya Publishing House, New Delhi, 2001.

165. Nabhi: *Compendium Buying Behaviour of Indian Families*, New Century Publication, New Delhi.

166. National Consumer Dispute Redressal Commission: *Landmark Judgments on Insurance Under Consumer Protection Act*, Universal Law Publishing Co. Pvt. Ltd., Delhi

167. Nolan-Haley, Jacqueline M.: *Alternative Dispute Resolution in a Nutshell*, Thomson, MN, 2008

168. Narasimhan Shakuntala: "Consumer Redressal Courts: Missing Commitment to Public Interest" in *Economic and Political Weekly*, Vol.27, No.22, 30 May, 1992, pp. 1129-1130.

169. Narula, Ruchira and Mythili Bhusnurmath: The Consumer in always Right...But Is He?", *Economic Times*, February 6, 1994

170. Nelson, A. Kim: "Consumer Decision Making and Image Theory: Understanding Value-Laden Decisions", *Journal of Consumer Psychology*, Vol. 14, No. ½, 2004, pp. 28-40.

171. NichollsandOpal: *Fair Trade*, Sage Publishers, New Delhi.

172. Nigam, Shalu: *Consumerism, Medicine and Law: Emerging Voices from India.*

173. Nijhawan, S.B.: *National Commission and Supreme Court on Consumer Cases-1986-2002*, Part-4th," International Law Books, Delhi.

174. Ohmae, Kenichi: *The Borderless World; Power and Strategy in the Interlinked Economy*, Harper Perrenial, New York, 1990

175. Otnescele and Tina M. Lowrey, L.J. Shrum: 'Toward an Understanding of Consumer Ambivalence", *The Journal of Consumer Research*, Vol. 24, No. 1, June 1997, pp. 80-93 (Published by: The University of Chicago).

176. Padberg, D. I.: "Consumer Protection for a Modern Industrialized Food System" in *American Journal of Agricultural Economics*, Vol. 52, No. 5, Proceedings Issue. Dec. 1970, pp. 821 -828.

177. Pai, M.R.: *Consumer Activism in India*, East West Books (Madras Pvt. Ltd., 2001.

178. Paney, Bhanu: "Are Consumer Courts Really Serving the Consumers", *The Economic Times,* 12 April, 2011.

179. Panwar, J.J.: *Beyond Consumer Marketing: Sectoral Marketing and Emerging Trends.*

180. Panwar, J.S., Navin Mathur and Darshana R. Dave(Eds.): *Consumers: Global and Indian Perspectives*

181. Papadopoulos, N. and L.A. Heslop: *Product-Country Images: Impact and Role in International Marketing,* The Haworth Press inc., New York, 1993

182. Pattanaik, Prasanta K. and Maurice Salles: *Social Choice and Welfare,* North-Holland, Amsterdam, 1982.

183. Paul, M.C.: *Problems of Consumer and Awareness of Consumer Rights: A Study of National Capital Region* (Unpublished), IIPA, New Delhi, 2006.

184. Paul, M.C. (Ed.): *Consumer Rights Protection in India: Issues and Challenges (An Interdisciplinary Studies of Consumer Courts and Mediation System in India),* (Unpublished Report). ^

185. Paul, M.C.: "Globalization and Protection of Consumer Rights in India" in Brig. R. S. Chhikara (Ed.): *Globalization Problems, Prospects and Perspectives,* Hope India Publications, Gurgaon (Haryana), 2009

186. Paul, M.C.: "A Report on Role of Consumer Disputes Redressal System in India: issues, Challenges and Opportunities", *Consumers Power,* Inaugural Issue, Vol. 1, No. 1, May 2010, pp. 19-22

187. Paul, M.C.:"Consumer Rights Protection: Role and Challenges of Consumer Courts in India", *Indian Journal of Youth Affairs,* Vol. 14, Number 2, July-December, 2010, pp. 88-96

188. Paul, M.C.:"Globalization of Markets and Consumer Rights: Challenges and Opportunities", *Yojana,* Vol. 58, Special Issue, April, 2014, pp. 28-36

189. Pavleen: *Consumer Decision Making,* Deep and Deep Publications, Delhi.

190. Philips Louis: *The Economics of Price Discrimination,* Cambridge University Press, New York, 1983

191. Pitofsky, Robert: "Beyond Nader: Consumer Protection and the Regulation of Advertising", *Harvard Law Review,* Vol. 90, No. 4, February 1977, pp. 661-701.

192. Pohit, Sanjib: "Liberalization of Consumer Goods: Issues, Status and Impact", *Paradigm,* Vol. 2, No.l, July, 1995, pp. 87-96

193. Polonsky, M. J. et al.: "Consumer Ethics in the European Union: A Comparison of Northern and Southern Views", *Journal of Business Ethics,* Vol.31, 2001.

194. Prasad, Rajendra, A.: "Historical Evolution of Consumer Protection and Law in India: A Bird's Eye View" in *Journal of Texas Consumer Law,* 2010

195. Provost, Colin: 'The Politics of Consumer Protection: Explaining State Attorney General Participation in Multi-State Lawsuits", *Political Research Quarterly,* Vol. 59, No.4, Dec. 2006, pp. 609-618.

196. Punj N. Girish and David W. Stewart: "An Interaction Framework of Consumer Decision Making", *The Journal of Consumer Research,* Vol. 10, No. 2 (Sep., 1983), pp. 181-196.

197. Rajamohan, S.: "Role of Voluntary Consumer Origination in Consumers Protection", *Rural India,* Vol. 65 Feb.-March 2002.

198. Ralph, L. Day (Ed): *Consumer satisfaction and Dissatisfaction and Complaining Behaviour,* Indiana University Press, Bloomington, Ind., 1977.

199. Rama, Jois M.: *Ancient Indian Law- Eternal Values in Manu Smriti,* Universal Law Publishing Co. Pvt. Ltd., Delhi, 2007.

200. Rangarajan, L. N. (Ed.): *Kautilya- The Arthashastra,* Penguin Books India, 1992

201. Rao, Mamta: *Public Utility Services under the Consumer Protection Act.* Deep & Deep Publications, New Delhi, 1999.

202. Rao, S.L.: "Consumer Markets: Myths and Reality", *Economic and Political Weekly,* Vol. 33, No. 44, Oct.31-Nov.6, 1998, pp. 2778-2781.

203. Rao, Suneeti: "Evolution of the Consumer Protection Law in India", *Journal of Indian School of Political Economy, 1* (3), July-Sept., 1995, pp. 433-512

204. Rasor, Paul B.: "Privacy Implications of Consumer Credit Protection Laws", *The John Marshall La\v Review*, Vol.19 (Summer 1986), pp. 941-957.

205. Rathor, N.S., A.S. Jhala, G.K. Mathur and S.S. Chasta (Ed.): *Consumer Awareness for Food and Dairy Products.*

206. Resnik J. Alan and Robert R. Harmon: "Consumer Complaints and Managerial Response: A Holistic Approach", *The Journal of Marketing*, Vot.47, No.l, 1986, pp. 86-97.

207. Roa, Mamta: Public Utility Services Under the Consumer Protection Act, Deep & Deep Publications, New Delhi, 1999.

208. Roa, Nageswara: *Conciliation Proceeding under the Indian Arbitration and Conciliation Act of 1996: An Overview*, *<www.lawcommissionofindia.nic.in/adr_conf/nageswararao10.pdf>.*

209. Roa, Rajyalakshmi: *Consumer Is King*\\, Universal Law Publishing Company, New Delhi, 2010 (2nd Edition)

210. Ross, H. Lawrence: *Settled out of Court: the Social Process of insurance Claims Adjustments*, Aldine, Chicago, 1970

211. Rothschild, P. Donal and Bruce C. Throne: "Criminal Consumer Fraud: A Victim-Oriented Analysis", *Michigan Law Review*, Vol. 74, No. 4 (Mar., 1976), pp. 661-707.

212. Ruskin, John: *Unto The Last: Four Essays on the First Principles of Political Economy (1860-61)*, London, 1898

213. Rustad, Michael L.: *Everyday Law for Consumers*,

214. Saraf, D.N.: *Law of Consumer Protection in India*, N.M. Tripathi Pvt. Ltd., Bombay, 1990

215. Sarjoo, Prasad: *Essential Commodities Act*," Law Publishers, Allahabad. 216.Sarkar, A.: *Problems of Consumers in Modern India*, Discovery Publishing House, 1989.

217. Sarma, Rajendra Nath: *Ancient India According to Manu*, 1980

218. Satyanarayanmurthy, P.V.V.: *Consumer Protection Act*, Indian Institute of Public Administration, Delhi.

219. Sawant, P.B. and Bandyopadhyay: *Advertisement Law and Ethics*, Universal Law Publishing Co. Pvt. Ltd., Delhi, 2002.

220. Schwartz, Anita: *Know Your Rights- A Guide to Consumer Protection,* Janus Book Publication, 1984

221. Seetharaman, Pravathy and Mohini Sethi: *Consumerism: strategies and Tactics.*

222. Sekhar, R.C.: *Ethical Choice in Business,* Sage.

223. Sen, Amartya K.: "Social Choice and Justice: A Review Article", *Journal of Economic Literature,* 23 December, 1985, pp. 1764-76

224. Sengupta, Soma: *Consumer Behaviour Dynamics of Building Brand Equity,* New Century, New Delhi.

225. Sharma, Chandrakant: *Role of Consumer Organizations in Consumer Protection,* Kanishka Publishers Distributors, Delhi. 1995.

226. Sharma, Jyoti: *Consumer Satisfaction and Loyalty in Indian Consumer Banking,* Universal Law Publishing Co. Pvt. Ltd., Delhi, 2010

227. Sharma, S.S.: *Consumer Behaviour,* Arihant Publishing House, Jaipur, 1995. 228.Shenoy, P.O.: P.D. *Shenoy Committee Report,* 2008, Government of India.

229. Sigurdson, Pamela and Larry A. Raine: *Consumer Redress Mechanisms,* Consumer Research Council Canada, Ottawa, 1977.

230. Silbey, S. Susan: "Case Processing: Consumer Protection in an Attorney General's Office", *Law and Society Review,* Vol.15, No.3/4, April 1967, Special Issue on Dispute Processing and Civil Litigation, pp. 849-882.

231. Singh, Avatar: *Law of Consumer Protection: Principles and Practice Being a Study of the Consumer Protection Act, 1986.*

232. Singh, Gurbax: *Digest of Consumer Protection Cases: 1986-1994,* Bharat Law Publications, Jaipur, 1994

233. Singh Gurjeet: *The Law of Consumer Protection in India: Justice Within Reach,* Deep & Deep Publications, Delhi, 1999.

234. Singh, Gurjeet: "The Problem of Consumer Protection in India: A Historical Perspective", *Consumer Protection Reporter,* 704 and 705, n.6 III, 1994

235. Singh, Gurjeet: "Business Self-Regulation and Consumer Protection in Jndia: A Critique" in *Journal Consumer Policy,* Publisher Springer Netherlands, Vol.16, 1st March 1993.

236. S. S. Singh and Sapana Chadah: *Consumer Protection Act,* Indian Institute of Public Administration, Delhi.

237. Singh, Mahendra Kumar: "Vacancies, Pending Cases Plague Apex Consumer Body", *The Times of India,* March 9, 2007

238. Singh, Randhir: "Limitations of the Market System: A Marxist Analysis"in *Mainstream,* December 25, 2004, pp. 53-63

239. S. S. Singh and Sapana Chadah: *Bharat Mein Upbhokta sanrakshan mahatwapoorn pehlu.* Indian Institute of Public Administration, Delhi.

240. Sisvaprakasham, P. and S. Rajamohan: *Consumer Empowerment: Rights and Responsib ilities.*

241. Smith, Adam: *The Wealth of Nations,* Chicago, 1976

242. Sobti, Renu: *Medical Services and Consumer Protection in India* (Cases reviewed up to April 2001), New Century Publications, New Delhi, 2001.

243. Sorian, R., and J. Feder: "Why We Need a Patients' Bill of Rights" in *Journal of Health Politics Policy and Law,* Vol. 24(5), (1999), pp. 1137-44.

244. South Asia Human Rights Documentation Centre Secretariat: *Introducing Human Rights: An Overview Including Issues of Gender Justice, Environmental and Consumer Law,* Oxford University Press, USA, 2006

245. Spanogle, John A., Ralph J. Rohner, Mary Dee Pridgen, Jeffrey Severn (Eds.): *Consumer Law,* Thomson West, 2007

246. Srinivas, Alam: *The Indian Consumer: One Billion Myths, One Billion Realities,* Wiley Publishers, 2008.

247. Srinivas, G., G. Srinivas Rao: *Rural Marketing in India: A Case Study,* Anmol Publishing Pvt, Ltd. New Delhi, 2006.

248. Srinivasan, K.: "A New Era in Consumerism", *The Hindu, Special Issue with Sunday Magazine,* October 31, 1999, pp. 1-5.

249. Srivastva, Sudha Rani: *Upbhokta Sanrakashan,"* Hindi Book Centre, Delhi.

250. Stearns, Peter: *Consumerism: A World History,* London, 2001
251.Steele, Eric H.: "Fraud, Disputes and the Consumer: Responding to Consumer Complaints" in 123 *University of Pennsylvania Law Review,* 1107, 1975

252. Stephen Edgell, Kevin Hetherington and Alan Warde: "Consumption Matters" Blackwell Publishers, *The Sociological Review.*

253. Stern, Louis L.: "Consumer Protection via Increased Information" in *The Journal of Marketing*, Vol. 31, No. 2, April, 1967, pp. 48-52.

254. Steven, Miles: *Consumerism As a Way of Life*, Sage Publication London, Thousand Oaks, New Delhi.

255. Subrahmanyam, Sanjay (Ed.): *Money and Market in India: 1100-1700*, 1998.

256. Sundarm, I.S.: *Consumer Protection in India*, B. R. Publishing House, New Delhi, 1980.

257. Sudhakaran, E.: *Doctor in Consumer Court: The Consumer Protection Act-1986*, 1996.

258. Supakar, Shraddhakar: *Law of Procedure and Justly in India*, 1986

259. Szmigin, Isabelle: *Understanding Consumer*, Response Books, New Delhi.

260. *The Banking Regulation Act, 1949*, Commercial Law Publishers Pvt. Ltd.

261. *The Consumer Protection Act, 1986*, Universal Law Publishing Company Pvt. Ltd., 2009

262. *The Drugs and Cosmetics Act, 1940*, Commercial Law Publishers Pvt. Ltd.

263. *The Negotiable Instruments Act 1881*, Universal Law Publishing Co. Pvt. Ltd., Delhi

264. *The Securitization and Reconstruction of Financial Assess and Enforcement of Security Interest Act, 2002*, Commercial Law Publishers Pvt. Ltd.

265. Thompson, Noel: *The Market and Its Critics: Socialist Political Economy in the Nineteenth Century*, London, 1998

266. UN: *Guidelines for Consumer Protection, 1985*, United Nations, New York, 1986

267. Uppal, R. K. and Rimpi Kaur: *Consumer Protection through Mass Awareness.*

268. Vats, R. M: *Law Relating to Electricity -with Special Reference to Consumer Protection Law,* Universal Law Publishing Co. Pvt. Ltd., Delhi, 2002

269. Vats, R. M.: *Law Relating to Telephones with Special reference to Consumer Protection Law,* Universal Law Publishing Co. Pvt. Ltd., Delhi, 2010.

270. Verma, S.K. and Kusum (Eds.): *Fifty Years of Supreme Court in India: Its Grasp and Reach*

271. Verma, S.K. and M.A. Wani (Eds.): *A Treatise on Consumer Protection Laws,* Universal Publishing Co. Pvt. Ltd., Delhi, 2004.

272. Verma, Y.S.: *Consumerism in India,* Anamika Prakashan, 1994.

273. Vogel, David: "Consumer Protection and Protectionism in Japan", *Journal of Japanese Studies,* Vol. 18, No. 1 (winter, 1992), pp. 119-154.

274. Wadhwa, D.P. Justice and N.L. Rajah (Eds.): *The Law of Consumer Protection (An Exhaustive Commentary on Consumer Protection Act, 1986),* Wadhwa & Company Nagpur, New Delhi, First Edition, 2006.

275. Wallendorf Melanie and Merrie Brack; "Introspection in Consumer Research: Implementation and Implications", *The Journal of Consumer Research,* Vol. 20, No. 3, Dec., 1993, pp. 339-359.

276. Walter, Adams: "Consumer Needs and Consumer Sovereignty in the American Economy", *The Journal of Business,* Vol. 35, No. 3 (Jul., 1962), pp. 264-277.

277. Warland, Rex H., Robert O. Hermann and Jane Willits: "Dissatisfied Consumers: Who Gets Upset and Who Takes Action", *Journal of Consumer Affairs,* 9 (148), 1975

278. Webster, F.E.: "Determining the characteristics of the socially conscious *consumer". Journal of Consumer Research,* Vol.2, 1975, pp. 188-196.

279. Wolfe S.M.: "Direct to Consumer Advertising Education or Promotion Emotion", *New England Journal of Medicine,* Vol. 334(7), 2002, pp. 524-26.

280. Woods Walter A.: *Consumer Behavior -Adopting and Experiencing,* Elesvier North Holland, New York, 1981

281. Yashoda: *Right to Information Act, 2005,* Tata McGraw Hill.

282. Zussman, David: "Consumer Complaint Behavior and Third Party Mediation", *Canadian Public Policy/ Analyse de Politiques,* Vol.9, No.2, Jun., 1983, pp. 223-235.

Index

E

N

O

List of Contributors

1. Sri RSN Sharma, Regional Project Officer (Asia and the Pacific), Consumers International, Lot 5-1 Wisma WIM, 7 Jalan Abang Haji Openg, TTDI, 60000 Kuala Lumpur, Malaysia
2. Prof. MC Paul, Professor, GAE, School of Social Sciences-I, Jawaharlal Nehru University, New Delhi.
3. Dr. Prem Lata, Former Member, District Consumer Redressal Forum, Shalimar Bagh, New Delhi
4. Mr. Patrick Von Braunmuehl, Former Senior Advisor, GTZ-ASEM, Consumer Protection & Sustainable Consumption, 12/2 Jamnagar House, Shahjahan Road, New Delhi
5. Dr. Sheetal Kapoor, Associate Professor, Department of Commerce, Kamla Nehru College, University of Delhi, Delhi
6. Sri Biraja Mahapatra, Advocate, Supreme Court of India, , New Delhi
7. Dr. Savita Hanspal, Associate Professor, Department of Commerce, Kamla Nehru College, University of Delhi, Delhi
8. Dr. Sapna Chadah and Pankaj Singh,Assistant Professor, Indian Institute of Public Administration, I.P. Estate, New Delhi
9. Sri B. Vaidyanathan, Chief Mentor, Consumer Protection Council, Rourkela (Odisa)
10. Dr. P.K. Agrawal, IAS (Retd),Writer, Advocate, Managing Partner of VAS Global, Law Firm at New Delhi.
11. Prof. Meenu Agrawal, Head, Economics Department,

G.D.M.C. (PG) College, Modinagar (U.P.)

12. Sri Atulesh Kumar, Advocate-On-Record, Supreme Court of India, New Delhi
13. Sri Parmarthy Venkataramana, Advocate, Supreme Court of India, New Delhi
14. Prof. Hari Dev Goyal, Director, RTI Centre, Dwarka, New Delhi-110075
15. Prof. M C Paul, Professor, #206, GAE, School of Social Sciences-I, Jawaharlal Nehru University, New Delhi.
16. Dr. Vinod Kumar, Assistant Professor, Department of Geography, University of Delhi, Delhi
17. Mr. Gerd Billen, Consumer Rights Advisor in Germany (c/o Patrick Von Braunmuehl, Former Senior Advisor, GTZ-ASEM, Consumer Protection & Sustainable Consumption)
18. Sri Shiv Kumar, Advocate and Mediator, Law & Options, Delhi Public School, King & Partridge, Solicitors, 70/3, I Floor, Miller's Road BANGALORE-560052
19. Sri Apurva Dave, Advocate, Gujarat High Court & Trustee, Consumer Education and Research Society, Sarkhej-Gandhinagar highway, Ahmedabad-380054, Gujarat.